Y0-BXQ-657

CD-ROM
RESEARCH
COLLECTIONS

Supplements to
COMPUTERS IN LIBRARIES

1. Essential Guide to dBase III+ in Libraries
   Karl Beiser
   ISBN 0-88736-064-5 1987
2. Essential Guide to Bulletin Board Systems
   Patrick R. Dewey
   ISBN 0-88736-066-1 1987
3. Microcomputers for the Online Searcher
   Ralph Alberico
   ISBN 0-88736-093-9 1987
4. Printers for Use with OCLC Workstations
   James Speed Hensinger
   ISBN 0-88736-180-3 1987
5. Developing Microcomputer Work Areas in Academic Libraries
   Jeannine Uppgard
   ISBN 0-88736-233-8 1988
6. Microcomputers and the Reference Librarian
   Patrick R. Dewey
   ISBN 0-88736-234-6 1988
7. Retrospective Conversion: A Practical Guide for Libraries
   Jane Beaumont and Joseph P. Cox
   ISBN 0-88736-352-0 1988
8. Connecting with Technology 1988: Microcomputers in Libraries
   Nancy Melin Nelson, ed.
   ISBN 0-88736-330-X 1989
9. The Macintosh ® Press: Desktop Publishing for Libraries
   Richard D. Johnson and Harriett H. Johnson
   ISBN 0-88736-287-7 1989
10. Expert Systems for Reference and Information Retrieval
    Ralph Alberico and Mary Micco
    ISBN 0-88736-232-X 1990
11. EMail for Libraries
    Patrick R. Dewey
    ISBN 0-88736-327-X 1989
12. 101 Uses of dBase in Libraries
    Lynne Hayman, ed.
    ISBN 0-88736-427-6 1990
13. FAX for Libraries
    Patrick R. Dewey
    ISBN 0-88736-480-2 1990
14. The Librarian's Guide to WordPerfect 5.0
    Cynthia LaPier
    ISBN 0-88736-493-4 1990
15. Technology for the 90's
    Nancy Melin Nelson, ed.
    ISBN 0-88736-487-X 1990
16. Microcomputer Management and Maintenance for Libraries
    Elizabeth S. Lane
    ISBN 0-88736-522-1 1990
17. Public Access CD-ROMS in Libraries: Case Studies
    Linda Stewart, Kathy Chiang, and Bill Coons, eds.
    ISBN 0-88736-516-7 1990
18. The Systems Librarian Guide to Computers
    Michael Schuyler and Elliott Swanson
    ISBN 0-88736-580-9 1990
19. Essential Guide to dBase IV in Libraries
    Karl Beiser
    ISBN 0-88736-530-2 1991
20. UNIX and Libraries
    D. Scott Brandt
    ISBN 0-88736-541-8 1991
21. Integrated Online Library Catalogs
    Jennifer Cargill, ed.
    ISBN 0-88736-675-9 1990
22. CD-ROM Retrieval Software: An Overview
    Blaine Victor Morrow
    ISBN 0-88736-667-8 1991
23. CD-ROM Licensing and Copyright Issues for Libraries
    Meta Nissley and Nancy Melin Nelson, editors
    ISBN 0-88736-701-1 1990
24. CD-ROM Local Area Networks: A User's Guide
    Norman Desmarais, ed.
    ISBN 0-88736-700-3 1991
25. Library Technology 1970-1990: Shaping the Library of the Future
    Nancy Melin Nelson, ed.
    ISBN 0-88736-695-3 1991
26. Library Technology for Visually and Physically Handicapped Patrons
    Barbara T. Mates
    ISBN 0-88736-704-6 1991
27. Local Area Networks in Libraries
    Kenneth Marks and Steven Nielsen
    ISBN 0-88736-705-4 1991
28. Small Project Automation for Libraries and Information Centers
    Jane Mandelbaum
    ISBN 0-88736-731-3 1991
29. Text Management for Libraries and Information Centers: Tools and Techniques
    Erwin K. Welsch and Kurt F. Welsch
    ISBN 0-88736-737-2 1992
30. Library Systems Migration: Changing Automated Systems in Libraries and Information Centers
    Gary M. Pitkin, ed.
    ISBN 0-88736-738-0 1991
31. From A - Z39.50: A Networking Primer
    James J. Michael
    ISBN 0-88736-766-6 1992
32. Search Sheets for OPACs on the Internet
    Marcia Henry, Linda Keenan, Michael Reagan
    ISBN 0-88736-767-4 1991
33. Directory of Directories on the Internet
    Ray Metz
    ISBN 0-88736-768-2 1991
34. Building Blocks for the National Network: InitiativesandIndividuals
    Nancy Melin Nelson
    ISBN 0-88736-769-0 1991
35. PublicInstitutions:Capitalizingonthe Internet
    Charles Worsely
    ISBN 0-88736-770-4 1991
36. A Directory of Computer Conferencing for Libraries
    Brian Williams
    ISBN 0-88736-771-2 1991
37. Optical Character Recognition: A Librarian's Guide
    Marlene Ogg and Harold Ogg
    ISBN 0-88736-778-X 1992
38. CD-ROM Research Collections
    Pat Ensor
    ISBN 0-88736-779-8 1992
39. Library LANs: Case Studies in Practice and Application
    Marshall Breeding
    ISBN 0-88736-786-0 1992
40. 101 Uses of Spreadsheets in Libraries
    Robert Machalow
    ISBN 0-88736-791-7 1992
41. Library Computing in Canada: Bilingualism, Multiculturalism, and Transborder Connections
    Nancy Melin Nelson and Eric Flower, eds.
    ISBN 0-88736-792-5 1991
42. CD-ROM in Libraries: A Reader
    Meta Nissley, ed.
    ISBN 0-88736-800-X 1992
43. Automating the Library with AskSam: A Practical Handbook
    Marcia D. Talley and Virginia A. McNitt
    ISBN 0-88736-801-8 1991

CD-ROM RESEARCH COLLECTIONS

An Evaluative Guide to Bibliographic and Full-Text CD-ROM Databases

PAT ENSOR

Meckler

Library of Congress Cataloging-in-Publication Data

Ensor, Pat.
CD-ROM research collections : an evaluative guide to bibliographic and full-text CD-ROM databases / Pat Ensor.
p. cm. -- (Supplements to Computers in libraries)
Includes bibliographical references and index.
ISBN 0-88736-779-8 (alk. paper) : $
1. Research libraries--Collection development. 2. Libraries--Special collections--Data bases. 3. Data libraries--Collection development. 4. Bibliography--Data bases--Directories. 5. Data bases--Directories. 6. CD-ROM--Directories. I. Title.
II. Series.
Z675.R45E57 1991
025.2 ' 1877 -- dc20 91-23710
CIP

British Library Cataloguing-in-Publication Data is available.

Meckler Publishing, the publishing division of Meckler Corporation,
11 Ferry Lane West, Westport, CT 06880.
Meckler Ltd., 247-249 Vauxhall Bridge Road,
London SW1V 1HQ, U.K.

Printed on acid free paper.
Printed and bound in the United States of America.

Table of Contents

Foreword

The idea for this book came from Meckler Publishing, which appreciated the need for an evaluative reference book about research-oriented CD-ROMs. Although numerous reviews are scattered throughout the CD-ROM periodical literature, there are almost no books that provide selected, evaluative CD-ROM listings, and none that focus on the kinds of databases needed by research organizations. This book attempts to remedy that lack of information.

CD-ROM Research Collections lists 114 CD-ROM databases chosen by the editor for their usefulness for bibliographic research. Although numeric, directory and other types of CD-ROM databases may certainly be used for research, for the purposes of this book, only bibliographic or full-text databases that are updated periodically are included. Beyond that, the primary judgment for inclusion was made based on database scope and coverage; search interface was a secondary consideration, although it was considered as it promoted or hindered research. The evaluation for each database considers geographic coverage of the database, the time period covered, variety of material formats covered, and breadth of subject area included. Reviews are quoted and listed when they are available.

I chose to deliberately exclude some categories of databases. I decided that research purposes were better served by national bibliographies, than by in-print bibliographies. I did decide to list two newspaper databases, but I chose two that I considered best for research purposes. There are so many popular magazine databases that, although I realize types of research can be done with them, I omitted them completely. I listed subfiles of major databases as separate entries, where I thought they could be uniquely useful for research institutions. I also listed all different vendors' versions of a database that I could find.

The ultimate choice of databases to be included was mine, but I appreciate the contributions of Becki Whitaker, information retrieval specialist at the Indiana Cooperative Library Services Authority; Pat Riesenman, reference librarian at Indiana University; Anthony Angiletta, chief reference librarian at Cecil H. Green Library at Stanford University; and Martin Courtois, science reference librarian at Michigan State University.

Not all desired information was obtainable for each database, but as much information as possible is included, and every attempt to verify accuracy was made. Correction of any errors found is welcome; changes will be made in future editions. I tried to make this directory the kind of tool that I have been looking for in my work, and I hope it turns out to be of value.

Pat Ensor

TITLE ABI/INFORM ONDISC

PUBLISHER Producer: University Microfilms International/Data Courier
Vendor: UMI/Data Courier

SCOPE AND CONTENT
ABI/INFORM Ondisc accesses over 800 business and management periodicals. It covers accounting and auditing, banking and international trade, data processing and information management, economics, finance and financial management, general management, health care, human resources, insurance, law and taxation, management science, marketing, advertising, and sales, real estate, and telecommunications.

The records themselves—about 200,000 to a disc—include succinct 150-word article abstracts in addition to full bibliographic citations. Over 800 journals are indexed. The current disc covers the last five years; backfiles are available to 1971. The database is updated monthly. (Publisher's brochure)

ABI/INFORM is the foremost index to business periodicals. The breadth of its coverage, as well as its international nature, the quality of its indexing, the scope of its coverage, and the completeness of its abstracts make it essential to businesses. International coverage is best for the United Kingdom, Germany, and the Pacific Rim. ABI/INFORM is valuable for its coverage of the long-lasting material in business and management journals, not simple company news. Its abstracts are true summaries of the articles they cover, not just descriptions. A very good backfile is available.

Stanger, cited below, reviewed ABI/INFORM based on a beta test at Eastern Michigan University. He concluded, "UMI's ABI/INFORM ONDISC has delighted most of its users at EMU since the installation of the test version in the spring of 1987. Even new users quickly retrieve records that seem pertinent. However, my observations suggest that most people do not use many of the very powerful and flexible searching capabilities built into this command-driven system nor do they really understand the structure of the database or how to construct a search that truly reflects their information needs....This situation provides a wonderful opportunity for the design and delivery of information-seeking skills instruction."

"What is the bottom line? ABI/INFORM ONDISC gets results for our users now, when many do not have much searching sophistication, and will get better results for them later, as they grow into the powerful search capabilities that are, in fact, currently available....I perceive the value of the product in our setting as excellent."

Another early review of ABI/INFORM by Nancy Karp noted that, "User response...has been very positive....All users said the system is easy to use....Most users accessed the system without help from library staff....Users reported a high degree of success in finding needed information and most rated the system excellent....the database is so useful for basic as well as more extensive research....The system is a welcome, valuable addition to the rapidly growing number of CD-ROM products."

The *Choice* review, cited below, notes that the UMI/Data Courier search software has some useful defaults that usually do what the reader intended. It is found, however, to be difficult to modify searches, and "Because ABI/INFORM is markedly slower than some other CDs, this awkwardness in modifying searches is irritating." The review concludes, "Although ABI/INFORM is very popular and not difficult to use, it should look toward further improvement of concealed decisions for users."

Wayne Kendrick, in reviewing ABI/INFORM in an item cited below, said, "The program is simple and easy to use. Those users who have never done computer database searching or who know nothing about computers will have no trouble using it." In looking at disadvantages, he noted, "The shortcomings are due to the fact that the program is menu-driven to make it easy to use and that it is used on a small computer which, in the case of commonly used search terms, will mean a good deal of waiting for a response."

Kendrick concludes, though, "In summary, this reviewer found the program to be straightforward and easy to use with simple commands. The only point of concern is the response time for heavily used terms and, if the search yields many items, the amount of time needed to peruse and print the results."

As the editor noted in her evaluation of ABI/INFORM, cited below, "...ABI/INFORM is fairly easy to use, yet, at the same time, it provides moderately sophisticated Boolean and other searching techniques....It is not as easy as systems that are primarily menu-driven, but the trade-off in sophistication of techniques and lack of cumbersome multi-step searches is worthwhile....As far as searching techniques are concerned, the main thing that keeps ABI/INFORM Ondisc from rivaling online systems in easy use of sophisticated search strategies, is the abysmally slow response time....This CD-ROM product has been a big hit with the patrons of a library at a medium-sized university with a sizable business school."

ABI/INFORM's research weaknesses are its coverage of only periodicals, and some lack in international areas. The UMI/Data Courier interface, while sophisticated and providing good research capabilities, can be clumsy to use and very slow.

Editor

REVIEWS

"Business and Economics: ABI/INFORM on Disc." *Preview* 1 (April 1989): 24.

CD-ROM Professional 3 (September 1990): 36-40.

Ensor, Pat. "ABI/INFORM Ondisc: Patron Evaluations in an Academic Library." *CD-ROM Librarian* 4 (October 1989): 25-30.

Foster, Ray. "CD-ROM in Brief: Business Periodicals Ondisc." *Laserdisk Professional* 3 (March 1990): 89-90.

Karp, Nancy S. "ABI/Inform on CD-ROM: a First Look." *Laserdisk Professional* 1 (May 1988): 28-34.

Kendrick, Wayne. "Software Reviews: ABI/INFORM ONDISC." *Technical Services Quarterly* 6 (issue 3/4, 1989): 137-142.

Plum, S. H. "Databases: ABI/Inform on Disc." *Choice* 26 (March 1989): 1134.

Stanger, Keith J. "Optical Product Review: ABI/INFORM ONDISC: a Review." *CD-ROM Librarian* 3 (May 1988): 25-30.

EQUIPMENT AND SOFTWARE REQUIREMENTS

Computer: IBM PC or compatible with hard disk and 640K RAM
Software: DOS 3.2 or higher, MS-DOS Extensions
CD-ROM Drive: Any IBM-compatible

PRICE Annual price: $4,950; Backfiles 1971-1980 and 1981-1986, one-time price, each: $3,750

ARRANGEMENT AND CONTROL

Record fields: title, author, journal title, citation, journal code, ISSN, subject headings, classification codes, date, abstract
Searchable: all fields

SEARCH SOFTWARE AND CAPABILITIES

Software: UMI/Data Courier

Capabilities: keyword, Boolean, search statement retention and back referencing, field searching, proximity searching, printing, downloading, index searching, truncation, automatic searching of singular and plural, nesting, varied display formats, library holdings display

PRINT/ONLINE/OTHER MEDIA COUNTERPARTS
Online: ABI/Inform — DIALOG, BRS, EPIC, NEXIS, Data-Star, Dialcom, ESA/IRS, Human Resource Information Network, ORBIT, SPENET, VU/TEXT

NETWORK LICENSING ARRANGEMENTS
Additional $150 per node/terminal.

TITLE AEROSPACE DATABASE

PUBLISHER Producer: American Institute of Aeronautics and Astronautics, National Aeronautics and Space Administration
Vendor: DIALOG

SCOPE AND CONTENT
Aerospace Database provides international coverage of scientific and technical literature related to aerospace engineering. It includes atmospheric and space sciences; aerodynamics; aircraft and aerospace systems; communications and navigation; propulsion; energy production and conversion; structural engineering and analysis; and laser and robotic technologies. Aerospace Database provides comprehensive coverage of these disciplines, including chemistry and materials, engineering, geosciences, life sciences, mathematical and computer sciences, physics, social sciences, and space sciences. Extensive coverage of related disciplines includes electronics, environmental studies, and computer sciences, plus economic and legal issues. Coverage is back to 1986.

Coproduced by the American Institute of Aeronautics and Astronautics Technical Information Service and NASA, DIALOG Ondisc Aerospace Database provides coverage of over 1600 worldwide sources in forty languages, including journal articles, conferences, books, theses, and unpublished report literature. Approximately 50 percent of these sources originate from more than 100 countries outside the United States, including Japan, China, and Soviet-bloc countries.

Each Aerospace Database record contains a complete bibliographic citation and summary abstract. Indexing terms are derived from the NASA Thesaurus, a comprehensive collection of aerospace terms, which ensures consistency with industry standards. Subject classifications assist in quickly reviewing everything available in a broad subject category. The database is updated quarterly. (Publisher's brochure)

The Aerospace Database is the world's most comprehensive bibliographic database in its field, and definitely the best source on CD-ROM for coverage of aerospace, aircraft, and related areas. For its abstracts, its international coverage, the variety of formats covered, the moderate-sized backfile, its subject comprehensiveness, and the excellent DIALOG interface, Aerospace Database is worthy of acquisition by any institution interested in aerospace research. Its only weakness as a research database is the lack of a longer backfile, but what it has provides a workable amount of information.

Editor

EQUIPMENT AND SOFTWARE REQUIREMENTS
Computer: IBM PC, XT, AT, PS/2, or compatible, 512K RAM minimum, 640K RAM recommended
Software: DOS 3.1 or higher, MS-DOS Extensions
CD-ROM Drive: any IBM-compatible

PRICE Annual price, current year plus four years backfile: $4,890; print subscribers discount: $3,912; annual price, current plus one-year backfile: $3,450; print subscribers discount: $2,760

ARRANGEMENT AND CONTROL
Record fields: abstract, accession number, author, availability, contract number, COSATI codes, COSATI code text, country of origin, country of publication, corporate source, corporate source code, descriptors, document type, ISBN, ISSN, journal announcement, journal name, language, notes, patent information, publication date, publication year, publisher data, report number, source, sponsoring organization code, subfile, subject category code, subject category text, summary language, title
Searchable: all

SEARCH SOFTWARE AND CAPABILITIES
Software: DIALOG Ondisc
Capabilities: keyword, Boolean, search statement retention and back referencing, field searching, field limiting, proximity searching, printing, down-

loading, index searching, novice mode, varied display formats, nesting, truncation, search saving, online updating, sorting, thesaurus.

PRINT/ONLINE/OTHER MEDIA COUNTERPARTS
Print: *Scientific & Technical Aerospace Reports*, *International Aerospace Abstracts*
Online: Aerospace Database — DIALOG

NETWORK LICENSING ARRANGEMENTS
Double the single user fee (above) for two to ten workstations

---

TITLE AGRICOLA

PUBLISHER Producer: National Agricultural Library
Vendor: OCLC, Quanta Press, SilverPlatter

SCOPE AND CONTENT
AGRICOLA contains citations of publications relating to all aspects of agriculture as compiled by the National Agricultural Library. The database catalogs and reviews books, periodicals, audiovisual materials, software, monographs, and technical reports. The database consists of over 2.5 million citations. A few of the subjects covered include general agriculture, pest control, veterinary medicine, aquaculture, chemistry, food science, agricultural engineering, agribusiness, forestry, pollution, law, economics, entomology, plant diseases, energy as related to agriculture, and rural sociology.

For the OCLC version, the current disc covers 1986 to present. Backfiles are available to 1978. For the Quanta Press version, backfiles are available to 1985. For SilverPlatter, the current disc includes the AGRICOLA database covering 1984 to present. The archival disc set includes AGRICOLA and CAIN (predecessor to AGRICOLA) with coverage from 1970 to 1983. All vendor versions are updated quarterly. (Publisher's brochure)

AGRICOLA is the most important American database covering agriculture. The number of documents included, the wide variety of subjects covered, the variety of formats of materials accessible, and the time span covered all make it essential for agricultural research. Its focus is inevitably more on American materials, and it does not have abstracts; these are its research-related weaknesses. The SilverPlatter and OCLC interfaces are about equivalent in their capabilities. The Quanta interface is almost unusable, especially for an inexperienced searcher, due to its complications and limited research capabilities.

Julia Tryon disagrees, although she had not seen the SilverPlatter and OCLC versions. She notes, "Unlike other retrieval engines, which permit one to search for a word or phrase in any or all fields, the ROMware software only allows for single word searching or exact field phrasing....Generally, this does not present much of a problem since most searchers at the college level, at least, do not need or want highly complex searching ability....Some searches may be frustrating with such limitations...."

She concludes, "Overall the Quanta version has merit. It does have limitations...but the price is great. It all boils down to a question of how valuable your time is to you. If you value your time and want a product that searches all the fields at the same time and that allows proximity searching, then this is not for you. However, one can argue that most people don't really need such sophistication....One can get by with the searching capability provided by ROMware. Once can actually create a search of a particular word in several fields—or all fields, if necessary; but this takes extra time and typing. This disc is worth the price. One can always go online if one needs to get fancy. I don't think the searching software provided by OCLC and SilverPlatter really justify the cost. I recommend this disc for all libraries that have an interest in agricultural topics."

DeForest Glendale reviewed the Quanta version of AGRICOLA, too, and he concluded, "Overall, this product receives an 'A' for presentation....the disc was fast; the software was easy to use—perhaps not quite as intuitive as I would have liked, but that may be a function of the documentation....I give the documentation a 'C,' about average. For convenience, I give the disc an 'A.' It's just 'put in the disc and go.'...So, overall, I give this product a solid 'B,' and I can't wait to get an updated version of this....I give them a big 'A+' for phone support. I was extremely happy to be so well-received."

Martin Courtois of the Science Library at Michigan State University puts AGRICOLA on his list of important research CD-ROM databases. He remarks, "Along with CAB Abstracts, I think this is one of the essential databases in agriculture....[It] provides the most thorough indexing of publications from USDA agencies, such as Cooperative Extension Service, Agricultural Experiment Stations, etc., which aren't covered as thoroughly in CAB Abstracts. I have heard criticism that AGRICOLA is not as comprehensive as CAB, doesn't include as many abstracts (which is true), the indexing is not as good, and it misses many publications which do show up in CAB....for nearly all searches in agriculture, unique citations can be found in both AGRICOLA and CAB Abstracts. The CD database is priced much lower than CABCD, which makes it the database of choice for agriculture schools on a budget."

The Colborne and Nicholls article, cited below, discusses the OCLC and SilverPlatter versions of AGRICOLA. It points out that "SilverPlatter's coverage is more comprehensive, going back to 1970." They concede that "In terms of coverage, SilverPlatter has the edge over OCLC, but much depends on other database requirements of the library." They note that "AGRICOLA...would be particularly appropriate for libraries with a strong plant or animal science program."

Ted Sibia, in evaluating SilverPlatter's version of AGRICOLA, noted that, "AGRICOLA on compact disk has been a very useful addition to our reference collection....The search station is very popular and in constant use." He continues, "Users are pleased to retrieve important literature in a short time. They are impressed with the powerful search language that permits access to topics by using multiple concepts. This would be impossible to do with the printed version." He concludes, "The CD-ROM edition of AGRICOLA has opened the way for many library patrons to find helpful material in a short time and with a great degree of confidence."

Editor

REVIEWS

OCLC

Colborne, David and Paul Nicholls. "Biology on Disc: CD-ROM Databases for the Non-Medical Academic Life Sciences Collection." *Laserdisk Professional* 3 (January 1990): 91-96.

Quanta Press

Glendale, DeForest. "Ergonomically Speaking: Agricola by Quanta Press." 1 (March 1990): 88-89.

Tryon, Julia R. "Optical Product Review: Agricola." *CD-ROM Librarian* 5 (June 1990): 32-34.

SilverPlatter

Charles, Susan K. and Katharine E. Clark. "Enhancing CD-ROM Searches with Online Updates: An Examination of End-User Needs, Strategies, and Problems." *College and Research Libraries* 51 (July 1990): 321-328.

Colborne, David and Paul Nicholls. "Biology on Disc: CD-ROM Databases for the Non-Medical Academic Life Sciences Collection." *Laserdisk Professional* 3 (January 1990): 91-96.

Sibia, T.S. "AGRICOLA." *Laserdisk Professional* 1 (May 1988): 100-101.

EQUIPMENT AND SOFTWARE REQUIREMENTS

OCLC
Computer: IBM PC or compatible with hard disk and 640K RAM; Macintosh
Software: DOS 3.2 or higher, MS-DOS Extensions
CD-ROM Drive: any IBM-compatible, Apple

Quanta Press
Computer: IBM PC, XT, AT, PS/2, or compatible with 512K RAM
Software: DOS 3.0 or higher, MS-DOS Extensions
CD-ROM Drive: any IBM-compatible

SilverPlatter
Computer: IBM PC XT, AT, PS/2, or 100 percent compatible with hard disk, 640K RAM; Macintosh Plus, SE, or II
Software: DOS 2.1 or higher, may use MS-DOS Extensions
CD-ROM Drive: Toshiba, Hitachi, Philips, Sony, DEC, or Apple

PRICE

OCLC annual price: $695, $595 for OCLC members, renewal $100 less; retrospective file, 1979-1982, one-time purchase: $350, $300 for OCLC members

Quanta Press annual price: $395; one-time cost, no updates: $99

SilverPlatter annual price: $650, current disc; current disc and archival set, first year: $1,200, subsequent years: $650; archival set, one-time purchase: $650

ARRANGEMENT AND CONTROL

OCLC
Record fields: accession number, added entry, added entry-series, additional physical form note, augmented title, author, conference name, contents note, contents type, corporate author, country of publication, current frequency, date of data collection note, date of publication, descriptors, dissertation note, edition statement, file characteristics, former frequency, former titles or variations, frequency, funding note, government document classification number, holding library/call number, host item entry, identifiers, imprint, ISBN, ISSN,

item number, key title, language, language of summary, linking entry complexity note, locally assigned LC-type class number, main series entry, mathematical map data, NAL call number, NAL subject category codes, nonspecific relationship entry, physical description, place of publication, preceding entry, publication type, publishing agency, publishing agency code, romanized title, series, short title, source of data file data, subseries, succeeding entry, summary note, supplement/special series entry, technical details, title, translation of title, uniform title, update date, variant access title, varying forms of title
Searchable: all but accession number, ISBN, ISSN, NAL call number, locally assigned LC-type class number, edition statement, mathematical map data, physical description, current frequency, frequency, former frequency, date of data collection note, additional physical form note, funding note, source of data file data, linking entry complexity note, holding library/call number, publishing agency code, update

Quanta Press
Record fields: accession number, author, call number, catalog code, CODEN, descriptors, language, notes, publication type, publication year, publishing agency, source, title, update code
Searchable: all

SilverPlatter
Record fields: abstract, accession number, author, author affiliation, call number, catalog code, notes, CODEN, content notes, corporate author, country of publication, descriptors, identifiers, interest level, ISSN, language, notes, original title, publication type, publication year, publishing agency, series title, source, subfiles, title, update
Searchable: all

SEARCH SOFTWARE AND CAPABILITIES

OCLC
Software: Search CD450
Capabilities: keyword, Boolean, search statement retention and back referencing, field searching, field limiting, proximity searching, printing, downloading, index searching, truncation, nesting, varied display formats

Quanta Press
Software: ROMware by Nimbus
Capabilities: keyword, Boolean, index searching, printing, downloading, field searching, sorting, varied display formats

SilverPlatter
Software: SilverPlatter
Capabilities: keyword, Boolean, search statement retention and back referencing, field searching, field limiting, proximity searching, printing, downloading, index searching, truncation, search saving, nesting, varied display formats

PRINT/ONLINE/OTHER MEDIA COUNTERPARTS
Print: *National Agricultural Library Catalog, Bibliography of Agriculture*
Online: AGRICOLA — DIALOG, BRS, DIMDI

NETWORK LICENSING ARRANGEMENTS

OCLC No additional charge

Quanta No additional charge

SilverPlatter No additional charge

TITLE AGRICULTURE LIBRARY

PUBLISHER Producer: OCLC
Vendor: OCLC

SCOPE AND CONTENT
A selected database compiled from the Online Union Catalog. Agriculture Library contains bibliographic records pertaining to agriculture, food production, forestry, fisheries, and veterinary medicine. It spans the twentieth century and includes references to materials printed as early as 1543. Coverage is international, and includes books, serials, sound recordings, musical scores, maps, manuscripts, audiovisual materials, and software. It contains over 300,000 bibliographic records. Updates are provided annually. (Publisher's brochure)

For its long-term span, broad coverage of material formats and range of agriculture topics, Agriculture Library is a highly desirable CD-ROM database for any library interested in agriculture. The breadth of coverage available in the OCLC Union Catalog is unmatched, and only in the last few years has this material been accessible by subject. Although the material is now accessible by subject through the EPIC online system, Agriculture Library provides the kind of focus that is difficult to get when doing subject searching of the entire OCLC catalog. The Search CD450 interface is quite acceptable for research purposes. The database's only weakness is its lack of abstracting, but this is understandable considering its origin from library cataloging.

Editor

EQUIPMENT AND SOFTWARE REQUIREMENTS
Computer: IBM PC or compatible with hard disk and 640K RAM; Macintosh
Software: DOS 3.2 or higher, MS-DOS Extensions
CD-ROM Drive: any IBM-compatible, Apple

PRICE Annual price: $350; OCLC members: $300

ARRANGEMENT AND CONTROL
Record fields: OCLC record number, title, author, LC call number, Dewey call number, government document number, report number, date, contents, language, publisher, place of publication, physical description, publication type, intellectual level, notes, series, subject code, subject headings
Searchable: all but physical description

SEARCH SOFTWARE AND CAPABILITIES
Software: Search CD450
Capabilities: keyword, Boolean, search statement retention and back referencing, field searching, field limiting, proximity searching, printing, downloading, index searching, truncation, nesting, varied display formats

PRINT/ONLINE/OTHER MEDIA COUNTERPARTS
Online: OCLC Online Union Catalog — EPIC

NETWORK LICENSING ARRANGEMENTS
No additional charge

TITLE AGRIS

PUBLISHER Producer: United Nations Food and Agricultural Organization
Vendor: SilverPlatter

SCOPE AND CONTENT
International information for the agricultural sciences and technology produced

by the AGRIS Coordinating Centre of the U.N. Food & Agricultural Organization. Covers all aspects of agriculture, including animal husbandry, aquatic sciences and fisheries and human nutrition from over 135 participating countries. The literature covered includes scientific and technical reports, theses, conference papers and more. There are 150,000 records added per year with keywords in French and Spanish. The archival disc covers from 1986 to 1988, the current from 1989. Updating is quarterly. (Publisher's brochure)

AGRIS is an important database covering the international agricultural literature, including a variety of formats and a backfile going back five years. The SilverPlatter interface is quite useful for research purposes. An added strength is the addition of keywords in French and Spanish. The weakness of AGRIS is its lack of abstracts, but it is still quite useful for libraries with a research interest in agriculture.

Paul Nicholls rates AGRIS, based on "...the database, the SilverPlatter system, and rather steep price tag...," giving it four out of a possible four stars. He gives data quality four stars, and search power and ease of use three stars.

Editor

REVIEWS
Nicholls, Paul T. *CD-ROM Collection Builder's Toolkit: the Complete Handbook of Tools for Evaluating CD-ROMS.* Weston, CT: Pemberton Press, 1990.

EQUIPMENT AND SOFTWARE REQUIREMENTS
Computer: IBM PC XT, AT, PS/2, or 100 percent compatible with hard disk, 640K RAM; Macintosh Plus, SE, or II
Software: DOS 2.1 or higher, may use MS-DOS Extensions
CD-ROM Drive: Toshiba, Hitachi, Philips, Sony, DEC, or Apple

PRICE Annual price: $750; archival disc: $700; both: $1,350

ARRANGEMENT AND CONTROL
Record fields: accession number, author, category codes, country of input, descriptors, language, notes, publication type, publication year, series/title information, source, title, update code
Searchable: all

SEARCH SOFTWARE AND CAPABILITIES
Software: SilverPlatter
Capabilities: keyword, Boolean, search statement retention and back refer-

encing, field searching, field limiting, proximity searching, printing, downloading, index searching, truncation, search saving, nesting, varied display formats.

PRINT/ONLINE/OTHER MEDIA COUNTERPARTS
Print: *AGRINDEX*
Online: AGRIS — DIALOG, DIMDI, ESA/IRS, FAO

NETWORK LICENSING ARRANGEMENTS
Contact vendor

TITLE AQUATIC SCIENCES AND FISHERIES ABSTRACTS

PUBLISHER Producer: Cambridge Scientific Abstracts
Vendor: Cambridge Scientific Abstracts

SCOPE AND CONTENT
Compiled from worldwide sources in both English and other languages. The disc includes abstracts from 5,000 journals, key reports, monographs, dissertations, gray literature and proceedings from United Nations sponsored ASFISS system. Backfiles to 1982 with updating provided quarterly. (Publisher's brochure)

Aquatic Sciences and Fisheries Abstracts has long been relied upon as an exemplary research database related to water resources and the water environment. Those interested in the public use of water, environmental health, and other related areas will find this database absolutely essential. The excellent research capabilities provided by Cambridge Scientific Abstracts make accessible an international database covering a wide variety of material formats. The backfile of material is extensive, and the subject focus makes for a usable body of information. In addition, abstracts are provided. This database has no real flaws as a research resource for those interested in the areas covered.

Martin Courtois of the Michigan State University Science Library puts Aquatic Sciences and Fisheries Abstracts on his list of important CD-ROM research databases. He points out, "This is a very comprehensive bibliographic database for the serious researcher on the science, technology, and management of marine or freshwater environments. I think it's best for aquaculture, aquatic biology, and environmental studies, and fisheries, but it covers a host of other areas: water pollution, coastal management, ocean technology, climatology, etc. Information is gathered from various U.N. agencies, so the undergraduate or casual researcher may be dismayed and disappointed at the number of foreign and/or difficult to find citations. But for someone doing a more comprehensive search, it's a good complement to other sources...."

Peter Brueggeman reviewed Aquatic Sciences and Fisheries Abstracts, describing its use at Scripps Institution of Oceanography. He pointed out, "The command mode uses the same commands as menus but with greater versatility....Searches are more quickly consummated with no menus to follow step by step....The command mode is learned quickly and is greatly preferred by continuing searchers." He concluded, "Reaction to the ASFA disks from the SIO's 190 graduate students and 270 academics has been extremely positive."

Colborne and Nicholls, cited below, note that, "One of the most attractive aspects of this search software is the consistency of the menu and command interfaces. End-users can progress smoothly from menu mode to the command mode." They also note "ASFA would serve the information needs of a library with a strong marine biology program."

Chuck Huber commented in his review that "ASFA-CD has become a very popular tool in our library, which serves a large marine science department. Its comprehensive coverage of any topic interacting with the freshwater or marine environments has made it useful to a wide range of patrons. Cambridge's menu system has proven both easy for new users and powerful enough to satisfy experienced users." He notes, "In practice, we've found the Menu mode to be identical in power to the Command mode and flexible enough that experienced users do not feel slowed by the Menu format." He concludes, "Judging from the high use of the ASFA-CD here, it can safely be recommended for any science library where patrons may have an interest in freshwater or oceanic studies of any kind."

James Harrington recently reviewed Aquatic Sciences and Fisheries Abstracts on CD, and concluded, "On a scale of 1 to 5, I would rate this product a 3. The DISPLAY layout is well done....The search software disappointed me most. As an experienced searcher, I had no trouble using the Command mode, but, in comparison to other products I have used, I found the Menus mode awkward." He continues, "On the plus side, I do like the way the program prompts the user to limit a search statement to particular fields."

David P. Allen, in his review, gave as pluses for Aquatic Sciences and Fisheries Abstracts, "Unique database available only from Cambridge Scientific Abstracts. Very efficient and powerful proprietary search software used with other CSA CD-ROM products." As minuses, he finds, "Confusing installation procedure not properly updated to accommodate latest hardware developments. Limited CD-ROM drive installation compatibility with poorly defined work-around."

Editor

REVIEWS

Allen, David P. "CD-ROM Title Reviews: Aquatic Sciences and Fisheries Abstracts." *CD-ROM EndUser* 2 (July 1990): 58-60.

Brueggeman, Peter. "ASFA on CD-ROM at Scripps Institution." *Laserdisk Professional* 1 (March 1988): 39-47.

Colborne, David and Paul Nicholls. "Biology on Disc: CD-ROM Databases for the Non-Medical Academic Life Sciences Collection." *Laserdisk Professional* 3 (January 1990): 91-96.

Harrington, James. "Optical Product Review: Aquatic Sciences and Fisheries Abstracts." *CD-ROM Librarian* 5 (November 1990): 41-45.

Huber, Chuck. "CD-ROM in Brief: Aquatic Sciences and Fisheries Abstracts." *CD-ROM Professional* 3 (July 1990): 100-101.

Marshall, K. E. "A Critique of Compact Cambridge Aquatic Sciences and Fisheries Abstract (ASFA) CD-ROM (2.1)." *Marine Science Information Throughout the World.* Miami: International Association of Marine Science Libraries and Information Centers, 1989, pp. 255-266.

EQUIPMENT AND SOFTWARE REQUIREMENTS

Computer: IBM PC, XT, AT, PS/2, or compatible with hard disk and 640K RAM
Software: DOS 3.1 or higher, MS-DOS Extensions
CD-ROM Drive: any IBM-compatible

PRICE Annual price: $2,495 for current year and last two years; $4,995 for current year and backfile to 1982; renewal for any of the above: $1,395

ARRANGEMENT AND CONTROL

Record fields: abstract, abstract language, author, author affiliation, classification code, conference date, conference location, conference name, corporate entry, descriptors, editor, environmental regime, language, new material,

note, number, original title, publication year, source, subfile, title
Searchable: all

SEARCH SOFTWARE AND CAPABILITIES
Software: Cambridge Scientific Abstracts
Capabilities: keyword, Boolean, field searching, printing, downloading, field limiting, index searching, varied display formats, search saving, search statement retention and back referencing, proximity searching, truncation, nesting

PRINT/ONLINE/OTHER MEDIA COUNTERPARTS
Print: *Aquatic Sciences and Fisheries Abstracts*
Online: Aquatic Sciences and Fisheries Abstracts — DIALOG, CAN/OLE, DIMDI, ESA/IRS

NETWORK LICENSING ARRANGEMENTS
No additional charge

TITLE ARCTIC & ANTARCTIC REGIONS (COLD REGIONS)

PUBLISHER Producer: Library of Congress, National Science Foundation, U.S. Army Cold Regions Research and Engineering Lab
Vendor: NISC—National Information Services Corporation

SCOPE AND CONTENT
Search the entire forty years of the bibliography on cold regions science and technology and twenty-seven years of Antarctic bibliography abstracts and titles. Compiled by the Library of Congress on behalf of the National Science Foundation and U.S. Army Cold Regions Research and Engineering Lab, Arctic & Antarctic Regions provides over 258,000 citations on one single disc. It now includes databases ASTIS (Arctic Science and Technology Information System), C-CORE, CITATION, SPRILIB (Scott Polar Research Institute Library), and AORIS. Backfiles are to 1950, updated semiannually. (Publisher's brochure)

Peter Brueggeman notes that, "Source items include journal articles, technical reports, books, conference papers, maps, and patents....The Cold Regions database contributes over 112,000 records and focuses on the physics and mechanics of snow, ice, glaciers, and frozen ground (permafrost) and all aspects of cold regions navigation and civil engineering, including materials science and equipment operation."

"The Antarctic Bibliography database contributes over 35,000 records and attempts to include all significant Antarctic material published worldwide in all disciplines. It covers Antarctic biology, geology, engineering, medicine, meteorology, oceanography, atmospheric physics, geophysics, and political and social science."

"The Arctic Science and Technology Information System (ASTIS) database, produced by the Arctic Institute of North America in Calgary, Alberta, Canada, contributes over 29,000 records. ASTIS emphasizes the Canadian Arctic, but it includes some material on other Arctic regions....The C-CORE database, produced by the Cold Ocean Resources Engineering Center, St. Johns, Newfoundland, Canada, contributes over 20,000 records. C-CORE focuses on ocean engineering in cold regions."

"The Citation database, produced by the World Data Center A for Glaciology, Boulder, Colorado, contributes over 25,000 records. It focuses on the physical properties and characteristics of ice, glaciers, and permafrost. The Scott Polar Research Institute Library (SPRILIB) database, produced by the Scott Library at the University of Cambridge, England, contributes over 30,000 records. SPRILIB covers polar regions worldwide (including Antarctica); it contains books and periodicals received and cataloged into the library's collection."

This database is an exemplar of focused subject coverage useful to research. Any institutions with research interests in the world environment, cold regions in particular, and cold conditions will find this database essential. The coverage is international, abstracts are provided for most items, the backfile is wonderfully long, and a variety of material formats are covered. On the down side, some of the citations do not have abstracts, but, generally, this is a highly useful database for research in its subject areas.

Peter Brueggeman noted in his review of A&AR, "Due to this amalgamation of individual databases, the Arctic & Antarctic Regions CD-ROM is quickly becoming the premier information source for north and south polar regions with no online or printed equivalent. If you need access to polar literature, this is it."

He concludes, "Overall the search software and database are very good. Most inexperienced searchers can readily use AAR; onscreen hints and ondisc F1 help will answer most questions. The search software has powerful and highly developed features. Particularly noteworthy is the capability to download in standardized record formats for subsequent importing into personal database software. AAR is indispensable for any individual or institution with Arctic or Antarctic research interests."

Editor

REVIEWS
Brueggeman, Peter. "Optical Product Review: Arctic & Antarctic Information." 5 *CD-ROM Librarian* (December 1990): 39-43.

EQUIPMENT AND SOFTWARE REQUIREMENTS
Computer: IBM PC, XT, AT, PS/2 Model 30, or compatible with 512K RAM
Software: DOS 3.1 or higher, MS-DOS Extensions
CD-ROM Drive: any IBM-compatible

PRICE Annual price: $795

ARRANGEMENT AND CONTROL
Record fields: bibliographic elements, keywords, language, broad disciplinary concepts, publication date, document type
Searchable: all

SEARCH SOFTWARE AND CAPABILITIES
Software: Dataware (customized), CD-Answer
Capabilities: keyword, Boolean, novice search mode, field searching, proximity searching, truncation, nesting, index searching, search saving, sorting, printing, downloading

PRINT/ONLINE/OTHER MEDIA COUNTERPARTS
Print: *Antarctic Bibliography*, *Current Antarctic Literature*, *Bibliography on Cold Regions Science and Technology*
Online: Cold Regions — ORBIT

NETWORK LICENSING ARRANGEMENTS
Contact vendor

TITLE ART INDEX

PUBLISHER Producer: H.W. Wilson Co.
Vendor: H.W. Wilson Co.

SCOPE AND CONTENT

Offers an international perspective on archaeology, architecture, art history, city planning, computer applications and computer graphics, crafts, film, folk art, graphic arts, industrial design, interior design, landscape architecture, museology, painting, photography, sculpture, television, textiles, and video. It covers 226 leading art publications from around the world. The disc indexes major English-language periodicals, yearbooks, and museum bulletins, as well as European periodicals published in French, Italian, German, Spanish, Dutch, and Swedish. It provides access to a wide range of bibliographies, notices of competitions and awards, reports of conferences, anthologies in periodicals, exhibition listings, review articles, interviews, and film reviews, as well as significant editorials and letters to the editor. Also, the disc serves as a comprehensive record of reproductions of works of art that appear anywhere in any of the publications indexed. Coverage back to 1984, updated quarterly. (Publisher's brochure)

Art Index is the only CD-ROM currently available that provides a reasonable basis for fine art research. It covers international periodicals, as well as other formats of materials. It has a fairly good sized backfile. Through the Wilsonline access method on Wilsondisc, complete, albeit not very user friendly, searching can be done to support research in the arts.

Art Index does not have abstracts and covers a comparatively small number of periodicals, but it is the primary source currently available in the fine arts on CD-ROM.

Editor

EQUIPMENT AND SOFTWARE REQUIREMENTS

Computer: IBM PC, XT, AT, 386, PS/2, or compatible with hard disk with 1 megabyte of space available and 640K RAM, Hercules graphics or better, modem for online updating
Software: DOS 3.1 or higher, MS-DOS Extensions
CD-ROM Drive: any IBM-compatible

PRICE Annual price: $1,495

ARRANGEMENT AND CONTROL

Record fields: author, title, journal title, citation, publication date, subject headings, special features
Searchable: all but citation

SEARCH SOFTWARE AND CAPABILITIES
Software: Wilsondisc
Capabilities: keyword, Boolean, search statement retention and back referencing, field searching, proximity searching, printing, downloading, truncation, thesaurus, online updating, novice search mode, search saving, automatic singular and plural, nesting, local holdings display

PRINT/ONLINE/OTHER MEDIA COUNTERPARTS
Print: *Art Index*
Online: Art Index — BRS, Wilsonline

NETWORK LICENSING ARRANGEMENTS
No additional charge for in-building access; contact Wilson for remote access charges.

TITLE BIBLIOGRAPHIE NATIONALE FRANÇAISE DEPUIS 1975 SUR CD-ROM

PUBLISHER Producer: Bibliothèque Nationale
Vendor: Chadwyck-Healey

SCOPE AND CONTENT
The first publication, in any form, of the cumulated national bibliography since 1975. The French National Bibliography on CD-ROM contains more than 390,000 records. The disc contains the records of all titles received by the Bibliothèque Nationale through legal deposit since 1975. Records are taken from the *Bibliographie de la France* (BGF), its supplement *Publications Officielles* and, for new titles not yet listed in the BGF, legal deposit. Updated quarterly. (Publisher's brochure)

Essential to research in any aspect of France, and areas covered in French publications in the last fifteen years, this bibliographic database provides data not accumulated anywhere else. By its very nature, this database provides access to an immensely broad array of materials in a variety of formats. The backfile is lengthy, and the searching interface provides adequate access to the materials listed.

On the other hand, the interface is sometimes awkward for complex searches, and, as one might expect, no abstracts are included. Naturally, researchers using this must be familiar with French. For institutions that support strong research programs concerning France, though, this database should be extremely useful.

Anthony Angiletta of Stanford University notes, "...the common software interface is a plus and the software itself is quite flexible and useful for both browsing and hard-citations searching by patrons and for collection development or management purposes by librarians....I have found [it] a boon to a collection evaluation project that I am conducting on West European social sciences and the hypothesis of a general decline in North American accessions. Subject and keyword searching in Bibliographie Nationale Française...ha[s] been essential to individual country studies as well as cross-national ones. In addition, assuming that work is completed on the postwar backfiles, one can trace authors or subjects or presses longitudinally, a task hopelessly filled with drudgery now."

Editor

EQUIPMENT AND SOFTWARE REQUIREMENTS
Computer: IBM PC, XT, AT, PS/2, or compatible with hard disk and 640K RAM
Software: DOS 3.1 or higher, MS-DOS Extensions
CD-ROM Drive: any IBM-compatible

PRICE Annual price: $1,000

ARRANGEMENT AND CONTROL
Record fields: author, title, series title, publisher, publication date, country of publication, language, bibliographic information, subject, place of publication, ISBN
Searchable: all

SEARCH SOFTWARE AND CAPABILITIES
Software: Chadwyck-Healey
Capabilities: keyword, Boolean, search statement retention and back referencing, field searching, field limiting, printing, downloading, index searching, truncation, varied display formats, nesting, thesaurus, menus and help messages in German, English, Italian, or French

PRINT/ONLINE/OTHER MEDIA COUNTERPARTS
Print: *Bibliographie de la France, Publications Officielles*

NETWORK LICENSING ARRANGEMENT
Contact publisher.

TITLE BIBLIOGRAPHY OF MEXICAN RESEARCH

PUBLISHER Producer: National University of Mexico
Vendor: Multiconsult SC

SCOPE AND CONTENT
Bibliography of Mexican research up to 1986 in the areas of history, literature, agronomy, chemistry, mathematics, astronomy, geophysics, nuclear engineering, oil engineering, industrial engineering, oceanography, health sciences, pharmaceutics, psychology, and zoology. The database is updated annually. Over 32,000 records are included. (Publisher's brochure)

Due to its specialized subject focus, this database may be of interest to organizations supporting research in Mexican topics. The subjects covered in this context are broad. Although, of course, the focus is on Mexico, within this context, it is a unique research support source.

Editor

EQUIPMENT AND SOFTWARE REQUIREMENTS
Computer: IBM PC, XT, AT, or compatible with 20MB hard disk and 512K RAM

PRICE Annual price: $420

NETWORK LICENSING ARRANGEMENTS
Contact vendor

TITLE BIOGRAPHY INDEX

PUBLISHER Producer: H.W. Wilson Co.
Vendor: H.W. Wilson Co.

SCOPE AND CONTENT
More than 2,700 periodicals of every kind are indexed. Current English-

language books including more than 1,800 works of individual and collective biography annually are also covered. Autobiographies, journals, memoirs, diaries, letters, interviews, bibliographies, and obituaries are indexed. Fiction (biographical novels), drama, pictorial works, poetry, juvenile literature, and biographical information from otherwise nonbiographical works round out the picture. Coverage is from July 1984 to present with updates provided quarterly. (Publisher's brochure)

Biography Index is the only purely biographical database on CD-ROM, and, as such, constitutes an important research source. Covering a large number of otherwise unindexed materials, this disc could be a useful acquisition for almost any institution. The strengths of the database include the coverage of a variety of material formats, the backfile, and the research capabilities of the Wilsondisc interface. The weaknesses include the lack of both abstracts and an international focus. Useful for historic and current research, Biography Index is worthy of consideration for a CD-ROM collection.

Carol Doyle commented about Biography Index, "The main use of BIOGRAPHY INDEX (BI) in any format is straightforward searching by a biographee's name. For such use, the disk format lends little advantage over the print besides covering multiple years in one search and giving the option to print citations. Considering the price, the short time span covered weakens this product's utility."

She concludes, "This product is recommended for school, public and academic libraries, whose need for finding biographical material from access points besides the biographee's name is sufficient to justify BIOGRAPHY INDEX ONDISC's relatively high-cost."

Editor

REVIEWS

Doyle, Carol. "CD-ROM in Brief: Biography Index Ondisc." *CD-ROM Professional* 4 (January 1991): 76-77.

EQUIPMENT AND SOFTWARE REQUIREMENTS

Computer: IBM PC, XT, AT, 386, PS/2, or compatible with hard disk with 1MB of space available and 640K RAM, Hercules graphics or better, modem for online updating

Software: DOS 3.1 or higher, MS-DOS Extensions

CD-ROM Drive: any IBM-compatible

PRICE Annual price: $1,095

ARRANGEMENT AND CONTROL
Record fields: author, title, journal title, citation, publication date, subject headings, special features
Searchable: all but citation

SEARCH SOFTWARE AND CAPABILITIES
Software: Wilsondisc
Capabilities: keyword, Boolean, search statement retention and back referencing, field searching, proximity searching, printing, downloading, truncation, thesaurus, online updating, novice search mode, search saving, automatic singular and plural, nesting, local holdings display

PRINT/ONLINE/OTHER MEDIA COUNTERPARTS
Print: *Biography Index*
Online: Biography Index — BRS, Wilsonline

NETWORK LICENSING ARRANGEMENTS
No additional charge for in-building access; contact Wilson for remote access charges.

TITLE BIOLOGICAL ABSTRACTS

PUBLISHER Producer: BIOSIS
Vendor: SilverPlatter

SCOPE AND CONTENT
Developed by BIOSIS, the world's largest abstracting and indexing service for the life sciences. This product is a basic research tool for those in the biological and biomedical fields. Entries include bibliographic citations and abstracts of current research reported in these fields. It provides searchable information on authors' institutional affiliations and language information for all citations. Over 9,000 periodicals are indexed for inclusion in the database. Approximately 250,000 records are indexed each year. Coverage starts with the 1990 calendar year; updates provided quarterly. (Publisher's brochure)

This is the world's most important database in the biological sciences. No CD-ROM collection of any institution interested in life science and medical research would be complete without it. The incredible breadth and scope of the subject coverage, the presence of abstracts, the international scope, and the capabilities of the SilverPlatter retrieval software all make this a well-developed database in the life sciences field. The weaknesses are the focus on periodical coverage (see next entry) and the lack of a backfile; the latter will, of course, change with time. This database is absolutely essential for biological research.

Martin Courtois, of Michigan State University's Science Library, feels Biological Abstracts belongs on a list of important research CD-ROMs, but has some reservations about it. "No one will argue that BA is the major life sciences database and that any library supporting graduate research in biology, biochemistry, microbiology, plant and animal science, or medicine will probably consider getting BA on CD. Yet we chose Cambridge Life Sciences Collection over BA for several reasons: a roller-coaster pricing strategy that made it difficult to determine what BA actually cost...; severely limited coverage of back-years...that has only recently been extended to 1989; and the fact that Life Sciences, while it covers just a little more than half of BA's 9000 journal titles, still provides access to the major publications in the life sciences. In a few years, when a decent backfile is built for BA on CD, it may be a more viable product."

Paul Nicholls calls Biological Abstracts "Probably the most important general bioscience database available...." As he notes, "Reviews are yet to appear, but on the basis of the database (not quite as complete as the online version) and well-known SilverPlatter system...," this rating would seem likely: four stars overall, of a possible four, four stars for data quality, and three stars for search power and ease of use.

Editor

REVIEWS
Nicholls, Paul T. *CD-ROM Collection Builder's Toolkit: the Complete Handbook of Tools for Evaluating CD-ROMS.* Weston, CT: Pemberton Press, 1990.

EQUIPMENT AND SOFTWARE REQUIREMENTS
Computer: IBM PC XT, AT, PS/2, or 100 percent compatible with hard disk, 640K RAM; Macintosh Plus, SE, or II
Software: DOS 2.1 or higher, may use MS-DOS Extensions
CD-ROM Drive: Toshiba, Hitachi, Philips, Sony, DEC, or Apple

PRICE Price: $8,325, non-U.S.: $9,155; print or microfilm subscribers: $4,100, non-U.S.: $4,510; subscribers to print or microfilm, and index: $2,300, non-U.S.: $2,530. 1990 price: $7,660, non-U.S.: $8,425; print or microfilm subscribers: $3,685, non-U.S.: $4,055; subscribers to print or microfilm, and index: $2,000, non-U.S.: $2,200. 1991 price: $7,190, non-U.S.: $7,910; print or microfilm subscribers: $3,475, non-U.S.: $3,820; subscribers to print or microfilm, and index: $1,900, non-U.S.: $2,090

ARRANGEMENT AND CONTROL

Record fields: abbreviated journal, abstract, author, author affiliation, biosystematic codes, CODEN, concept codes, corporate source, descriptors, journal announcement, language, language of summary, major concept codes, minor concept codes, publication year, source, super taxa, title, update
Searchable: all

SEARCH SOFTWARE AND CAPABILITIES

Software: SilverPlatter
Capabilities: keyword, Boolean, search statement retention and back referencing, field searching, field limiting, proximity searching, printing, downloading, index searching, truncation, search saving, nesting, varied display formats

PRINT/ONLINE/OTHER MEDIA COUNTERPARTS

Print: *Biological Abstracts*
Online: BIOSIS — DIALOG, BRS, CAN/OLE, Data-Star, DIMDI, ESA/IRS, Japan Information Center of Science and Technology, JIPNET, STN

NETWORK LICENSING ARRANGEMENTS

$1,500 additional for up to eight workstations

TITLE BIOLOGICAL ABSTRACTS/RRM

PUBLISHER Producer: BIOSIS
Vendor: SilverPlatter

SCOPE AND CONTENT

Biological Abstracts/RRM was developed by BIOSIS, the world's largest abstracting and indexing service for the life sciences. RRM stands for "Reports, Reviews, Meetings." BA/RRM on CD contains citations in English that identify research literature in biology and biomedicine.

BA/RRM on CD provides extensive and unique references to papers from international meetings and symposia, books, book chapters, and review publications. Citations from this state-of-the-art reference tool are derived from the world's largest life science database—BIOSIS Previews—which includes references from approximately 9,000 serials worldwide. In 1991, an estimated 260,000 invaluable references will be recorded on BA/RRM on CD. Plus, a backfile will be available on CD-ROM, covering references recorded in 1989 and 1990. Updates are quarterly.

For 1990 the geographical breakdown was as follows: 48 percent from Europe and the Middle East, 28 percent from North America, 16 percent from Asia and Australia, 6 percent South and Central America, and 2 percent from Africa. (Publisher's brochure)

BA/RRM remedies one of the weaknesses of the Biological Abstracts database on its own (see previous entry). This database provides access to much literature other than periodicals in the broad areas of biology and biomedicine. This increases access to much otherwise fugitive literature in these vital areas. Any institution supporting medical and life sciences research could profit from this database. The coverage is international, and the SilverPlatter interface is useful for research.

The database does have some drawbacks; it may well be more difficult than usual to retrieve the literature cited. The backfile is small, and abstracts are not included. This will still be useful for serious biological research.

Editor

EQUIPMENT AND SOFTWARE REQUIREMENTS
Computer: IBM PC XT, AT, PS/2, or 100 percent compatible with hard disk, 640K RAM; Macintosh Plus, SE, or II
Software: DOS 2.1 or higher, may use MS-DOS Extensions
CD-ROM Drive: Toshiba, Hitachi, Philips, Sony, DEC, or Apple

PRICE 1991 disc: $4,240, non-U.S.: $4,665; for BA/RRM print subscribers: $2,105, non-U.S.: $2,315; for BA/RRM and BA/RRM Cumulative subscribers: $1,175, non-U.S.: $1,290; 1989-90 disc: $7,805, non-U.S.: $8,585; for BA/RRM print subscribers: $3,870, non-U.S.: $4,255; for BA/RRM and BA/RRM Cumulative Index subscribers: $2,215, non-U.S.: $2,435

ARRANGEMENT AND CONTROL
Record fields: abstract, author, biosystematic codes, book source, CODEN,

concept codes, corporate source, descriptors, document type, ISBN, journal announcement, language, language of summary, major concept codes, meeting information, minor concept codes, original title, publication year, publisher information, source, super taxa, title, update code
Searchable: all

SEARCH SOFTWARE AND CAPABILITIES
Software: SilverPlatter
Capabilities: keyword, Boolean, search statement retention and back referencing, field searching, field limiting, proximity searching, printing, downloading, index searching, truncation, search saving, nesting, varied display formats

PRINT/ONLINE/OTHER MEDIA COUNTERPARTS
Print: *Biological Abstracts/RRM*
Online: BIOSIS — DIALOG, BRS, CAN/OLE, Data-Star, DIMDI, ESA/IRS, Japan Information Center of Science and Technology, JIPNET, STN

NETWORK LICENSING ARRANGEMENTS
$1,500 additional for up to eight workstations

TITLE BRITISH LIBRARY GENERAL CATALOGUE OF PRINTED BOOKS TO 1975 ON CD-ROM

PUBLISHER Producer: SAZTEC Europe Ltd., The British Library
Vendor: Chadwyck-Healey

SCOPE AND CONTENT
If the sum of human knowledge could be found anywhere it would probably be The British Library. No other library can match the riches and variety of its resources for research into every aspect of human thought and achievement. It is one of the world's very few general and universal libraries with sufficiently comprehensive collections to satisfy the specialist, and it has the scale and depth of the collections that underlie the importance of the catalogue.

The British Library contained (at 1975) over 8,500,000 volumes of which only 53 percent were in English. Almost every book published in the United Kingdom is represented on the shelves of The British Library through copyright deposit and through collections, such as the Royal Library given by George II and the great collections that came from George IV, Joseph Banks, and Thomas Grenville.

It has the largest number of pre-1914 imprints of any library in the world and some of its special foreign collections of pre-twentieth-century works are more complete than in any country of origin. Percentages of other major languages are French (14 percent), German (6 percent), Slavonic and East European (4 percent) and Spanish and Portuguese (4 percent). Titles in Cyrillic, Greek and Hebrew and other non-Roman alphabets comprise 3 percent of the total.

The CD-ROM publication consists of a set of three CD-ROM discs, which can now be accessed on an inexpensive personal computer. The catalogue includes all entries for pre-1975 imprints acquired and catalogued by The British Library prior to 1976 and all pre-1971 imprints acquired and catalogued before the end of 1982. (Publisher's brochure)

The British Library is one of the foremost libraries of the western world. Its collections in English and other languages are an incredibly varied research resource in all subject fields. This CD-ROM now makes this bibliographic treasure widely available.

The General Catalogue does not, of course, abstract its materials, and this database only comes up to 1975 in its coverage. The search interface has some awkwardness in dealing with complicated searches. That said, however, this database is an excellent research source, especially for the humanities and social sciences. The international coverage is amazingly broad, the time period covered is vast, and the variety of material formats is quite useful. The search interface does provide sufficient access for such a bibliographic database. Any research institution should consider acquisition of this database.

Pat Riesenman, reference librarian at Indiana University, notes that the General Catalogue has the "same general system as Bowker stuff, but system drawbacks [are] less bothersome than with PAIS [original version]—fairly useful for research."

Editor

EQUIPMENT AND SOFTWARE REQUIREMENTS
Computer: IBM PC, XT, AT, PS/2, or compatible with hard disk and 640K RAM; Hercules Extended Graphics Plus card or compatible
Software: DOS 3.1 or higher, MS-DOS Extensions
CD-ROM Drive: any IBM-compatible

PRICE Price: $16,500; payment over three years: $19,500 in three payments of $6,500 each

ARRANGEMENT AND CONTROL
Record fields: author, title, publisher, publication date, bibliographic information, subject, place of publication, shelfmark, ISBN
Searchable: all

SEARCH SOFTWARE AND CAPABILITIES
Software: Chadwyck-Healey
Capabilities: keyword, Boolean, search statement retention and back referencing, field searching, field limiting, printing, downloading, index searching, truncation, varied display formats, nesting, thesaurus

PRINT/ONLINE/OTHER MEDIA COUNTERPARTS
Print: *General Catalogue of Printed Books*

NETWORK LICENSING ARRANGEMENTS
No additional charge for multiusers

TITLE BRITISH NATIONAL BIBLIOGRAPHY ON CD-ROM

PUBLISHER Producer: The British Library
Vendor: Chadwyck-Healey

SCOPE AND CONTENT
Easy and rapid access to British publishing since 1950. Contains more than one million detailed and authoritative records. The backfile contains all records from the BNB for the period 1950-1985 and is complete on two discs. The current file covers the period 1986 onwards. Updating is provided quarterly. (Publisher's brochure)

For those interested in almost any topic, especially one that has a British focus or slant, the British National Bibliography on CD-ROM provides a wealth of bibliographic information on items published in Britain in the last forty years. The coverage, of course, because of the scope of the database, is focused on British imprints, and no abstracts are provided, but a vast variety of materials are covered, and the backfile is large. The software provided can be a bit clumsy for elaborate searches, but is suitable for this type of bibliographic database.

Anthony Angiletta of Stanford University notes, "...the common software interface is a plus and the software itself is quite flexible and useful for both browsing and hard-citations searching by patrons and for collection development or management purposes by librarians....I have found [it] a boon to a collection evaluation project that I am conducting on West European social sciences and the hypothesis of a general decline in North American accessions. Subject and keyword searching in...the BNB on CD-ROM...ha[s] been essential to individual country studies as well as cross-national ones. In addition, assuming that work is completed on the postwar backfiles, one can trace authors or subjects or presses longitudinally, a task hopelessly filled with drudgery now."

Editor

EQUIPMENT AND SOFTWARE REQUIREMENTS
Computer: IBM PC, XT, AT, PS/2, or compatible with hard disk and 640K RAM
Software: DOS 3.1 or higher, MS-DOS Extensions
CD-ROM Drive: any IBM-compatible

PRICE Annual price: $1,900; backfile, one-time purchase: $6,900

ARRANGEMENT AND CONTROL
Record fields: author, title, series title, publisher, publication date, country of publication, language, bibliographic information, subject, place of publication, ISBN
Searchable: all

SEARCH SOFTWARE AND CAPABILITIES
Software: Chadwyck-Healey
Capabilities: keyword, Boolean, search statement retention and back referencing, field searching, field limiting, printing, downloading, index searching, truncation, varied display formats, nesting, thesaurus

PRINT/ONLINE/OTHER MEDIA COUNTERPARTS
Print: *British National Bibliography*
Online: BLAISE-LINE
Other Media: Books in English — microfiche

NETWORK LICENSING ARRANGEMENTS
No additional charge for multiusers

TITLE BRITISH NEWS INDEX

PUBLISHER Producer: Research Publications
Vendor: Research Publications

SCOPE AND CONTENT
Now available on one CD-ROM disc. Fast, reliable access to indexes for *The Times of London, The Sunday Times of London, The Sunday Times of London Magazine, The Times of London Higher Education Supplement, The Times of London Literary Supplement, The Times of London Educational Supplement* (English and Scottish editions), *The Financial Times, The Independent,* and *The Independent on Sunday.*

Browse a complete day's news reports in minutes. Search instantaneously by headline, title, keywords, journalist, subject, indexing terms, month, and day. Search across all news sources or just within one source. View the information...Print it out...Download it; create a thorough media bibliography in minutes.

Find names, subjects, topics faster, easier, and more precisely with root-word and adjacency search features. Researchers can now perform high-speed searches on precisely assigned index terms, concise article summaries, article titles, journalist's name, and issue dates to locate pertinent information.

Searches can be of a sole news source or across many or all current media. In seconds, the exact location of relevant articles—by publication name, date, page number, and column position—is displayed for all retrieved items.

The first British News Index CD-ROM disc covers 1990 and the first three months of 1991. Cumulatively updated BNI discs are sent quarterly by subscription—eventually, about five years' indexing will be accessible on one disc. (Publisher's brochure)

Newspapers are a necessary research source in some fields, although they may not be the first source one thinks of using. Newspapers can provide useful information for researchers in history, political science, international affairs, sociology, public affairs, criminology, health, business, education, and the humanities. The British News Index could be of use to researchers in all of these areas, especially, of course, to those interested in the United Kingdom and the Commonwealth. The British News Index should also provide vital information to those who are interested in other parts of Europe and those who might want to research how the United States is viewed overseas.

The database is easy to install and use, and provides an amazing number of research capabilities, considering the simplicity of its software. The editor was able to learn to use it fairly easily with an occasional glance at the documentation in about fifteen minutes. One especially nice feature is the ability to download records in a variety of formats, not just ASCII. One can also save search strategies to disc and rerun them.

Due to its scope, of course, this CD-ROM only covers newspapers, but factors that make it of interest for research are the article summaries it provides (although they are brief), its international scope, its unique subject and material coverage, and the searching capabilities of the software. Of course, the backfile is very short now, but will increase. This CD-ROM database should be of interest to those institutions supporting researchers in aspects of the United Kingdom, the Commonwealth, and the rest of Europe.

Editor

EQUIPMENT AND SOFTWARE REQUIREMENTS
Computer: IBM PC or compatible with hard disk and 640K RAM
Software: DOS 3.2 or higher, MS-DOS Extensions
CD-ROM Drive: any IBM-compatible

PRICE Annual price: $1,750

ARRANGEMENT AND CONTROL
Record fields: abstract, column, date, index terms, journalist, newspaper, page, publication code, title
Searchable: all but publication code

SEARCH SOFTWARE AND CAPABILITIES
Software: Dataware
Capabilities: keyword, Boolean, field searching, proximity searching, printing, downloading, index searching, truncation, search saving, varied display formats, sorting

PRINT/ONLINE/OTHER MEDIA COUNTERPARTS
Print: Print indexes to *The Times of London, The Sunday Times of London, The Sunday Times of London Magazine, The Times of London Higher Education Supplement, The Times of London Literary Supplement, The Times of London Educational Supplement* (English and Scottish editions), *The Financial Times, The Independent, The Independent on Sunday.*

NETWORK LICENSING ARRANGEMENTS
Two to four local network nodes: 2 x license fee; five to seven nodes: 3 x license fee; eight to ten nodes: 4 x license fee; over ten nodes: 5 x license fee

---

TITLE BUSINESS DATELINE ONDISC

PUBLISHER Producer: University Microfilms International/Data Courier
Vendor: UMI/Data Courier

SCOPE AND CONTENT
Business Dateline Ondisc contains articles from more than 180 regional business journals, daily newspapers, and business wire services. Researchers can use the database to locate over 150,000 hard-to-find articles about the companies, people, and events shaping the regional and national business scene. The database gives your researchers business information they might otherwise have missed. Each Business Dateline Ondisc record contains full bibliographic and indexing information, plus the complete text (in ASCII format) of articles about mergers, acquisitions, expansions, and failures; business executives; new products and new trends in marketing and production; business and industries in particular areas; business conditions in selected cities, states, or regions; niche markets; smaller divisions of large corporations; and much more.

Business Dateline Ondisc features the same easy-to-use software as other UMI Ondisc products, including a powerful "tab" function that allows researchers to quickly pinpoint their search subject in the database's full-text records.

Business Dateline Ondisc includes the current disc, backfile discs from 1985 forward, which are yours to keep, and updated discs every month. (Publisher's brochure)

Business Dateline is a prime example of a database that is misunderstood and underrated by many who believe they know what it contains. It does contain "merely" regional business information, but the world of business is made up of what happens in regions. Small business forms a much larger part of the world of business than do large nationally known corporations; even large corporations have regional aspects.

Regional business journal articles often include invaluable information as to what business people actually do in their work, background statistics about national industries, hard-to-find information about business people, and little known aspects of nationwide companies. This database not only indexes such material; it provides full texts of it. This is a prime example of the value a database can provide.

Researchers in business may have to be persuaded to believe it, but this CD-ROM will provide them with a world of otherwise hard-to-find information and is an end source in itself. Obviously due to its scope, it is not trying to provide international coverage, nor does it cover anything but periodicals and 3 wire services. The nature of the database, the unique information it provides, and the length of the backfile all make it, nonetheless, invaluable in business research.

Editor

EQUIPMENT AND SOFTWARE REQUIREMENTS
Computer: IBM PC or compatible with hard disk and 640K RAM
Software: DOS 3.2 or higher, MS-DOS Extensions
CD-ROM Drive: any IBM-compatible

PRICE Annual price: $2,950

ARRANGEMENT AND CONTROL
Record fields: article text, author, codes, companies, date, dateline, document type, issue, journal, journal code, length, names, section, SIC, terms, title, volume
Searchable: all

SEARCH SOFTWARE AND CAPABILITIES
Software: UMI/Data Courier
Capabilities: keyword, Boolean, search statement retention and back referencing, field searching, proximity searching, printing, downloading, index searching, truncation, automatic searching of singular and plural, nesting, varied display formats, library holdings display

PRINT/ONLINE/OTHER MEDIA COUNTERPARTS
Online: Business Dateline — DIALOG, BRS, Dow Jones, Human Resource Information Network, NEXIS, VU/TEXT

NETWORK LICENSING ARRANGEMENTS
Additional $100 per node/terminal

TITLE CAB ABSTRACTS

PUBLISHER Producer: Commonwealth Agricultural Bureau
Vendor: SilverPlatter

SCOPE AND CONTENT
The only major agricultural database with abstracts. Over 10,000 journals are scanned for inclusion in CAB Abstracts as well as books, conference reports and other kinds of literature published worldwide. Subjects covered include: animal and crop husbandry, animal and plant breeding and plant protection, genetics, forestry engineering, economics, veterinary medicine, human nutrition, rural development, leisure and tourism. Approximately 130,000 records are added annually. International coverage is from 1984; updating is annual. (Publisher's brochure)

CAB Abstracts is the premiere research database in the field of agriculture. It covers the contents of over fifty abstracting journals in all areas of agriculture. Its coverage is international, and includes a wide number of formats of material. It has a fairly good size backfile, and the SilverPlatter searching capabilities are excellent for serious research. The abstracts are more extensive than those of any comparable agriculture database. CAB Abstracts has no weaknesses as a research database, and it should be in an library supporting agriculture research.

Martin Courtois of Michigan State University's Science Library says about CAB Abstracts, "This is the major database in agriculture, and also provides excellent coverage in nutrition and veterinary medicine....CAB seems to have much more of a research focus than AGRICOLA. The emphasis in CAB is on research journals, and one seldom finds citations to the more ephemeral materials such as reports, technical bulletins, circulars, etc., that are more common in AGRICOLA. Still, it is my experience that unique citations on most agriculture research topics can be found in both CAB and AGRICOLA. CAB is the primary research database on CD, but with its price at 4-5 times that of AGRICOLA, I think many libraries that are forced to choose only one CD-ROM in this area will select AGRICOLA."

Paul Nicholls says, "Reviews are yet to appear, but likely to be positive and approximate..." these ratings: an overall four stars of a possible four, with four stars for data quality, and three stars for search power and ease of use.

Editor

REVIEWS

Nicholls, Paul T. *CD-ROM Collection Builder's Toolkit: the Complete Handbook of Tools for Evaluating CD-ROMS.* Weston, CT: Pemberton Press, 1990.

EQUIPMENT AND SOFTWARE REQUIREMENTS

Computer: IBM PC XT, AT, PS/2, or 100 percent compatible with hard disk, 640K RAM; Macintosh Plus, SE, or II
Software: DOS 2.1 or higher, may use MS-DOS Extensions
CD-ROM Drive: Toshiba, Hitachi, Philips, Sony, DEC, or Apple

PRICE Annual price: $2,750, Vol. III (1990-1992); Vol. 1 (1984-1986) one-time fee: $2,750; Vol. II (1987-1989) one-time fee: $5,500; Vol. III (1990-1992), prepaid, one-time fee: $6,600

ARRANGEMENT AND CONTROL

Record fields: abstract, accession number, address of author, author, availability, CAB Abstracts publication data, corporate author, descriptors, geographic headings, ISBN, language, language of summary, original title, publication type, publication year, secondary journal citation, source, subjects, title
Searchable: all but availability and secondary journal citation

SEARCH SOFTWARE AND CAPABILITIES

Software: SilverPlatter
Capabilities: keyword, Boolean, search statement retention and back referencing, field searching, field limiting, proximity searching, printing, downloading, index searching, truncation, search saving, nesting, varied display formats

PRINT/ONLINE/OTHER MEDIA COUNTERPARTS

Print: *AgBiotech News and Information, Agricultural Engineering Abstracts, Agroforestry Abstracts, Animal Breeding Abstracts, Animal Disease Occurrence, Apicultural Abstracts, Arid Lands Development Abstracts, Biocontrol News and Information, Biodeterioration Abstracts, Crop Physiology Abstracts, Dairy Science Abstracts, Faba Bean Abstracts, Field Crop Abstracts, Forest Products Abstracts, Forestry Abstracts, Helminthological Abstracts, Herbage Abstracts, Horticultural Abstracts, Index Veterinarius, Irrigation*

and Drainage Abstracts, Leisure, Recreation and Tourism Abstracts, Maize Abstracts, Nematological Abstracts, Nutrition Abstracts and Reviews Series A—Human and Experimental, Nutrition Abstracts and Reviews Series B—Livestock Feeds and Feeding, Ornamental Horticulture, Pig News and Information, Plant Breeding Abstracts, Plant Growth Regulator Abstracts, Postharvest News and Information, Potato Abstracts, Poultry Abstracts, Protozoological Abstracts, Review of Agricultural Entomology, Review of Medical and Veterinary Entomology, Review of Medical and Veterinary Mycology, Review of Plant Pathology, Rice Abstracts, Rural Development Abstracts, Rural Extension, Education and Training Abstracts, Seed Abstracts, Soils and Fertilizers, Sorghum and Millets Abstracts, Soyabean Abstracts, Sugar Industry Abstracts, Veterinary Bulletin, Weed Abstracts, Wheat, Barley and Triticale Abstracts, World Agricultural Economics and Rural Sociology Abstracts
Online: CAB Abstracts — DIALOG, BRS, CAN/OLE, DIMDI, ESA/IRS, Japan Information Center of Science and Technology

NETWORK LICENSING ARRANGEMENTS
1984-1990: two to ten users — $24,000; eleven plus users — $30,000. 1987-1990: two to ten users — $18,000; eleven plus users — $22,500. 1991-1992: two to ten users — $8,000; eleven plus users — $10,000. 1990 only: two to ten users — $6,000; eleven plus users — $7,500

TITLE CAB ABSTRACTS—ANIMAL SCIENCE

PUBLISHER Producer: Commonwealth Agricultural Bureau
Vendor: SilverPlatter

SCOPE AND CONTENT
A comprehensive new CD product covering the field of animal science. It includes all thirteen of CABI's abstract journal series pertaining to veterinary medicine, animal health, and animal production from the CAB Abstracts database. It consists of two CDs spanning the years 1973 to the present, and contains a total of approximately 700,000 records. Annual updates will deliver approximately 50,000 additional records. (Publisher's brochure)

Veterinary and animal science research facilities will welcome this focused subset of the vitally important CAB Abstracts database. As a whole, CAB Abstracts has virtually no flaws as a research database, with its abstracts, international coverage, decent-sized backfile, coverage of a variety of material formats, and use of the widely accepted SilverPlatter interface. This subset has those features and is limited down to the material useful in animal science. This should be an exciting product for researchers in that area.

Editor

EQUIPMENT AND SOFTWARE REQUIREMENTS
Computer: IBM PC XT, AT, PS/2, or 100 percent compatible with hard disk, 640K RAM; Macintosh Plus, SE, or II
Software: DOS 2.1 or higher, may use MS-DOS Extensions
CD-ROM Drive: Toshiba, Hitachi, Philips, Sony, DEC, or Apple

PRICE Annual price for updates: $1,700; one-time purchase price, 1973 to mid-1991: $7,500

ARRANGEMENT AND CONTROL
Record fields: abstract, accession number, address of author, author, availability, CAB Abstracts publication data, corporate author, descriptors, geographic headings, ISBN, language, language of summary, original title, publication type, publication year, secondary journal citation, source, subjects, title
Searchable: all but availability and secondary journal citation

SEARCH SOFTWARE AND CAPABILITIES
Software: SilverPlatter
Capabilities: keyword, Boolean, search statement retention and back referencing, field searching, field limiting, proximity searching, printing, downloading, index searching, truncation, search saving, nesting, varied display formats

PRINT/ONLINE/OTHER MEDIA COUNTERPARTS
Print: *Animal Breeding Abstracts*, *Animal Disease Occurrence*, *Apicultural Abstracts*, *Dairy Science Abstracts*, *Helminthological Abstracts*, *Index Veterinarius*, *Nematological Abstracts*, *Nutrition Abstracts and Reviews Series B—Livestock Feeds and Feeding*, *Pig News and Information*, *Poultry Abstracts*, *Protozoological Abstracts*, *Review of Agricultural Entomology*, *Review of Medical and Veterinary Entomology*, *Review of Medical and Veterinary Mycology*, *Veterinary Bulletin*
Online: CAB Abstracts — DIALOG, BRS, CAN/OLE, DIMDI, ESA/IRS, Japan Information Center of Science and Technology

NETWORK LICENSING ARRANGEMENTS
Contact vendor

TITLE CANADIAN BUSINESS AND CURRENT AFFAIRS

PUBLISHER Producer: Micromedia Limited
Vendor: DIALOG

SCOPE AND CONTENT
DIALOG Ondisc Canadian Business and Current Affairs gives you instant access to information on Canadian national and local activities, news, business, politics, education, social issues, arts, sports and leisure. This comprehensive source of important information, covering 1981 through the current year, is available on a single compact disc, updated quarterly.

The information in DIALOG Ondisc Canadian Business and Current Affairs is compiled by Micromedia Limited of Toronto. Each year, Micromedia indexes 220,000 articles from 200 business periodicals, 340 magazines, and ten newspapers, including the *Globe and Mail*, the *Toronto Star*, and the *Montreal Gazette*.

In addition, the database combines five key Canadian reference sources: *Canadian Business Index*, *Canadian News Index*, *Canadian Magazine Index*, *Bibliography of Works on Canadian Foreign Relations*, and the *Ontario Securities Commission Filings*. (Publisher's brochure)

Since this is the only database that devotes itself to Canadian matters, it is worthy of consideration as a research resource for any library supporting inquiry about this vital country. Since it covers a broad topic area, it should be of interest to anyone studying North American business, public affairs, foreign relations, sociology, humanities, and many other areas.

It uses the excellent DIALOG searching interface, has an excellent geographic focus for its purpose, covers a variety of material formats, and is unique in its material indexing. Although it does not have abstracts, for its purpose it is unique and essential.

Paul Nicholls, in *CD-ROM Collection Builder's Toolkit*, says "...CBCA offers the most comprehensive coverage of this literature available and is indispensable for any public, school, academic or special library needing access to Canadian sources." He gives it four out of a possible four stars.

Editor

REVIEWS
CD-ROM Professional 3 (issue 4, 1990): 105-107.

Nicholls, Paul T. *CD-ROM Collection Builder's Toolkit: the Complete Handbook of Tools for Evaluating CD-ROMS.* Weston, CT: Pemberton Press, 1990.

EQUIPMENT AND SOFTWARE REQUIREMENTS
Computer: IBM PC, XT, AT, PS/2, or compatible, 512K RAM minimum, 640K RAM recommended
Software: DOS 3.1 or higher, MS-DOS Extensions
CD-ROM Drive: any IBM-compatible

PRICE Annual price: $1,450

ARRANGEMENT AND CONTROL
Record fields: author, availability, CanCorp number, company, corporate source, descriptors, ISSN, journal name, language, named person, note, publication date, publication type, publisher, special features, title, trade name
Searchable: all

SEARCH SOFTWARE AND CAPABILITIES
Software: DIALOG Ondisc
Capabilities: keyword, Boolean, search statement retention and back referencing, field searching, field limiting, proximity searching, printing, downloading, index searching, novice mode, varied display formats, nesting, truncation, search saving, online updating, sorting, online document ordering, thesaurus

PRINT/ONLINE/OTHER MEDIA COUNTERPARTS
Print: *Canadian Business Index, Canadian News Index, Canadian Magazine Index, Bibliography of Works on Canadian Foreign Relations, Ontario Securities Commission Filings.*
Online: Canadian Business and Current Affairs — DIALOG, CAN/OLE, QL Systems Ltd.

NETWORK LICENSING ARRANGEMENTS
Double the single user fee (above) for two to ten workstations.

TITLE CANCER-CD

PUBLISHER Producer: Elsevier Science Publishers, Year Book Medical Publishers, National Cancer Institute
Vendor: SilverPlatter

SCOPE AND CONTENT
References, abstracts, and commentaries of the world's literature in cancer and related subjects from Elsevier Science Publishers, Year Book Medical Publishers, and the complete CANCERLIT file from the National Cancer Institute in conjunction with the National Library of Medicine. Contains material from more than 3000 journals in both English and other languages along with conference papers, books, symposia reports, monographs, dissertations, and doctoral theses. SilverPlatter has merged duplicate citations into one record while preserving information that is unique to each Information Provider. Updated quarterly, the database covers current year plus five previous years. (Publisher's brochure)

Fryer, Baratz, and Helenius found that Cancer-CD "...is easy to use despite the multifile aspects. However, searching the descriptor field can be tricky, because Elsevier/EMBASE and the National Library of Medicine assign different subject headings." They concluded, "CANCER-CD is an important tool for those involved in cancer treatment, research, and education. It is appropriate to a variety of settings such as oncologists' offices, Comprehensive Cancer Centers, and health science libraries. This CD-ROM version includes more information than the online CANCERLIT file. CANCER-CD is a good choice for comprehensive cancer information."

Cancer-CD is the epitome of an excellent combined research source in oncology. The combination of several sources, including the broad CANCERLIT database, into one CD-ROM research collection makes this a vital source in the area of cancer studies. The international coverage, the breadth of access to cancer topics, the inclusion of a variety of formats, the good-size backfile, the inclusion of abstracts, and the capabilities of the SilverPlatter software all make this an essential database in its field. It would be vital to any medical research institution. It really has no weaknesses as a research source.

Editor

REVIEWS
CD-ROM Lab Report 1 (June 1988): 16-17.

Fryer, R.K., N. Baratz, and M. Helenius. "Beyond Medline: a Review of Ten Non-Medline CD-ROM Databases for the Health Sciences." *Laserdisk Professional* 2 (May 1989): 27-39.

MD Computing 6 (issue 1, 1989): 12-19.

EQUIPMENT AND SOFTWARE REQUIREMENTS
Computer: IBM PC XT, AT, PS/2, or 100 percent compatible with hard disk, 640K RAM; Macintosh Plus, SE, or II
Software: DOS 2.1 or higher, may use MS-DOS Extensions
CD-ROM Drive: Toshiba, Hitachi, Philips, Sony, DEC, or Apple

PRICE Annual price: $1,500

ARRANGEMENT AND CONTROL
Record fields: address of author, author's abstract, CANCERLIT accession number, CANCERLIT subset, CODEN, contributing database, country of publication, EMBase accession number, EMBase descriptors, EMTags, ISSN, language, major MeSH headings, Medical Subject Headings, original title, publication type, publication year, source, title
Searchable: all

SEARCH SOFTWARE AND CAPABILITIES
Software: SilverPlatter
Capabilities: keyword, Boolean, search statement retention and back referencing, field searching, field limiting, proximity searching, printing, downloading, index searching, truncation, search saving, nesting, varied display formats

PRINT/ONLINE/OTHER MEDIA COUNTERPARTS
Print: *Excerpta Medica, Section 16: Cancer*, *Year Book of Cancer*, *CANCERGRAMS*
Online: CANCERLIT — DIALOG, BRS, Data-Star, DIMDI, Japan Information Center of Science and Technology, Karolinska Institutets Bibliotek och Informationscentral, MEDLARS

NETWORK LICENSING ARRANGEMENTS
$2,500 for multiusers

TITLE CERAMIC ABSTRACTS

PUBLISHER Producer: American Ceramic Society
Vendor: NISC—National Information Services Corporation

SCOPE AND CONTENT
Over 100,000 citations and abstracts from the American Ceramic Society, Inc. covers all the world's scientific, engineering, and commercial literature pertaining to ceramics and related materials, including processing and manufacturing aspects. Subjects include abrasives, art, design, cements, plasters, glass, clay, semiconductors, superconductors, ferroelectrics, magnetic materials, nuclear materials, production processes and equipment, etc. Coverage is back to 1976, with semiannual updates. (Publisher's brochure)

Ceramic science is a vitally important area in current technology, and this database provides an essential focus for those doing research in this area. It combines international coverage, abstracts, a very good backfile, an easy to use, yet powerful, interface, and an excellent subject focus. It also covers all formats of materials. In short, it has no real weaknesses as a research database. Ceramic Abstracts is highly recommended to institutions interested in this area.

Editor

EQUIPMENT AND SOFTWARE REQUIREMENTS
Computer: IBM PC, XT, AT, PS/2, or compatible with 512K RAM
Software: DOS 3.1 or higher; MS-DOS Extensions
CD-ROM Drive: any IBM-compatible

PRICE Annual price: $695

ARRANGEMENT AND CONTROL
Record fields: abstract, abstract number, author, CODEN, descriptor, document type, ISBN, journal announcement, journal name, language, patent assignee, patent country, patent number, publication year, publisher, section heading, source information, title
Searchable: all

SEARCH SOFTWARE AND CAPABILITIES
Software: Dataware CD-Answer
Capabilities: keyword, Boolean, novice search mode, field searching, proximity searching, truncation, nesting, index searching, search saving, sorting, printing, downloading

PRINT/ONLINE/OTHER MEDIA COUNTERPARTS
Print: *Ceramic Abstracts*
Online: Ceramic Abstracts — DIALOG, ORBIT

NETWORK LICENSING ARRANGEMENTS
Contact vendor

TITLE CHICANO DATABASE

PUBLISHER Producer: Chicano Studies Library, University of California, Berkeley
Vendor: Chicano Studies Library

SCOPE AND CONTENT
Contains bibliographic citations on the Chicano experience. Includes segments of the *Chicano Periodicals Index* (1967-1988), *The Chicano Index* (1989-present), *Arte Chicano: An Annotated Bibliography of Chicano Art* (1965-1981), and *The Chicano Anthology Index.* (*CD-ROMs in Print*, Meckler Publications, 1991)

The Chicano Database fills a niche in the CD-ROM research world, and should be of great interest to almost any organization supporting research in sociology, psychology, public affairs, political science, art, literature—any area which needs to research the vital subject area of Chicanos. Although the database does not have abstracts, it is broad in coverage of types of material, has a lengthy backfile, and uses a research-capable interface.

In a recent review of Chicano Database, Salvador Guerena comments, "This is a long-awaited milestone in the effort to improve access to the growing interdisciplinary body of literature in the field of Chicano studies. The Chicano Database is unique in its culturally sensitive, uniform subject access to the sources it indexes. Indexing terms are based on the Chicano Thesaurus, which was designed to overcome the inadequacies prevalent in many traditional indexing sources."

He feels, "Novices should have few problems getting it because of the simple searching structure, yet the software is flexible enough to accommodate the demands of more sophisticated searchers wishing to create and manipulate sets with Boolean operators."

He concludes, "This product has been developed in response to a specialized information need involving the growing Chicano/Latino population. The *Chicano Periodical Index*, which makes up much of the database, is endorsed by the National Association for Chicano Studies and by the Chicano Information Management Consortium of California."

"There is no other like product on the market. The producers plan to continue the practice of selectively indexing articles published in mainstream or non-Chicano journals and magazines. Owing to the broad range of sources indexed, libraries should consider purchasing The Chicano Database, even if their holdings of Chicano periodicals are minimal."

Editor

REVIEWS
Guerena, Salvador. "CD-ROM in Brief: Chicano Database on CD-ROM." *CD-ROM Professional* 4 (March 1991): 88-89.

EQUIPMENT AND SOFTWARE REQUIREMENTS
Computer: IBM PC, AT, XT, or compatible with 640K RAM
Software: DOS 3.1 or higher, MS-DOS Extensions
CD-ROM Drive: any IBM-compatible

PRICE Annual price: $495

ARRANGEMENT AND CONTROL
Record fields: author, date, index terms, language, supplementary terms, title
Searchable: all

SEARCH SOFTWARE AND CAPABILITIES
Software: KAware2
Capabilities: keyword, Boolean, search statement retention and back referencing, field searching, index searching, printing, varied display formats

PRINT/ONLINE/OTHER MEDIA COUNTERPARTS
Print: *Chicano Periodicals Index, The Chicano Index, Arte Chicano: An Annotated Bibliography of Chicano Art, The Chicano Anthology Index*

NETWORK LICENSING ARRANGEMENTS
Contact vendor

TITLE CITIS CD-ROM

PUBLISHER Producer: CITIS, Ltd.
Vendor: CITIS, Ltd.

SCOPE AND CONTENT

International Civil Engineering Abstracts (40,000 records) and software abstracts for engineers (4,000 plus records). It covers Civil/Environmental Engineering and computer program abstracts with three search modes: novice, intermediate, and expert. The disc indexes over 400 journals. The CITIS CD-ROM is the only CD-ROM database providing details of commercially available computer programs for the construction industry. An English/German thesaurus is incorporated, which enables keyword searching in English or German. Updating is semiannual with backfiles available to 1972. (Publisher's brochure)

Crucial for any engineering research institution, CITIS is an important source in civil and environmental engineering. It is international in scope and indexes journals and software—it is unique in its coverage of the latter. Abstracts are provided, and the backfile is extensive. The BRS/Search software has long been tested as a searching interface, and supports research well. In fact, this database is completely useful as a research resource in civil engineering and is recommended to all engineering institutions.

Kathy Jackson reviewed this database at length, and concluded, "When making the purchasing decision, we were primarily interested in ICEA. However, we also purchased SAFE for one year, more or less as a trial, because of the special pricing available. I do not think that SAFE will be as popular as ICEA. Computer technology is advancing so rapidly, that the information on software in SAFE will quickly become outdated, especially since it will be updated only annually. Also, the European focus makes it less attractive than other software directories and databases."

"Most users will quickly move past the novice mode and will generally search in the intermediate mode. A few users will graduate to the expert mode. Those who do should not have trouble searching in the expert mode if they have used other online systems."

"I do think, however, that librarians will have to provide more support to users when they are printing, downloading, or displaying from these databases, because of the nature of these functions. I hope that the producers of the databases will review these features. They should look at other products...which have more direct and simpler methods for displaying and manipulating search results. The search software is adequate, but not failsafe. I managed to crash the system several times—once by simply not having the printer online."

"I look forward to introducing our civil engineers to ICEA, because some of their questions are difficult to deal with, and we do not always find satisfactory answers in the traditional tools to which we normally turn. Architects should also be interested in this database. While many of the publications included are European, the major American civil engineering and construction publications are indexed. Test searches on difficult topics were very productive."

Editor

REVIEWS
Jackson, Kathy. "International Civil Engineering Abstracts and Software Abstracts for Engineers—Two European Imports Which Use Modified BRS Search Software." *Laserdisk Professional* 2 (November 1989): 115-128.

EQUIPMENT AND SOFTWARE REQUIREMENTS
Computer: IBM PC, AT, XT, or compatible with 640K RAM
Software: DOS 3.0 or higher, MS-DOS Extensions
CD-ROM Drive: any IBM-compatible

PRICE Annual price: $1,125, $2,250 for archival file; for International Civil Engineering Abstracts only: $825 annual price, $1,650 for archival file; for software abstracts for engineers only: $600 annual price, $975 for archival file

ARRANGEMENT AND CONTROL
Record fields: author, title, abstract, descriptor, language, country of origin, year of publication, journal, name of program, name and address of software firm, computers supported, program summary, price, keywords
Searchable: all

SEARCH SOFTWARE AND CAPABILITIES
Software: BRS/Search
Capabilities: keyword, Boolean, search statement retention and back referencing, field searching, field limiting, proximity searching, printing, downloading, truncation, novice search mode, sorting, varied display formats, nesting, index searching, English/German thesaurus

PRINT/ONLINE/OTHER MEDIA COUNTERPARTS
Print: *International Civil Engineering Abstracts*, *Software Abstracts for Engineers*

NETWORK LICENSING ARRANGEMENTS
Contact vendor

TITLE COMPACT LIBRARY: AIDS

PUBLISHER Producer: San Francisco General Hospital, National Library of Medicine, Bureau of Hygiene and Tropical Diseases (U.K.), American Foundation for AIDS Research, Medical Publishing Group
Vendor: Maxwell Electronic Publishing

SCOPE AND CONTENT
Compact Library: AIDS holds a complete library of medical information on AIDS, including a growing list of respected sources. It includes:

AIDS Knowledge Base — An electronic reference book written and continually updated by over fifty clinicians at the San Francisco General Hospital and the University of California, San Francisco.

AIDS-Related Citations from MEDLINE — More than 25,000 AIDS-related bibliographic citations and abstracts from the National Library of Medicine's MEDLINE database.

AIDS Database from the Bureau of Hygiene and Tropical Diseases (London) — Bibliographic references and critical abstracts of papers on all viruses in the HIV/HTLV family and AIDS-related retroviruses and associated infections.

American Foundation for AIDS Research AIDS/HIV Experimental Treatment Directory — A directory of compounds being tested in the treatment of AIDS and HIV infection. A listing of current clinical trials follows a detailed description of each compound.

Articles from leading publications — More than 5,000 full-text articles about AIDS selected from the leading biomedical journals.

About 3,400 journals are indexed and the database is updated quarterly. (Publisher's brochure)

This database provides incredible research value for its cost in a vitally important research area for any biomedical/life sciences program. Exemplifying what a well-rounded and useful database can be, Compact Library: AIDS combines a number of useful databases that include a lot of full-text material, which can all be searched simultaneously. Full-text and directory information is included, as well as journal article citations. The focus is international and the backfile extends to the relevant time period for AIDS research. Obviously, abstracts and full text are provided. There is no more well-rounded source of AIDS information available, and the searching interface, which is sufficiently sophisticated and user-friendly, completes the picture of an unparalleled database.

A producer of Compact Library: AIDS, Bart Rubenstein, said in an interview in *Database*, "We most definitely employ hypertext on our discs. The most innovative feature is that they link together related information from full-text and bibliographic databases. We make it very easy for a user who lands in one place, either because he did a search and found a hit or because he is browsing through text, to move directly to related information without executing an independent search. All he has to do is hit a key or click the mouse to immediately call up the related information."

Fryer, Baratz, and Helenius, in evaluating Compact Library: AIDS' search software, find that, "The Medical Publishing Group has put together a user-friendly and innovative product that makes searching easy by utilizing function keys, windows, and menus." For ease of use, "Compact Library: AIDS allows sophisticated searching with a user-friendly interface. Its 'linking' ability is at present unique, but should be incorporated in all multi-database CD-ROMs."

They conclude, "This CD-ROM will be an instant hit with anyone involved in AIDS research, AIDS patient care, and AIDS issues. It represents CD-ROM technology at its best; one can search for information on one part of the disk and in many cases find full-text articles on another part of the disc. It will be used extensively in medical, hospital, or departmental libraries."

The review in *CD-ROM EndUser*, cited below, lists as Compact Library: AIDS' pluses, "Thorough collection of virtually all published information on the nature of AIDS and treatment of those afflicted. Excellent product support; 800 number service. Supports use of mouse as option. De-install software also provided." There were no minuses that are currently in effect.

The review continues, "...the treatment of the subject is exhaustive." It finds that the "...unrehearsed 'look and lead' method of exploring a database is to be applauded for its virtue of making highly technical information much more easily available and useful to the casual non-professional in the AIDS field....it is clear that the publishers are working diligently to add to the benefit of the search software with more powerful features."

Reinhard Wentz evaluated Compact Library: AIDS and concluded, "The direct or indirect involvement of four renowned institutions would appear to guarantee the future development and maintenance of this important database. It represents an example of a well-organized, current and easy-to-use computerized information system with impeccable credentials of authority. It has been received at the Kobler Centre with great enthusiasm by all health-care workers requiring information on AIDS-related subjects."

"Interestingly, the versatility and comprehensiveness of Compact Library: AIDS suggested to some clinicians that it might be used as an expert system (although not specifically designed for this purpose) and actually assist in different diagnosis and evaluation of treatment options."

Norman Desmarais reviewed Compact Library: AIDS in detail, and concluded, "Compact Library: AIDS offers extensive information from a variety of sources on its subject. It uses powerful search software and demonstrates impressive hypertext capabilities. As a pioneer in the use of hypertext on CD-ROM, the product shows some rough edges in this area. Undoubtedly, future editions will refine these features and add new ones as we learn more about hypertext and its capabilities."

In the *Bulletin of the Medical Library Association*, Regina Fryer notes, "Compact Library: AIDS is a comprehensive collection of the most recent AIDS research and clinical material from around the world. It offers a new and exciting approach to information retrieval without the financial burden of online fees....The Medical Publishing Group has put together a user-friendly, innovative product that makes searching easy by employing a combination of function keys, windows, and menus."

"Compact Library: AIDS is easy to use and provides clear explanations. The online 'help' screens are very good and can be invoked at any point in the program. The system makes superb use of color. The user manual is well written and contains a tutorial, and demonstration diskette is available. Dial-up support via an '800' number is available Monday through Friday from 9:00 A.M. to 5:00 P.M."

"In summary, Compact Library: AIDS offers an electronic textbook, bibliographic information, full-text journal articles, and an experimental treatment directory all on one disc. The rich contents of this CD-ROM, the financial savings over online systems, and the time savings to end users combine to make this a valuable resource. It will be used extensively by anyone involved in AIDS research, AIDS patient care, or AIDS issues. One of its major advantages is its ability to enrich information sought in one database by linking it with relevant information or full-text articles in other database on the disc. Compact Library: AIDS is CD-ROM technology at its best."

Editor

REVIEWS

"CD-ROM Title Reviews: Compact Library: AIDS." *CD-ROM EndUser* 2 (May 1990): 91-92.

"Compact Library: AIDS: Medical Literature Moves Toward Its Future." *Annals of Internal Medicine* 109 (November 1, 1988).

Desmarais, Norman. "Compact Library: AIDS — a Librarian's Opinion." *CD-ROM Librarian* 4 (November/December 1989): 46-51.

Fryer, Regina Kenny. "Book Reviews: Compact Library: AIDS." *Bulletin of the Medical Library Association* 77 (October 1989): 393-395.

Fryer, R.K., N. Baratz, and M. Helenius. "Beyond Medline: a Review of Ten Non-Medline CD-ROM Databases for the Health Sciences." *Laserdisk Professional* 2 (May 1989): 27-39.

Van Camp, Ann J. "Electronic Publishing at the Massachusetts Medical Society: an Interview with Bart Rubenstein." *Database* 12 (October 1989): 112-117.

Wentz, Reinhard. "Information Technology." *Health Libraries Review* 6 (September 1989): 187-189.

EQUIPMENT AND SOFTWARE REQUIREMENTS
Computer: IBM PC XT, AT, or PS/2 with hard disk with at least 1 megabyte of space (preferably 2) available and 640K RAM; mouse optional
Software: DOS 3.1 or higher, MS-DOS Extensions
CD-ROM Drive: any IBM-compatible

PRICE Annual price: $875

ARRANGEMENT AND CONTROL
Record fields: author, title, source (journal citation — abbreviated journal title), institution, major Medical Subject Headings, minor Medical Subject Headings, edition of journal, abstract, full text
Searchable: all

SEARCH SOFTWARE AND CAPABILITIES
Software: BRS/Search
Capabilities: keyword, Boolean, search statement retention and back referencing, field searching, field limiting, proximity searching, printing, downloading, truncation, simultaneous searching of all databases

PRINT/ONLINE/OTHER MEDIA COUNTERPARTS
Print: *AIDS*, *Annals of Internal Medicine*, *British Medical Journal*, *Journal of Infectious Diseases*, *Lancet*, *MMWR: Morbidity & Mortality Weekly Report*, *Nature*, *New England Journal of Medicine*, *Science*, *Index Medicus*, *AIDS/HIV Experimental Treatment Directory*
Online: MEDLINE AIDS Subset — DIALOG, BRS, MEDLARS; MEDLINE DIALOG, BRS, MEDLARS, Data-Star, PaperChase, Mead Data Central, Questel, DIMDI; AIDS Knowledge Base — BRS; Bureau of Hygiene and Tropical Diseases AIDS Database — BRS, Data-Star

NETWORK LICENSING ARRANGEMENTS
Contact vendor

TITLE COMPACT LIBRARY: VIRAL HEPATITIS

PUBLISHER Producer: National Library of Medicine
Vendor: Maxwell Electronic Publishing

SCOPE AND CONTENT
A comprehensive collection of information on hepatitis research from around

the world. Includes a unique, textbook-like database of references developed by physician editors. More than 33,000 bibliographic citations from Medline and complete text of related articles from selected core journals. It is updated semiannually.

Compact Library: Viral Hepatitis contains a comprehensive collection of information on hepatitis research from around the world. The compact disc contains the Hepatitis Knowledge Base, a unique textbook-like database of references to the hepatitis literature developed by physician editors. It is based on abstracts of seminal articles published in the literature since 1930. The Knowledge Base contains the equivalent to a comprehensive 1,000-page textbook.

The disc also includes more than 33,000 bibliographic citations and abstracts from the National Library of Medicine's Medline database as well as the complete text of related articles from core journals including *The New England Journal of Medicine*, *The Lancet*, *The British Medical Journal*, *Annals of Internal Medicine*, *Hepatology*, *Journal of Allergy and Clinical Immunology*, *MMWR*, *American Journal of Public Health*, *The Medical Letter*, *Seminars in Liver Disease*, *Gastroenterology*, and *Journal of Infectious Disease*.

The collection will grow as other publishers participate. The CD-ROM collection is edited by Raymond S. Koff, M.D., Chairman, Department of Medicine at Framingham Union Hospital (Framingham, MA) and Professor of Medicine at Boston University School of Medicine. The data is accessible using software from Compact Library and BRS Information Technologies. Commenting on the need for a resource on hepatitis, Koff said, "A comprehensive disc of information on hepatitis will be invaluable to clinicians, researchers, and public health specialists worldwide working to treat and control the spread of this disease. This CD-ROM offers them a single source for reliable and digested information." (Publisher's brochure)

Like its longer-established sister product, Compact Library: AIDS, this CD-ROM database combines specialized Medline entries with full text of an electronic "textbook" and selected journal articles to focus on one important disease. It also uses the user-friendly interface based on BRS/Search software. It is international in scope and does provide abstracts and full text. It is an excellent research database. For institutions supporting intensive research in the important area of viral hepatitis, this database should be invaluable.

Editor

EQUIPMENT AND SOFTWARE REQUIREMENTS
Computer: IBM PC XT, AT, or PS/2 with hard disk with at least 1MB of space (preferably 2) available and 640K RAM; mouse optional
Software: DOS 3.1 or higher, MS-DOS Extensions
CD-ROM Drive: any IBM-compatible

PRICE Annual price: $595

ARRANGEMENT AND CONTROL
Record fields: author, title, source (journal citation — abbreviated journal title), institution, major Medical Subject Headings, minor Medical Subject Headings, edition of journal, abstract, full text
Searchable: all

SEARCH SOFTWARE AND CAPABILITIES
Software: BRS/Search
Capabilities: keyword, Boolean, search statement retention and back referencing, field searching, field limiting, proximity searching, printing, downloading, truncation, simultaneous searching of all databases

PRINT/ONLINE/OTHER MEDIA COUNTERPARTS
Print: *Index Medicus*, *The New England Journal of Medicine*, *The Lancet*, *The British Medical Journal*, *Annals of Internal Medicine*, *Hepatology*, *Journal of Allergy and Clinical Immunology*, *MMWR*, *American Journal of Public Health*, *The Medical Letter*, *Seminars in Liver Disease*, *Gastroenterology*, *Journal of Infectious Disease*.
Online: MEDLINE — DIALOG, BRS, MEDLARS, Data-Star, PaperChase, Mead Data Central, Questel, DIMDI

NETWORK LICENSING ARRANGEMENTS
Contact vendor

TITLE COMPENDEX PLUS

PUBLISHER Producer: EI: Engineering Information Inc.
Vendor: DIALOG

SCOPE AND CONTENT
Compendex contains abstracts of the world's significant scientific and technological literature. Engineering fields covered include: civil, energy, envi-

ronmental, geological, and bioengineering; electrical, electronics, and control engineering; mechanical, automotive, transportation, nuclear, and aerospace engineering; computer and communications engineering; robotics and industrial robots; and materials science, among others.

Worldwide coverage of approximately 4,500 journals and selected government reports and books is provided, as well as records of significant published proceedings of engineering and technical conferences. Each record in Compendex Plus is a reference to a journal article, technical report, engineering society publication, book, conference proceeding, or individual conference paper in engineering or a related field. Each record includes a concise abstract with an engineering viewpoint. Approximately 150,000 records a year are incorporated into the database. Coverage is back to 1986 and updating is quarterly. (Publisher's brochure)

Compendex Plus is the world's foremost engineering database. Any institution interested in engineering-related research should subscribe to this CD-ROM database. It has international coverage, covers a wide variety of material formats, has a decent-sized backfile, focuses on one broad subject area, and has abstracts. As Becki Whitaker, information retrieval specialist at the Indiana Cooperative Library Services Authority, points out, Compendex is part of a "core of databases that have been online for almost twenty years and now find themselves on CD-ROM."

Martin Courtois, from the Science Library at Michigan State University, feels that Compendex should be on any list of research databases. He comments, "Compendex is the major databaes to world-wide literature in all areas of engineering and technology. The CD-ROM version should prove much more useful than the print equivalent *Engineering Index*, which in my experience suffered from subject indexing that was too broad and difficult to use. The high price and the fact that subscribers cannot build a backfile of discs, i.e., have to keep getting the paper copy, unfortunately, make this a database that only the largest engineering libraries can consider."

Chuck Huber in his review of Compendex Plus commented, "Compendex Plus is one of the first of the giant scientific bibliographic databases to come to CD-ROM, providing powerful access where the corresponding print tool can be very difficult to use. While the basic system is easy to use in both menu and command modes, attempts to perform more complex searches or combine features can lead to confusing displays."

He concludes, "Compendex Plus is worthy of attention in any engineering library. The database coverage is vast and the software far more powerful and easy to use than the printed version. The user interface is flawed but DIALOG has demonstrated a commitment to upgrading the software which leads me to hope that most of these flaws will be remedied in the near future."

The DIALOG Ondisc interface does at least make Compendex usable for research purposes. This database is highly recommended for any institution doing research in any engineering-related subject area; as a research tool, it is close to perfect.

Editor

REVIEWS

Huber, Chuck. "COMPENDEX Plus." *CD-ROM Professional* 3 (September 1990): 105-106.

EQUIPMENT AND SOFTWARE REQUIREMENTS

Computer: IBM PC, XT, AT, PS/2, or compatible, 512K RAM minimum, 640K RAM recommended
Software: DOS 3.1 or higher, MS-DOS Extensions
CD-ROM Drive: any IBM-compatible

PRICE Annual price: $3,450, for current year plus previous year (two discs); for current year plus four previous years (five discs): $4,920

ARRANGEMENT AND CONTROL

Record fields: abstract, author, CAL classification code, CAL classification heading, CODEN, conference date, conference location, conference number, conference sponsor, conference title, conference year, corporate source, descriptors, document type, identifiers, ISBN, ISSN, journal announcement, journal name, language, monthly abstract number, publication year, source publication, title, treatment code, yearly abstract number
Searchable: all

SEARCH SOFTWARE AND CAPABILITIES

Software: DIALOG Ondisc
Capabilities: keyword, Boolean, search statement retention and back referencing, field searching, field limiting, proximity searching, printing, downloading, index searching, novice mode, varied display formats, nesting, truncation, novice mode, varied display formats, nesting, truncation, search saving, online updating, sorting, online document ordering, thesaurus

PRINT/ONLINE/OTHER MEDIA COUNTERPARTS
Print: *Engineering Index, Bioengineering and Biotechnology Abstracts, Energy Abstracts*
Online: Compendex Plus — DIALOG, BRS, STN, Data-Star, ORBIT
Other media: Engineering Index Annual — microfiche

NETWORK LICENSING ARRANGEMENTS
Double the single user fee (above) for two to ten workstations

---

TITLE COMPUTER LIBRARY

PUBLISHER Producer: OCLC
Vendor: OCLC

SCOPE AND CONTENT
This disc lists over 250,000 records that cover the subject of computers from the earliest days of computer development to the microchip revolution that's made the supercomputers of today possible. Government, academic, and private industry sources are all utilized to provide you with the most comprehensive body of information available on the computer industry. Coverage is international and includes books, serials, sound recordings, musical scores, maps, manuscripts, audiovisual materials, and software. The database is updated annually. (Publisher's brochure)

Similar to its parallel OCLC products, such as Education Library, Computer Library taps resources heretofore inaccessible by subject, and only otherwise available now through the online vendor, EPIC. The OCLC Computer Library allows much more focusing onto a research area more easily than EPIC, in addition to allowing end-user/researcher access. This resource is especially essential for covering the history of computers and computer science. Coverage is international and spans all formats of materials. The Search CD450 interface is quite suitable to research usage, providing wide access to the materials cited. This database would not, of course, be suitable for research in cutting edge topics, since it is updated annually, and it does not have abstracts—its only weaknesses.

Editor

EQUIPMENT AND SOFTWARE REQUIREMENTS
Computer: IBM PC or compatible with hard disk and 640K RAM; Macintosh

Software: DOS 3.2 or higher, MS-DOS Extensions
CD-ROM Drive: any IBM-compatible, Apple

PRICE Annual price: $350; OCLC members: $300

ARRANGEMENT AND CONTROL
Record fields: OCLC record number, title, author, LC call number, Dewey call number, government document number, report number, date, contents, language, publisher, place of publication, physical description, publication type, intellectual level, notes, series, subject code, subject headings
Searchable: all but physical description

SEARCH SOFTWARE AND CAPABILITIES
Software: Search CD450
Capabilities: keyword, Boolean, search statement retention and back referencing, field searching, field limiting, proximity searching, printing, downloading, index searching, truncation, nesting, varied display formats

PRINT/ONLINE/OTHER MEDIA COUNTERPARTS
Online: OCLC Online Union Catalog — EPIC

NETWORK LICENSING ARRANGEMENTS
No additional charge

TITLE CONGRESSIONAL MASTERFILE

PUBLISHER Producer: Congressional Information Service
Vendor: Congressional Information Service

SCOPE AND CONTENT
CIS's Congressional Masterfile harnesses state-of-the-art CD-ROM technology to CIS's current and retrospective congressional databases. Congressional Masterfile provides the detailed indexing and thorough coverage of CIS's printed index services, but adds the speed and flexibility of computerized searching. Congressional Masterfile offers the most comprehensive access to congressional information available anywhere.

Congressional Masterfile 1 allows users to search all of CIS's major historical congressional indexes—covering almost 200 years—with just one lookup. Now researchers can find congressional information in more ways and with greater precision than ever before.

Congressional Masterfile 1 incorporates all the detailed indexing and other features of *CIS US Serial Set Index (1789-1969)*, *CIS US Congressional Committee Hearings Index (1833-1969)*, *CIS Index to Unpublished US Senate Committee Hearings (1823-1964)*, *CIS US Congressional Committee Prints Index (1830-1969)*, *CIS Index to US Senate Executive Documents & Reports (1817-1969)*, *CIS Index to Unpublished US House of Representatives Committee Hearings (1833-1946)*, and *CIS Index to Unpublished US Senate Committee Hearings (1965-1968).*

Congressional Masterfile 1 purchasers may select the complete multiple index database or select individual indexes. Libraries that have already purchased one or more print editions of the CIS retrospective congressional indexes may deduct the full list price from the price of Congressional Masterfile 1.

Congress generates over half a million pages of information a year during the course of its investigative, oversight, and legislative activities. With its virtually unlimited power to summon witnesses and commission studies, Congress explores a phenomenal range of subjects of both historical and current interest. They include: AIDS, terrorism, acid rain, oil spills, abortion, air safety, drug testing, the space programs, bank failures, chemical weapons, obscenity and pornography, crime, atomic energy and nuclear weapons, the American Nazi Party, child care, homelessness, computer crime, and virtually every country in the world—from Afghanistan and Zimbabwe. Congressional Masterfile 2 makes this rich source of information more accessible than ever before.

Congressional Masterfile 2 also offers a unique Legislative History feature, providing a summary CIS-prepared legislative history for any public law since 1970 in seconds, along with all the abstracts for the congressional publications in the legislative history.

Congressional Masterfile 2 provides comprehensive access to the award-winning *CIS/Index.* With a few keystrokes, users can pinpoint information contained in hearings, reports, documents, committee prints, Senate executive reports and documents, and Senate treaty documents—from 1970 to the present.

Both a current service and a retrospective set are available. Current service subscribers receive quarterly CD-ROM disc updates. (Publisher's brochure)

The Congressional Information Service has been providing excellent indexing and coverage of Congressional information for over twenty years now, and they have now carried their wonderful information sources over to CD-

ROM. For any institution supporting research in history, political science, public affairs, sociology, science, or any number of other subjects Congress has ever dealt with in its wide-ranging deliberations, this database is an unparalleled, unique source of information.

Sanderson, Williams, and Taylor, in reviewing Congressional Masterfile, find, "For some time CIS indexing has been a standard by which one can judge other print sources....As might be expected, the CD-ROM versions improve even on 'perfection.'" They conclude, "...the search technique is learned easily....The CIS Masterfile series are highly recommended for purchase for libraries with extensive requests for searches in Congressional publications. Those libraries which have the CIS print volumes will appreciate the additional benefits of the CD-ROM capability."

Cary Griffith, in a survey of legal CD-ROMs, noted, "These CIS products are some of the most comprehensive, detailed and well indexed U.S. Congressional...reference materials available. Users who are already familiar with their printed versions will appreciate the added search and information management capabilities of their CD-ROM offerings." He continues, "The search software engine that drives the use of these CIS products sounds fairly powerful....The Congressional Masterfile CD-ROM titles will be of most interest to attorneys and legal researchers."

Kellough and Gomez, in their extensive review of Congressional Masterfile, did find that it has some drawbacks—"A major drawback to the Congressional Masterfile on CD-ROM is slow response time. There are a number of techniques that can be used to reduce response time including limiting fields and using logical operators. The use of punctuation and spacing is critical for retrieving records by date or numbers....Inserted internal spaces and punctuation will prevent the system from correctly recognizing your search entry. Another drawback is the incompatibility of the database terminology. Because the Serial Set uses keyword-in-context and the Hearings and Prints indexes controlled vocabulary, search strategy in one may not work in the other."

They concluded, "The Congressional Masterfile on CD-ROM is expensive. However, even non-depository libraries may find it useful to identify documents in order to obtain them through interlibrary loan....We...found that our staff and users required more time to learn to use this software effectively than was required for other products in the Documents Division....The search software for Congressional Masterfile is powerful but geared toward the sophisticated end-user. The database itself really has increased our ability to answer user inquiries in a timely and effective manner."

Herbert Somers notes, "Despite the many useful features of Congressional Masterfile, the program suffers from somewhat complicated and nonintuitive procedures for altering display and print formats. Although on-screen help is plentiful, printed system documentation is rather meager and novice users will find that a good deal of experimentation and practice is necessary to gain expertise with the many intricacies of the system. Regardless, researchers who persevere and successfully familiarize themselves with this unique product will be rewarded with unparalleled access to this substantial body of significant historical congressional documents."

"Congressional Masterfile is an exceptionally powerful and versatile system, allowing users the unprecedented ability to track issues or individuals over a wide range of years and variety of legislative materials. Certainly, libraries with extensive retrospective congressional publications collections or, who have purchased the corresponding CIS microfiche sets of unpublished and non-depository materials, will find Congressional Masterfile an indispensable electronic reference tool for facilitating use of these important and often neglected retrospective documents."

Due to its scope, of course, Congressional Masterfile only covers a special subset of government documents, and it has a United States focus, although the whole world is covered, in relation to the United States. Within its purpose and constraints, however, it is a wonderful collection of data. It covers over 200 years of information, provides descriptive information on the items it lists, and has an acceptable search interface for research. Within its stated limits, it is an excellent research collection, and provides access to information that is not otherwise available on CD-ROM.

Editor

REVIEWS

"Government Information: CIS Congressional Masterfile, 1789-1969." *Preview* 2 (January 1990): 8.

Griffith, Cary. "Legal Information on CD-ROM: a Survey." *CD-ROM Professional* 3 (May 1990): 80-85.

Kellough, Jean, and Joni Gomez. "Congressional Masterfile 1 & 2 on CD-ROM: a Door Opener to Congressional Publications." *CD-ROM Professional* 3 (issue 3, 1990): 73-79.

Sanderson, Rosalie M., Pamela D. Williams, and Betty W. Taylor. "CD-ROM as an Information Medium: CIS Masterfile on CD-ROM." *Microform Review* 18 (Fall 1989): 210-216.

Somers, Herbert A. "Reviews: CIS Congressional Masterfile, 1789-1969." *Government Publications Review* (September/October 1989): 507-508.

EQUIPMENT AND SOFTWARE REQUIREMENTS
Computer: IBM PC or compatible with 640K RAM
Software: DOS 3.1 or higher, MS-DOS Extensions
CD-ROM Drive: any IBM-compatible

PRICE Congressional Masterfile 1, complete set, maximum price: $40,990; price will be reduced for owners of corresponding print indexes. Congressional Masterfile 2, current service (1991), maximum price for largest budget class of library: $5,640; price will be reduced for CIS/Index print subscribers and for smaller budget class of library. CM2, retrospective (1970-1990) price: $13,060; for current CM2 subscribers: $7,820. Contact vendor for further detail.

ARRANGEMENT AND CONTROL
Record fields: abstract, CIS number, collation, congress session, date, document type, item number, LC card number, monthly catalog entry number, source, SUDOC number, title
Searchable: all

SEARCH SOFTWARE AND CAPABILITIES
Software: Quantum Leap
Capabilities: keyword, Boolean, field searching, index searching, proximity searching, printing, downloading, truncation, thesaurus, novice mode

PRINT/ONLINE/OTHER MEDIA COUNTERPARTS
Print: *CIS US Serial Set Index (1789-1969), CIS US Congressional Committee Hearings Index (1833-1969), CIS Index to Unpublished US Senate Committee Hearings (1823-1964), CIS US Congressional Committee Prints Index (1830-1969), CIS Index to US Senate Executive Documents & Reports (1817-1969), CIS Index to Unpublished US House of Representatives Committee Hearings (1833-1946), CIS Index to Unpublished US Senate Committee Hearings (1965-1968), CIS/Index.*
Online: CIS Index — DIALOG

NETWORK LICENSING ARRANGEMENTS
Contact vendor

TITLE CROSS-CULTURAL CD

PUBLISHER Producer: Human Relations Area Files
Vendor: SilverPlatter

SCOPE AND CONTENT
Cross-Cultural CD is a series of full-text files from the Human Relations Area Files (HRAF). The texts are extracts from over 1,000 anthropological, sociological, and psychological books and articles on life in sixty different societies around the world in the nineteenth and twentieth centuries. The CD-ROM series consists of ten topical databases. The first CD covers human sexuality, to be followed semiannually by databases on marriage, family life, crime and social problems, old age, death and dying, childhood and adolescence, socialization and education, religious beliefs, and religious practices. Subscribers to the series enjoy membership in HRAF. Additions will come semiannually.

Starting in Spring 1989, SilverPlatter has published two databases each year. Each database contains from 6,000 to 12,000 pages of text, citations to the source documents, and summaries providing basic descriptive information on each of the sixty societies covered. Topics on each of the ten databases, in order of publication, are:

Human Sexuality—sexuality, sexual stimulation, sexual relations, sexual practices, premarital sex, extramarital sex, sex restrictions, homosexuality, celibacy

Marriage—reasons for marriage, types of marriage, economic transactions and marriage, arranged marriages, ceremonies, divorce, remarriage, irregular marriages

Family—postmarital residence, family authority, family relationships, adoption, nuclear family, polygynous family, extended family

Crime and Social Problems—sanctions, homicide, rape, assault, sex crimes, property offenses, offenses against the state, alcohol and drug abuse, disasters, invalidism, poverty, delinquency

Old Age—variable definitions of old age, longevity, rejuvenation, activities of the aged, treatment of the aged

Death and Dying—life force, causes of death, suicide, funeral practices, mourning, funeral specialists, adjustments to death, cult of the dead

Childhood and Adolescence—naming, ceremonies, infant care, child care, development and maturation, childhood activities, puberty, adolescent activities, age of majority

Socialization and Education—techniques of inculcation, weaning and food training, cleanliness training, sex training, aggression training, independence training, transmission of norms, skills, and beliefs, educational system, teachers

Religious Beliefs—types of religion, role of religion, cosmology, mythology, animism, the soul, spirits, gods, luck and chance, sacred objects and places, theological systems

Religious Practices—religious experiences, rituals, propitiation, purification, atonement, avoidance, taboo, asceticism, orgies, revelation, divination (Publisher's brochure)

The Human Relations Area Files have long been a source of hard-to-find anthropological and sociological information about a variety of cultures around the world. Putting them in a CD-ROM format has vastly increased their utility for research. The subject focus of each CD makes optimizes the time of the researcher. The international focus, the variety of materials covered, the time span, the presence of full text, and the SilverPlatter interface make this essential for research in sociology, anthropology, cross-cultural studies, education, religion, criminology, psychology, and related areas.

In a lengthy article about the parent Human Relations Area Files and the Cross-Cultural CD, Ellen Sutton finds that "Cross-Cultural CD clearly demonstrates added value to the subset of the HRAF archive covered in the series, since the contents of the archive have been available until now only in print and microfiche formats. Information retrieval of a small but well-chosen set of subject categories on a carefully selected sample of the world's societies is greatly enhanced by its availability in machine-readable form." She continues, "Access to the portion of the HRAF Archive available via Cross-Cultural CD is far easier than access to the archive itself, whether in paper or microfiche format. The compact disk system allows a tremendous potential for time saving in general exploratory searching for ethnographic information."

Sutton concludes, "...Cross-Cultural CD promises to be a rich and accessible source of ethnographic information that can stand alone without its parent archive....persons researching a particular society should find in the set of databases a reasonable amount of cultural and social information in a readily accessible form, by means of a flexible, well-designed system."

Editor

REVIEWS

Sutton, Ellen D. "The Human Relations Area Files and Cross-Cultural CD: Enhanced Access to Selected Subjects." *Reference Services Review* 19 (Spring 1991): 57-70.

EQUIPMENT AND SOFTWARE REQUIREMENTS

Computer: IBM PC XT, AT, PS/2, or 100 percent compatible with hard disk, 640K RAM; Macintosh Plus, SE, or II
Software: DOS 2.1 or higher, may use MS-DOS Extensions
CD-ROM Drive: Toshiba, Hitachi, Philips, Sony, DEC, or Apple

PRICE Annual price: $1,495; full set, one-time charge: $5,980

ARRANGEMENT AND CONTROL

Record fields: author, cultural summaries note, cultural summary citations, descriptors, full text of excerpt, geographic focus, outline of cultural materials subject codes, page numbers in source, period of time measured, publication date, publisher information, record control number, society , title
Searchable: all

SEARCH SOFTWARE AND CAPABILITIES

Software: SilverPlatter
Capabilities: keyword, Boolean, search statement retention and back referencing, field searching, field limiting, proximity searching, printing, down-

loading, index searching, truncation, search saving, nesting, varied display formats

PRINT/ONLINE/OTHER MEDIA COUNTERPARTS
Print: *Human Relations Area Files*
Other Media: Human Relations Area Files — microfiche

NETWORK LICENSING ARRANGEMENTS
No additional charge

TITLE CUMULATIVE BOOK INDEX

PUBLISHER Producer: H.W. Wilson Co.
Vendor: H.W. Wilson Co.

SCOPE AND CONTENT
Cumulative Book Index is a permanent record of accurate, complete, and timely information on English-language books published each year around the world. CBI indexes English-language works published around the world, including foreign-language dictionaries, phrase books, and other aids to language learning that contain some English. This CD-ROM version includes the out-of-print status for both clothbound and paperback editions. Coverage is from January 1982 to present; updating is quarterly.

Nearly half of all CBI records are based on an examination of the actual book; the remainder are derived from U.S. and British MARC records, Canadian, Australian National Bibliography, and Library of Congress Accessions Lists. This procedure eliminates partial or approximate information, and greatly reduces inaccuracies. CBI uses Wilson's Name Authority File to ensure that all variant forms of authors' names and names used as subjects are cross-referenced to the preferred form. In addition, authority files for subjects and publishers are also used, guaranteeing an overall consistency in CBI entries. (Publisher's brochure)

Cumulative Book Index is a unique resource on CD-ROM for researching any topic covered in English-language books for most of the 1990s. Not limited to in-print books and covering all subject areas, this database could be useful in any area of research. Although its scope means that it does not provide full international coverage or cover more than one material format, and it does not have abstracts, CBI has a good backfile and covers all subject areas.

Paul Kahn, in comparing different CD-ROM searching interfaces, called Wilsondisc "...the best example of the seamless integration of CD-ROM and telecommunications capabilities in a single application currently on the market." He notes, however, "With the exception of the Browse facility, the product offers the same interface options for searching information on the CD-ROM or online. This 'one size fits all' approach is convenient for the command interface, but is seriously inadequate in the case of the Wilsearch menu interface...."

He finds, "Doing a search using the Wilsearch menu is visually structured, but it is no less complex than using the Wilsonline command language. Complexity is, in fact, increased since the system performs transformations of the user's input that may or may not be helpful. Although the transformations performed and the special syntax required is documented in the help files, they are not explained in the menu interface itself." He notes, "The part of the interface that does not use commands is Wilsearch. Once users have selected Wilsearch, they are presented with a full screen form in which to fill in search terms. The problem here is that the form itself does not really tell users what to do or what the results of an action will be....Users will not necessarily get the desired result by typing what they have in mind....As a result, the syntax of filling in this form is just as complex as any command interface."

Although there are problems with the Wilsondisc interface, Cumulative Book Index has an interface that make its contents accessible for research. It should be considered for any research collection.

Editor

REVIEWS

Kahn, Paul. "Making a Difference: a Review of the User Interface Features in Six CD-ROM Database Products." *Optical Information Systems* 8 (July/August 1988): 169-183.

EQUIPMENT AND SOFTWARE REQUIREMENTS

Computer: IBM PC, XT, AT, 386, PS/2 or compatible with hard disk with

1MB of space available and 640K RAM, Hercules graphics or better, modem for online updating
Software: DOS 3.1 or higher, MS-DOS Extensions
CD-ROM Drive: any IBM-compatible

PRICE Annual price: $1,295

ARRANGEMENT AND CONTROL
Record fields: author, binding, compiler, distributor, edition, illustrations, illustrator, ISBN, LC card number, pagination, price, publication date, publisher, series note, size, special features, subject headings, subtitle, title, translator
Searchable: all

SEARCH SOFTWARE AND CAPABILITIES
Software: Wilsondisc
Capabilities: keyword, Boolean, search statement retention and back referencing, field searching, proximity searching, printing, downloading, truncation, thesaurus, online updating, novice search mode, search saving, automatic singular and plural, nesting, local holdings display

PRINT/ONLINE/OTHER MEDIA COUNTERPARTS
Print: *Cumulative Book Index*
Online: Cumulative Book Index — BRS, Wilsonline

NETWORK LICENSING ARRANGEMENTS
No additional charge for inbuilding access; contact Wilson for remote access charges

---

TITLE DEUTSCHE BIBLIOGRAPHIE AKTUELL CD-ROM

PUBLISHER Producer: Buchhaendler-Vereinigung GmbH
Vendor: Chadwyck-Healey

SCOPE AND CONTENT
The German National Bibliography on CD-ROM contains over 500,000 records taken from the following series: booktrade publications, non-

booktrade publications, maps, dissertations, and CIP data for new titles not yet catalogued. The CD-ROM contains all records of the Deutsche Bibliothek from January 1986 to the present, and is updated quarterly. (Publisher's brochure)

For institutions with research programs dealing with Germany, the German view of things, German language material, and general topics covered in German, this CD-ROM database is an invaluable source. Covering a variety of material formats, although limited by its scope to German publications, this database has a workable backfile, although it will become more valuable as time goes on. No abstracts are included, of course, and the search interface is not as well suited to complicated searches as others are, but the interface is adequate for the bibliography searching needed with this disc. Any well-rounded research program covering this important Western European country will want to consider this database.

Anthony Angiletta of Stanford University notes, "...the common software interface is a plus and the software itself is quite flexible and useful for both browsing and hard-citations searching by patrons and for collection development or management purposes by librarians....I have found [it] a boon to a collection evaluation project that I am conducting on West European social sciences and the hypothesis of a general decline in North American accessions. Subject and keyword searching in ...Deutsche Bibliographie ha[s] been essential to individual country studies as well as cross-national ones. In addition, assuming that work is completed on the postwar backfiles, one can trace authors or subjects or presses longitudinally, a task hopelessly filled with drudgery now."

Editor

EQUIPMENT AND SOFTWARE REQUIREMENTS
Computer: IBM PC, XT, AT, PS/2, or compatible with hard disk and 640K RAM
Software: DOS 3.1 or higher, MS-DOS Extensions
CD-ROM Drive: any IBM-compatible

PRICE Annual price: $1,450

ARRANGEMENT AND CONTROL
Record fields: author, title, series title, publisher, publication date, country of

publication, language, bibliographic information, subject, place of publication, ISBN
Searchable: all

SEARCH SOFTWARE AND CAPABILITIES
Software: Chadwyck-Healey
Capabilities: keyword, Boolean, search statement retention and back referencing, field searching, field limiting, printing, downloading, index searching, thesaurus, truncation, varied display formats, nesting, menus and help messages in German, English or French

PRINT/ONLINE/OTHER MEDIA COUNTERPARTS
Print: *German National Bibliography*
Online: BIBLIODATA — STN

NETWORK LICENSING ARRANGEMENTS
Contact publisher

TITLE DISSERTATION ABSTRACTS ONDISC

PUBLISHER Producer: University Microfilms International
Vendor: UMI/Data Courier

SCOPE AND CONTENT
Dissertation Abstracts Ondisc contains bibliographic citations and abstracts for doctoral dissertations as well as some masters theses completed at accredited North American colleges and universities. Some international dissertations are also included. Backfiles are available to 1861, and updating is semiannual. Citations prior to 1980 do not include abstracts. (Publisher's brochure)

Dissertation Abstracts Ondisc is an essential CD-ROM for any library supporting graduate-level study. It is a unique source, providing a breadth of subject coverage in dissertations and theses that cannot be matched elsewhere. The fact that the entire run of *Dissertation Abstracts* is available in this format makes it even more useful. It provides some coverage of other nations also.

The UMI/Data Courier interface is sophisticated enough for indepth research, and the nature of DAO means that it is not as slow in operation as it can be with more specialized databases. DAO has comparatively little information on each disc, and it covers all subject areas, so that any search terms being used will not have so many postings that it can slow down the search.

DAO's weaknesses are that its international coverage is not broad enough, and that the abstracts are not included until 1980. It is a unique source, however, for what it does cover.

Pat Riesenman, reference librarian at Indiana University, finds Dissertation Abstracts to be "quite useful—the system is by no means my favorite, but it's much less awful than" some others.

Colborne and Nicholls evaluate Dissertation Abstracts as a life sciences research tool and conclude, "Dissertation Abstracts is an expensive tool requiring specific needs on the part of the library to justify purchase. These include large numbers of comprehensive searches, particularly at the graduate and postgraduate level and the presence of other faculties with similar needs." They point out "...Dissertation Abstracts will probably be of special interest in libraries serving a range of scientific disciplines."

Reese reviewed DAO as an education research tool. She concluded "Dissertation Abstracts Ondisc provides a quick and efficient means to explore the dissertation literature. Most of our users are graduate students working on their own dissertation. Results of a preliminary survey show 100 percent were at least satisfied with its ease of use....Sixty percent found the 'Ease of Use' 'excellent,' while the remaining 40 percent was split evenly between 'very good' and 'satisfactory'....We feel Dissertation Abstracts Ondisc, with its improved user friendliness will offer a sophisticated tool for searching which will help greatly with the research needs of our patrons."

Royal Purcell looks at use of Dissertation Abstracts Ondisc at Indiana University, and concludes, "...Dissertation Abstracts is a distinctive resource that makes research results of graduate-level dissertations widely available. The computerized version, DAO, is now available in convenient size on compact disc stored on a small computer....In the library, increased use of these CD-ROM offerings can help turn their present, initial effectiveness into increased appeal and usefulness."

Kathy Jackson looked at Dissertation Abstracts Ondisc after University Microfilms updated its software in 1989. She concluded, "Version 1.5 certainly is an improvement over the previous University Microfilms software. For the user, it is excellent software....DA Ondisc is a valuable asset to graduate students. At the Evans Library we encourage every graduate student who comes in for one of our comprehensive, no-cost searches for those working on theses or dissertations to search DA Ondisc and other end-user databases first. When we can talk students into doing this before a librarian conducts a mediated search in a subject database, the mediated search has been much more fruitful because the students have perfected their search strategies. For this and many other reasons, we highly recommend Dissertation Abstracts to institutions where Ph.D.-level work is done."

Editor

REVIEWS

Colborne, David, and Paul Nicholls. "Biology on Disc: CD-ROM Databases for the Non-Medical Academic Life Sciences Collection." *Laserdisk Professional* 3 (January 1990): 91-96.

Jackson, Kathy. "Diskware: New University Microfilms Software Provides Ease of Use." *Laserdisk Professional* 2 (May 1989): 85-88.

Purcell, Royal. "Dissertation Abstracts on CD-ROM: the Indiana University Experience." *CD-ROM Librarian* 3 (November/December 1988): 18-20.

Reese, Jean. "Dissertation Abstracts Ondisc in the Education Library: a Preliminary Review." *Laserdisk Professional* 1 (May 1988): 56-61.

EQUIPMENT AND SOFTWARE REQUIREMENTS

Computer: IBM PC or compatible with hard disk and 640K RAM
Software: DOS 3.2 or higher, MS-DOS Extensions
CD-ROM Drive: any IBM-compatible

PRICE Annual price: $1,695; backfile, 1861-1984, two discs, one-time fee: $5,495

ARRANGEMENT AND CONTROL

Record fields: title of dissertation, DAI location, publication number, number of pages, author, school name and school code, subject and subject code, date, abstract
Searchable: all but DAI location, publication number, number of pages

SEARCH SOFTWARE AND CAPABILITIES
Software: UMI/Data Courier
Capabilities: keyword, Boolean, search statement retention and back referencing, field searching, proximity searching, printing, downloading, index searching, truncation, automatic searching of singular and plural, nesting, varied display formats

PRINT/ONLINE/OTHER MEDIA COUNTERPARTS
Print: *Comprehensive Dissertation Index, Dissertation Abstracts International, Masters Theses Abstracts*
Online: Dissertation Abstracts International — DIALOG, BRS

NETWORK LICENSING ARRANGEMENTS
Additional $200 per node/terminal

TITLE DISSERTATION ABSTRACTS ONDISC-A

PUBLISHER Producer: University Microfilms International
Vendor: UMI/Data Courier

SCOPE AND CONTENT
As mentioned in the previous entry, Dissertation Abstracts Ondisc contains bibliographic citations and abstracts for doctoral dissertations as well as some masters theses completed at accredited North American colleges and universities. Some international dissertations are also included. Announced in *Advanced Technology/Libraries*, Dissertation Abstracts Ondisc-A contains over 500,000 citations and abstracts to doctoral dissertations and masters theses in the humanities and social sciences.

DAO includes citations and 350-word abstracts for British dissertations published since July 1988, and citations and 150-word abstracts for masters theses published since spring 1988. Backfiles are available to 1861, and updating is semiannual. Citations prior to 1980 do not include abstracts. The current edition dates back to 1986; the archival disc covers 1861 to 1985. (Publisher's brochure and *Advanced Technology/Libraries*)

Dissertation Abstracts Ondisc is essential to any academic library, with its greatly expanded access to this tedious-to-use index. Access to the dissertation and thesis literature is vital, and this disc brings it in a more narrowed subject focus than the entire DAO. This can be quite useful for libraries that only need to support the social sciences and humanities, or that need to have the database divided by broad subject interest, so that it can be located in appropriate separate libraries.

Although the database, of course, focuses on a small number of material formats, it does have some international coverage, and can provide good interdisciplinary subject coverage. It has a lengthy backfile, and abstracts since 1980. The UMI Proquest interface can be slow and clumsy for complicated searches, but it does provide research capabilities.

The database's weaknesses are the relative lack of international coverage for the entirety of the database, and the fact that abstracts are not available prior to 1980. This is a subset of an essential research database.

Editor

REVIEWS
"UMI to Offer Dissertation Abstracts Ondisc Subsets." *Advanced Technology/Libraries* 20 (March 1991): 9.

EQUIPMENT AND SOFTWARE REQUIREMENTS
Computer: IBM PC or compatible with hard disk and 640K RAM
Software: DOS 3.2 or higher, MS-DOS Extensions
CD-ROM Drive: any IBM-compatible

PRICE Annual price, archival or current editions: $2,995; archival and current editions: $5,495

ARRANGEMENT AND CONTROL
Record fields: title of dissertation, DAI location, publication number, number of pages, author, school name and school code, subject and subject code, date, abstract
Searchable: all but DAI location, publication number, number of pages

SEARCH SOFTWARE AND CAPABILITIES
Software: UMI/Data Courier
Capabilities: keyword, Boolean, search statement retention and back referencing, field searching, proximity searching, printing, downloading, index searching, truncation, automatic searching of singular and plural, nesting, varied display formats

PRINT/ONLINE/OTHER MEDIA COUNTERPARTS
Print: *Comprehensive Dissertation Index, Dissertation Abstracts International, Masters Theses Abstracts*
Online: Dissertation Abstracts International — DIALOG, BRS

NETWORK LICENSING ARRANGEMENTS
Additional $200 per node/terminal

TITLE DISSERTATION ABSTRACTS ONDISC-B

PUBLISHER Producer: University Microfilms International
Vendor: UMI/Data Courier

SCOPE AND CONTENT
As mentioned in previous entries, Dissertation Abstracts Ondisc contains bibliographic citations and abstracts for doctoral dissertations as well as some masters theses completed at accredited North American colleges and universities; some international dissertations are also included. Announced in *Advanced Technology/Libraries*, Dissertation Abstracts Ondisc-B contains over 600,000 citations and abstracts to doctoral dissertations and masters theses in the sciences and engineering.

DAO includes citations and 350-word abstracts for British dissertations published since July 1988, and citations and 150-word abstracts for masters theses published since spring 1988. Backfiles are available to 1861, and updating is semiannual. Citations prior to 1980 do not include abstracts. The current edition dates back to 1986; the archival disc covers 1861 to 1985. (Publisher's brochure and *Advanced Technology/Libraries*)

Dissertation Abstracts Ondisc is vitally important for any academic library; the computerized form makes its previously almost inaccessible print version usable for the average end user. This science and engineering subset will be very useful for libraries that only cover these areas, and may want to be able to locate the other subset of DAO in another library, or not get it at all.

As mentioned above, this database provides some international coverage, although it does not extend very far back. It also has abstracts, although not prior to 1980. It limits itself, of course, to theses and dissertations. It is an essential research database, for an academic library, and it is unique and irreplaceable.

Although the UMI interface can be somewhat awkward and slow for complicated searches, it does provide all of the needed research capabilities.

Editor

REVIEWS
"UMI to Offer Dissertation Abstracts Ondisc Subsets." *Advanced Technology/Libraries* 20 (March 1991): 9.

EQUIPMENT AND SOFTWARE REQUIREMENTS
Computer: IBM PC or compatible with hard disk and 640K RAM
Software: DOS 3.2 or higher, MS-DOS Extensions
CD-ROM Drive: any IBM-compatible

PRICE Annual price, archival or current editions: $2,995; archival and current editions: $5,495

ARRANGEMENT AND CONTROL
Record fields: title of dissertation, DAI location, publication number, number of pages, author, school name and school code, subject and subject code, date, abstract
Searchable: all but DAI location, publication number, number of pages

SEARCH SOFTWARE AND CAPABILITIES
Software: UMI/Data Courier
Capabilities: keyword, Boolean, search statement retention and back referencing, field searching, proximity searching, printing, downloading, index searching, truncation, automatic searching of singular and plural, nesting, varied display formats

PRINT/ONLINE/OTHER MEDIA COUNTERPARTS
Print: *Comprehensive Dissertation Index, Dissertation Abstracts International, Masters Theses Abstracts*
Online: Dissertation Abstracts International — DIALOG, BRS

NETWORK LICENSING ARRANGEMENTS
Additional $200 per node/terminal

TITLE DRUG INFORMATION SOURCE

PUBLISHER Producer: Cambridge Scientific Abstracts, American Society

of Hospital Pharmacists, American Hospital Formulary Service
Vendor: Cambridge Scientific Abstracts

SCOPE AND CONTENT

Database contains American Society of Hospital Pharmacists References, American Hospital Formulary Service Drug Information, International Pharmaceutical Abstracts (1970 to date), and Handbook on Injectable Drugs. It contains full-text data on drug indications, uses and administrative options, dosages, regimens and more. Over 700 journals are indexed; updating is semiannual. (Publisher's brochure)

In the area of drugs and pharmaceuticals, this database forms a prime research source. Institutions supporting research in medicine and psychology will find this a highly useful database. It combines several formats of material, including full texts of some books. It is international in scope, and abstracts are provided for most materials where full text is not given. The backfile is quite extensive. The Cambridge interface is quite suitable to research. In fact, for institutions concerned with research in this area, this database exemplifies the kind of value that can be added to a CD-ROM database to make it much more useful for research.

David P. Allen finds the pluses of Drug Information Source to be, "Single source for quick information on virtually every drug available in the U.S. today. Efficient and powerful Cambridge Scientific proprietary search software." The minuses include, "Confusing installation process not properly updated to accommodate latest hardware developments. Limited CD-ROM player installation compatibility with poorly defined work-around." He comments, "The Drug Information Source provides easy access to drug monographs and bibliographic information relating to the drugs."

B.S. Brizuela commented about Drug Information Source, "DIS contains the text of the current editions of AHFS and HID and citations and abstracts since 1970 from IPA. Note that not all of IPA is included, but only those references providing drug information. This single source of basic information, such as dosage, administration, interactions, pharmacokinetics, and toxicity, on virtually all currently marketed U.S. drugs along with citations and abstracts from the professional literature should prove useful in a clinical setting. However, many of our patrons found the lengthy AHFS and HID monographs somewhat cumbersome. In an academic environment such as ours IPA is a welcome adjunct to our Medline CD-ROM system and would prove even more useful if all of IPA were included. One particularly valuable feature is the ability to limit search results to a single database or combination of the three."

She concludes, "The biggest complaint from our patrons was the poor instructions. The new manual will alleviate this difficulty to some extent, but an abbreviated 'cheat sheet' would be a big help. Those who did figure out how to use DIS were usually able to locate the information they wanted and were generally satisfied with the results."

Editor

REVIEWS

Allen, David P. "CD-ROM Title Reviews: Drug Information Source." *CD-ROM EndUser* 2 (May 1990): 88-90.

Brizuela, B. Sue. "Drug Information Source." *Laserdisk Professional* (November 1989): 109-110.

EQUIPMENT AND SOFTWARE REQUIREMENTS

Computer: IBM PC, XT, AT, PS/2, or compatible with hard disk and 640K RAM
Software: DOS 3.1 or higher, MS-DOS Extensions
CD-ROM Drive: any IBM-compatible

PRICE Annual price: $2,750; renewal: $1,495

ARRANGEMENT AND CONTROL

Record fields: abbreviated name, abstract, additional text, AHFS classification number, AHFS classification term, author, author affiliation, CAS Registry Number, chemical name, CODEN, concept tags, descriptors, document type, drug name, footnote, generic name, human indicator, investigational drug identifier, journal name, language, language of summary, major headings, major section headings, manufacturer, minor section headings, molecular formula, monograph title, new material, primary text, publication year, source book name, synonym name, table data, table heading, title, trade name, unique number
Searchable: all

SEARCH SOFTWARE AND CAPABILITIES

Software: Cambridge Scientific Abstracts
Capabilities: keyword, Boolean, field searching, printing, downloading, field limiting, index searching, varied display formats, search saving, search statement retention and back referencing, proximity searching, truncation, nesting

PRINT/ONLINE/OTHER MEDIA COUNTERPARTS
Print: *Handbook on Injectable Drugs, AHFS Drug Information*
Online: Drug Information Fulltext — BRS, DIALOG, Chemical Information Systems, MEDIS; International Pharmaceutical Abstracts — DIALOG, BRS, Data-Star, DIMDI, ESA/IRS
Other Media: International Pharmaceutical Abstracts — microfiche

NETWORK LICENSING ARRANGEMENTS

Cambridge — no additional charge

TITLE ECONLIT

PUBLISHER Producer: American Economic Association
Vendor: SilverPlatter

SCOPE AND CONTENT
Covering international material, EconLIT includes bibliographic citations and abstracts to selected articles from 326 journals; citations and abstracts to single-author books; and citations to dissertations and edited chapters or papers in books, conference proceedings, and similar collected works. Approximately 100 publications are from outside of the United States. Most journals are indexed cover to cover, including articles, comments, and replies. The database contains over 170,000 records.

Topics covered in EconLIT reflect the breadth of the field of economics, including: economic theory and history, econometrics, fiscal theory, public finance, economic forecasting, managerial economics and industrial relations, monetary theory and financial institutions, business finance and investment, law and economics, demography, international, regional, and urban economics, agricultural and natural resource economics, labor economics, welfare programs, country studies, and economic growth and development.

While similar to the online database, EconLIT on CD provides greater coverage of the world's economic literature by introducing abstracts of books, citations to dissertations, and author affiliations. One CD-ROM disc covers 1969 to present, and is updated quarterly. (Publisher's brochure)

EconLit is the foremost database for economics available on CD-ROM. Its extensive coverage of economics and related topics, its coverage of a variety of material formats, the extensive backfile, the provision of abstracts since 1986, the international scope, and the SilverPlatter interface all combine to make this database essential for institutions supporting economic research. It has no weaknesses as far as suitability for research purposes.

In a recent review of EconLIT, Mary Cahill commented, "The SilverPlatter search software used by EconLit allows those engaged in serious economics research the opportunity to access quickly the contents of the JEL and IEA with greater accuracy than that afforded by the printed version. However, unlike other SilverPlatter databases EconLit has no ondisk tutorial (a printed general tutorial comes with the database documentation) and certain features of the system make this a package it takes some time and effort to learn to use effectively."

She noted, "...this is a very enjoyable database to search and most of our users (faculty and undergraduates) have been satisfied with their results. Those few who were not were often looking for information outside the scope of the database (applied economics and business.)" She concludes, "Searching EconLit is still by far a more efficient means of exploring the economic literature than using the printed JEL or untimely IEA, although users need to be aware that there are problems in executing large searches and in some lateral searching. EconLit would be a beneficial addition in any academic environment."

Editor

REVIEWS

Cahill, Mary. "CD-ROM in Brief: EconLit on CD." *CD-ROM Professional* 4 (March 1991): 86-88.

EQUIPMENT AND SOFTWARE REQUIREMENTS

Computer: IBM PC XT, AT, PS/2, or 100 percent compatible with hard disk, 640K RAM; Macintosh Plus, SE, or II
Software: DOS 2.1 or higher, may use MS-DOS Extensions
CD-ROM Drive: Toshiba, Hitachi, Philips, Sony, DEC, or Apple

PRICE Annual price: $1,600

ARRANGEMENT AND CONTROL

Record fields: abstract, abstract indicator, accession number, affiliation, author, descriptors, document type, festschrift, geographic location, ISSN, ISBN, names, publication year, source, title
Searchable: all

SEARCH SOFTWARE AND CAPABILITIES
Software: SilverPlatter
Capabilities: keyword, Boolean, search statement retention and back referencing, field searching, field limiting, proximity searching, printing, downloading, index searching, truncation, search saving, nesting, varied display formats

PRINT/ONLINE/OTHER MEDIA COUNTERPARTS
Print: *Journal of Economic Literature, Index to Economic Articles*
Online: EconLIT — DIALOG

NETWORK LICENSING ARRANGEMENTS
$2,400 for multiusers

TITLE EDUCATION LIBRARY

PUBLISHER Producer: OCLC
Vendor: OCLC

SCOPE AND CONTENT
Selected from the OCLC Online Union Catalog, this database consists of over 450,000 records pertaining to education. Records are for English- and foreign-language materials published in all bibliographic formats, including books and journals, newspapers, A/V materials, recordings, videocassettes, archival material, manuscripts, filmstrips, microforms, and slides. The database spans the twentieth century and also includes records describing materials printed as early as 1543. Records are selected by a combination of Library of Congress and Dewey Decimal classification numbers. The database is updated annually. (Publisher's brochure)

Just as its companion products (Agriculture Library, etc.) from OCLC do, Education Library covers a long-time span, a wide variety of material formats, and a great range of education topics. The Search CD450 interface is a useful research tool for this unique compilation of bibliographic listings, which was unavailable for subject access until it became searchable on the online vendor, EPIC. For libraries supporting serious education research, Education Library is quite an improvement over EPIC, however, since it provides unlimited usage at a fixed, low cost, allowing researchers to do their own searching, and since it allows focusing of the tremendous OCLC database down to the education field. If it has a weakness, it is the absence of abstracts.

Philbin and Ryan describe Education Library briefly in their article about recommended databases for education. They also compare its features to other education bibliographic databases in a chart.

Linda Sabelhaus reviewed Education Library and commented, "The EMIL CD is fairly easy to use since there is no command language, the appropriate function keys are always defined on the screen, and for a problem, the help menu can be retrieved....One of the EMIL CD's best features is subject searching....OCLC has done a very good job creating this database and is making good use of the vast amount of data in the OCLC catalog."

"The EMIL database can be of value to a library if used as a supplementary source of information on education. The greatest value is that it is one of the best listings of books available for the education field. It is rather inexpensive, and if a library had any need for this type of information at all it would be valuable to purchase it. Hopefully OCLC will produce other subsets of their Union Catalog for CD-ROM in the future."

Editor

REVIEWS

Electronic Library 7 (April 1989): 94-97.

Online 11 (September 1987): 42-54.

Philbin, Paul and Joe Ryan. "ERIC and Beyond: a Survey of CD-ROMs for Education Collections." *Laserdisk Professional* 1 (November 1988): 17-27.

Sabelhaus, Linda J. "OCLC Search CD450: Education Materials in Libraries (EMIL)." *RQ* 27 (Spring 1988): 416-419.

EQUIPMENT AND SOFTWARE REQUIREMENTS

Computer: IBM PC or compatible with hard disk and 640K RAM; Macintosh
Software: DOS 3.2 or higher, MS-DOS Extensions
CD-ROM Drive: any IBM-compatible, Apple

PRICE Annual price: $350; OCLC members: $300

ARRANGEMENT AND CONTROL

Record fields: OCLC record number, title, author, LC call number, Dewey call number, government document number, report number, date, contents, language, publisher, place of publication, publication type, physical descrip-

tion, intellectual level, notes, series, subject code, subject headings
Searchable: all but physical description

SEARCH SOFTWARE AND CAPABILITIES
Software: Search CD450
Capabilities: keyword, Boolean, search statement retention and back referencing, field searching, field limiting, proximity searching, printing, downloading, index searching, truncation, nesting, varied display formats

PRINT/ONLINE/OTHER MEDIA COUNTERPARTS
Online: OCLC Online Union Catalog — EPIC

NETWORK LICENSING ARRANGEMENTS
No additional charge

TITLE EI CHEMDISC

PUBLISHER Producer: EI: Engineering Information Inc.
Vendor: DIALOG

SCOPE AND CONTENT
Over one million records from chemical engineering journals, records of the significant published proceedings of engineering and technical conferences, and chemical abstracts written from the point of view of applied engineering are included. Emphasis is on the technical challenges of process control, measurement, and analysis in virtually every field, and it also covers environmental impact, pollution and hazardous wastes, preventive maintenance and quality control, geology and geophysics, heat and thermodynamics, lasers, metallurgy and metallography, refrigeration and cryogenics, solid fuels, and more. Search applications include monitoring technology, tracking the competition, evaluating new products and new ideas, and minimizing development time and costs. Approximately 4,500 journals are indexed. The database is updated quarterly and coverage is back to 1980. (Publisher's brochure)

This database focuses on the chemical aspects of engineering, but also covers a wide range of related material. Drawn from Compendex, the world's foremost engineering database, this particular combination of material is only found on CD-ROM. EI Chemdisc combines international coverage of several materials formats, a good-sized backfile, a comparatively focused subject coverage, good abstracts, and an excellent searching interface to support research in any institution interested in chemistry and engineering. The database has no real weaknesses in the research area. Becki Whitaker, information retrieval specialist at the Indiana Cooperative Library Services Authority, is correct in pointing out that Compendex is part of a "core of databases that have been online for almost twenty years and now find themselves on CD-ROM."

Editor

EQUIPMENT AND SOFTWARE REQUIREMENTS
Computer: IBM PC, XT, AT, PS/2, or compatible, 512K RAM minimum, 640K RAM recommended
Software: DOS 3.1 or higher, MS-DOS Extensions
CD-ROM Drive: any IBM-compatible

PRICE Annual price: $6,750

ARRANGEMENT AND CONTROL
Record fields: abstract, author, CAL classification code, CAL classification heading, CODEN, conference date, conference location, conference number, conference sponsor, conference title, conference year, corporate source, descriptors, document type, identifiers, ISBN, ISSN, journal announcement, journal name, language, monthly abstract number, publication year, source publication, title, treatment code, yearly abstract number
Searchable: all

SEARCH SOFTWARE AND CAPABILITIES
Software: DIALOG Ondisc
Capabilities: keyword, Boolean, search statement retention and back referencing, field searching, field limiting, proximity searching, printing, downloading, index searching, novice mode, varied display formats, nesting, truncation, search saving, online updating, sorting, online document ordering, thesaurus

PRINT/ONLINE/OTHER MEDIA COUNTERPARTS
Print: *Engineering Index*
Online: Compendex Plus — DIALOG, BRS, STN, Data-Star, ORBIT
Other media: Engineering Index Annual — microfiche

NETWORK LICENSING ARRANGEMENTS
Double the single user fee (above) for two to ten workstations

TITLE EI EEDISC

PUBLISHER Producer: EI: Engineering Information Inc.
Vendor: DIALOG

SCOPE AND CONTENT

Computer, electronics, and electrical engineers will find DIALOG Ondisc EI EEDisc tailored specifically to their needs. Containing abstracts to significant engineering and technological literature from around the world, EI EEDisc covers such topics as electric transmission and distribution, electronic components, telephone and line communications, computer hardware and software, optics and optical devices, lasers acoustics, instrumentation, and more. Coverage is back to 1985, and will eventually be back to 1980. About 4,500 journals are indexed and updating is quarterly. (Publisher's brochure)

EI EEDisc is taken from the comprehensive engineering database, Compendex Plus, and this particular subject-focused combination of material is available only on CD-ROM. In institutions where the focus is on computers, electronics, and electrical engineering, this database would be excellent to support research. Becki Whitaker, Information Retrieval Specialist at the Indiana Cooperative Library Services Authority, points out that Compendex is part of a "core of databases that have been online for almost twenty years and now find themselves on CD-ROM."

Its international focus, the coverage of a variety of material formats, the decent-sized backfile, the subject focus, and the excellent DIALOG searching interface all combine to provide a premiere research tool in EI EEDisc. The database also has useful abstracts. In short, it has no research weaknesses, and is highly recommended.

Editor

EQUIPMENT AND SOFTWARE REQUIREMENTS

Computer: IBM PC, XT, AT, PS/2, or compatible, 512K RAM minimum, 640K RAM recommended
Software: DOS 3.1 or higher, MS-DOS Extensions
CD-ROM Drive: any IBM-compatible

PRICE Annual price, 1980 to present: $6,750; 1985 to present: $3,850

ARRANGEMENT AND CONTROL

Record fields: abstract, author, CAL classification code, CAL classification

heading, CODEN, conference date, conference location, conference number, conference sponsor, conference title, conference year, corporate source, descriptors, document type, identifiers, ISBN, ISSN, journal announcement, journal name, language, monthly abstract number, publication year, source publication, title, treatment code, yearly abstract number
Searchable: all

SEARCH SOFTWARE AND CAPABILITIES
Software: DIALOG Ondisc
Capabilities: keyword, Boolean, search statement retention and back referencing, field searching, field limiting, proximity searching, printing, downloading, index searching, novice mode, varied display formats, nesting, truncation, search saving, online updating, sorting, online document ordering, thesaurus

PRINT/ONLINE/OTHER MEDIA COUNTERPARTS
Print: *Engineering Index*
Online: Compendex Plus — DIALOG, BRS, STN, Data-Star, ORBIT
Other media: Engineering Index Annual — microfiche

NETWORK LICENSING ARRANGEMENTS
Contact vendor

TITLE EI ENERGY AND ENVIRONMENT DISC

PUBLISHER Producer: EI: Engineering Information Inc.
Vendor: DIALOG

SCOPE AND CONTENT
From DIALOG and Engineering Information comes comprehensive coverage of the world's literature on energy and the environment. EI Energy and Environment Disc covers a broad range of topics, including: meteorology, air and water pollution, sewage and industrial wastes treatment, geology and geophysics, petroleum and other fuels, power plants and generators, nuclear technology, thermodynamics, refrigeration and cryogenics, hydroelectric power and more. Articles are abstracted from an applied engineering viewpoint, and are valuable to both academic and corporate engineers and researchers. Coverage is back to 1985, and will eventually be back to 1980. Approximately 4,500 journals are indexed; updating is quarterly. (Publisher's brochure)

EI Energy and Environment Disc is a subject-focused abstraction from Compendex Plus, the world's foremost engineering database, and this particular combination of data is available only on CD-ROM. For institutions interested in energy and the environment, this database should prove an excellent research collection. As Becki Whitaker, Information Retrieval Specialist at the Indiana Cooperative Library Services Authority, points out, Compendex is part of a "core of databases that have been online for almost twenty years and now find themselves on CD-ROM."

It has an international breadth, focuses on a manageable subject area, covers a variety of material formats, has a decent-sized backfile, and includes abstracts. The excellent DIALOG searching interface rounds out the research picture. This database has no real research weaknesses, for institutions supporting study in the increasingly vital areas of energy and the environment.

Editor

EQUIPMENT AND SOFTWARE REQUIREMENTS
Computer: IBM PC, XT, AT, PS/2, or compatible, 512K RAM minimum, 640K RAM recommended
Software: DOS 3.1 or higher, MS-DOS Extensions
CD-ROM Drive: any IBM-compatible

PRICE Annual price, 1980 to present: $4,500; 1985 to present: $2,500

ARRANGEMENT AND CONTROL
Record fields: abstract, author, CAL classification code, CAL classification heading, CODEN, conference date, conference location, conference number, conference sponsor, conference title, conference year, corporate source, descriptors, document type, identifiers, ISBN, ISSN, journal announcement, journal name, language, monthly abstract number, publication year, source publication, title, treatment code, yearly abstract number
Searchable: all

SEARCH SOFTWARE AND CAPABILITIES
Software: DIALOG Ondisc
Capabilities: keyword, Boolean, search statement retention and back referencing, field searching, field limiting, proximity searching, printing, downloading, index searching, novice mode, varied display formats, nesting, truncation, search saving, online updating, sorting, online document ordering, thesaurus

PRINT/ONLINE/OTHER MEDIA COUNTERPARTS

Print: *Engineering Index*
Online: Compendex Plus — DIALOG, BRS, STN, Data-Star, ORBIT
Other media: Engineering Index Annual — microfiche

NETWORK LICENSING ARRANGEMENTS

Contact vendor

TITLE EMERGINDEX

PUBLISHER Producer: Micromedex
Vendor: Micromedex

SCOPE AND CONTENT

Emergindex is a referenced clinical information system that presents pertinent data for the practice of acute care medicine. It is designed to help those who deal with acute medical/surgical and traumatic injuries to more quickly and efficiently diagnose and treat the multitude of problems encountered daily. The system includes Clinical Reviews, Clinical Abstracts, and Pre-Hospital Care Protocols. The database is indexed by a 40,000 keyword medical thesaurus. (*CD-ROMs in Print*, Meckler Publications, 1991)

Fryer, Baratz, and Helenius point out, "Emergindex collects information for the practice of acute care medicine. It includes full-text information on case presentations, laboratory and radiologic analyses, differential diagnoses, and treatment modalities. It also includes citations and abstracts in emergency and critical care medicine." Emergindex is part of the Computerized Clinical Information Systems, which also includes information on drugs and poisoning.

Fryer, Baratz, and Helenius find that "CCIS is a menu-driven system that easily guides users to relevant information...The CCIS interface is so easy to learn that the lack of a manual is not a problem. Menus have clear instructions and help screens." They conclude "CCIS will be used extensively in emergency rooms, intensive care units, drug information centers, health science libraries, poison-control centers, and pharmaceutical companies. It is a most impressive database that gives clinicians and drug information professionals quick and efficient access to valuable information."

Although Emergindex is aimed primarily at acute care practitioners, it also constitutes a research resource in this area, since it has a bibliographic element. It provides a subject-focused view of the medical literature, covers a decent-sized backfile (going back to 1985), and has abstracts. For institutions wanting to provide a database focused on the critical/emergency care area, this is a suitable subset of the literature.

The St. Louis Medical Center Library tried Emergindex and found, "These components contain a great deal of information on...emergency procedures....MICROMEDEX is an informational tool designed to give specific answers to specific questions, without the questioner needing to go to additional sources." Emergindex was "...well received by the users of the library...." They conclude, "In the case of MICROMEDEX, the price alone made it prohibitive, although it continues to occupy a prominent place on our wish list. The Hospital Pharmacy, which got its first exposure to MICROMEDEX through our evaluation, subsequently obtained the system for its own use."

Editor

REVIEWS

CD-ROM Lab Report 1 (June 1988): 20-23.

Fryer, R.K., N. Baratz, and M. Helenius. "Beyond Medline: a Review of Ten Non-Medline CD-ROM Databases for the Health Sciences." *Laserdisk Professional* 2 (issue 3, 1989): 27-39.

Plutchak, T. Scott. "New Approaches to Access: CD-ROM at the St. Louis University Medical Center Library." in *Public Access CD-ROMs in Libraries: Case Studies*, Linda Stewart. Katherine S. Chiang, and Bill Coons. eds. Westport, CT: Meckler Publications, 1990, p. 111.

EQUIPMENT AND SOFTWARE REQUIREMENTS

Computer: IBM PC or compatible with hard disk and 512K RAM; 100 percent Epson-compatible printer
Software: DOS 3.1 or higher, MS-DOS Extensions
CD-ROM Drive: any IBM-compatible

PRICE Annual subscription to Computerized Clinical Information System required; contact vendor for details.

SEARCH SOFTWARE AND CAPABILITIES

Software: MICROMEDEX

PRINT/ONLINE/OTHER MEDIA COUNTERPARTS
None

NETWORK LICENSING ARRANGEMENTS
Contact vendor

TITLE ENERGY LIBRARY

PUBLISHER Producer: OCLC
Vendor: OCLC

SCOPE AND CONTENT
Energy Library lists over 290,000 records on hundreds of energy-related topics taken from the OCLC Online Union Catalog. It provides information on such energy resources as oil, nuclear, coal, and solar that you won't find anywhere else. From federal studies on the feasibility of solar power to the future of nuclear energy, political and economic aspects of energy consumption, the importance of the profit motive in the development of new energy resources—these are sample topics. Formats covered include books, serials, videocassettes, sound recordings, software, microforms, A/V materials, filmstrips and more. Coverage is pre-1900 to the present. Updating is done annually. (Publisher's brochure)

The databases that focus on a portion of the vast OCLC Online Union Catalog are a rich and invaluable resource for researchers. Energy Library provides such a resource for any library interested in energy research, due to its wide range of energy topics, its coverage of a variety of formats, its date coverage, and its international scope. The Search CD450 interface allows research-type searching, providing the kind of access needed. The OCLC Online Catalog has finally become subject-accessible through the online vendor EPIC, but, for focused research, the Energy Library provides much more cost effective and complete access.

Editor

EQUIPMENT AND SOFTWARE REQUIREMENTS
Computer: IBM PC or compatible with hard disk and 640K RAM; Macintosh
Software: DOS 3.2 or higher, MS-DOS Extensions
CD-ROM Drive: any IBM-compatible, Apple

PRICE Annual price: $350. OCLC members: $300.

ARRANGEMENT AND CONTROL
Record fields: OCLC record number, title, author, LC call number, Dewey call number, government document number, report number, date, contents, language, publisher, place of publication, physical description, publication type, intellectual level, notes, series, subject code, subject headings
Searchable: all but physical description

SEARCH SOFTWARE AND CAPABILITIES
Software: Search CD450
Capabilities: keyword, Boolean, search statement retention and back referencing, field searching, field limiting, proximity searching, printing, downloading, index searching, truncation, nesting, varied display formats

PRINT/ONLINE/OTHER MEDIA COUNTERPARTS
Online: OCLC Online Union Catalog — EPIC

NETWORK LICENSING ARRANGEMENTS
No additional charge

TITLE ENVIRO/ENERGYLINE ABSTRACTS PLUS

PUBLISHER Producer: Bowker A&I Publishing
Vendor: R.R. Bowker

SCOPE AND CONTENT
Featuring the complete backfile and all current abstracts and citations from *Environment Abstracts*, *Energy Information Abstracts*, and *Acid Rain Abstracts*, this one disc delivers critical, current data on all aspects of the environment, acid rain, and energy. Coverage of both policy and technology issues serves a broad base of user needs. Advanced CD-ROM technology, allowing keyword and subject searching across databases, enhances the natural affinity between energy and environmental issues.

The database currently contains 180,561 articles, with an estimated 12,120 items to be added in 1990. Backfiles are available to 1971. With the push of a few buttons and virtually no staff assistance, patrons will research topics from global warming to nuclear fusion to the deforestation of Brazil. Sources include research journals, conference proceedings, technical reports (including government, corporate and academic), laboratory studies, monographs, patents, periodicals and daily newspapers and worldwide investment banking research. The database is updated quarterly.

Review categories in environment include: air pollution, toxicology and environmental safety, energy, environmental education, environmental design and urban ecology, food and drugs, general, international, land use and pollution, noise pollution, non-renewable resources, oceans and estuaries, population planning and control, radiological contamination, renewable resources—terrestrial, renewable resources—water, waste management, transportation, water pollution, weather modification and geophysical change, wildlife, and business watch.

Review categories in energy include: U.S. economics, U.S. policy and planning, international, research and development, general, resources and reserves, petroleum and natural gas resources, coal resources, unconventional resources, solar energy, fuel processing, fuel transport and storage, electrical power generation, electric power storage and transmission, nuclear resources and power, thermonuclear power, consumption and conservation, industrial consumption, transportation consumption, residential consumption, environmental impact, and business watch.

Review categories in acid rain includes: sources, atmospheric processes, deposition monitoring, aquatic impacts, terrestrial impacts, general, economics and health, control technologies, U.S. policy and planning, and international. (Publisher's brochure)

This combination of databases about the environment and energy contains data that will provide an excellent resource to any institution supporting research in these areas. The combination of several databases provides more value for cost, and the abstracts included also make it more useful for research purposes. The search interface provides at least the minimum required support for research purposes.

On the other hand, the database does not go back far in time, although, of course, this will change. The focus is solely on periodical articles, and the search interface can be somewhat awkward for complicated searches in a database with abstracts. The database should still prove quite useful in supporting research, however, and should be considered by anyone doing research in the environment and/or energy.

Martin Courtois, science librarian at Michigan State University, says of this product, "Environment Abstracts in particular provides very broad coverage of environmental topics, including the scientific, technical, political, and social aspects. Sources indexed include conference papers, government documents, and newspaper articles as well as journal articles. A reasonable price...and coverage back to 1971 make Enviro/Energyline Abstracts an attractive package for libraries that currently receive one or more of the print equivalents."

Editor

EQUIPMENT AND SOFTWARE REQUIREMENTS
Computer: IBM PC, XT, AT, PS/2, or compatible with hard disk (strongly suggested) or two 5.25- or one 3.5-inch floppy diskette drive, 640K RAM
Software: DOS 3.0 or higher, MS-DOS Extensions
CD-ROM Drive: any IBM-compatible

PRICE Annual price: $1,295; $3,690 for three-year subscription; for subscribers to Bowker A&I microfiche: $695; $1,410 for three-year subscription.

ARRANGEMENT AND CONTROL
Record fields: database, review classification, accession number, title, author, author affiliation, source, date, number of pages, document type, abstract, subjects, SIC codes, special features
Searchable: all except number of pages

SEARCH SOFTWARE AND CAPABILITIES
Software: Bowker
Capabilities: keyword, Boolean, search statement retention and back referencing, field searching, proximity searching, printing, downloading, index searching, truncation, novice search mode, thesaurus, OCLC-type 4.4, author, title searching, online vendor ordering, varied display formats

PRINT/ONLINE/OTHER MEDIA COUNTERPARTS
Print: *Environment Abstracts*, *Energy Information Abstracts*, *Acid Rain Abstracts*
Online: Energyline — Data-Star, DIALOG, ORBIT Enviroline — Data-Star, DIALOG, ORBIT
Other media: Bowker A&I microfiche

NETWORK LICENSING ARRANGEMENTS
$3,885 for multiusers; $11,073 for multiusers, three years

TITLE ENVIRONMENT LIBRARY

PUBLISHER Producer: OCLC
Vendor: OCLC

SCOPE AND CONTENT
Environment Library contains over 400,000 records taken from the OCLC Online Union Catalog that touch upon every facet of the environment. Sample topics include: effects of pollutants on the food chain, the extinction of animals, depletion of the ozone layer, and hundreds of others. Formats covered include: books, serials, videocassettes, sound recordings, software, microforms, A/V materials, filmstrips and more. Coverage is pre-1900 to the present. The database is updated annually. (Publisher's brochure)

For its long-time span, broad coverage of material formats and range of environment topics, Environment Library is a highly desirable CD-ROM database for any library interested in the environment. The breadth of coverage available in the OCLC Union Catalog is unmatched, and only in the last few years has this material been accessible by subject. Although the material is now accessible by subject through the EPIC online system, Environment Library provides the kind of focus that is difficult to get when doing subject searching of the entire OCLC catalog. The Search CD450 interface is quite acceptable for research purposes. The database's only weakness is its lack of abstracting, but this is understandable considering its origin from library cataloging.

Editor

EQUIPMENT AND SOFTWARE REQUIREMENTS
Computer: IBM PC or compatible with hard disk and 640K RAM; Macintosh
Software: DOS 3.2 or higher, MS-DOS Extensions
CD-ROM Drive: any IBM-compatible, Apple

PRICE Annual price: $350; OCLC members: $300

ARRANGEMENT AND CONTROL
Record fields: OCLC record number, title, author, LC call number, Dewey call number, government document number, report number, date, contents, language, publisher, place of publication, physical description, publication type, intellectual level, notes, series, subject code, subject headings
Searchable: all but physical description

SEARCH SOFTWARE AND CAPABILITIES
Software: Search CD450
Capabilities: keyword, Boolean, search statement retention and back referencing, field searching, field limiting, proximity searching, printing, downloading, index searching, truncation, nesting, varied display formats

PRINT/ONLINE/OTHER MEDIA COUNTERPARTS
Online: OCLC Online Union Catalog — EPIC

NETWORK LICENSING ARRANGEMENTS
No additional charge

TITLE ENVIRONMENTAL PERIODICALS BIBLIOGRAPHY

PUBLISHER Producer: Environmental Studies Institute
Vendor: NISC—National Information Services Corporation

SCOPE AND CONTENT
More than 400,000 citations, collected since 1972, make EPB the world's most extensive collection of bibliographic records focused on environmental issues and research. The user can complete an environmental impact statement, know what chemicals are in the food we eat, study the effects of oil spills on the food chain, or research the abuse of our environment on a global scale.

The following disciplines are covered in depth: human ecology, including federal, state, and local government planning laws, programs, policies and regulations, recycling and management of world wastes, ecological and biological environmental pollution, environmental education and information, and transportation studies; energy, including fossil fuels and synthesis, nuclear power generation, chemical, fission, and fusion energy, solar, geothermal, wind, wave, and tide energy, hydroelectric and pumped storage energy, and handling and disposal of radioactive materials; water resources, including fertilizer and phosphate eutrophication, detergents, sewage and waste, treatment systems and processes, agricultural effluents, and thermal, oil, and chemical pollution; air, including air quality control, emissions and detection, thermal air pollution, climatic change, meteorology, and atmospheric chemistry; land resources, including animal habitats, wilderness preservation, hunting and fishing, soil erosion and conservation, mining and land reclamation, and agriculture and forestry; and nutrition and health, including drug use and abuse, food poisoning and contamination, population planning and control, public health, and toxicological studies. This database covers 360 periodicals. It is updated semiannually and coverage is back to 1973. (Publisher's brochure)

The Environment Periodicals Bibliography has long been a useful research database online. It is now possible to make it widely available to end users in CD-ROM format. Any institution supporting research in environmental studies should consider subscribing to it. It is one of the most extensive databases covering environmental periodical literature. The focus is wide, and the backfile is lengthy, although there are no abstracts, and only periodicals are indexed. The focus of indexing is valuable, however, to environmental research institutions.

Editor

EQUIPMENT AND SOFTWARE REQUIREMENTS
Computer: IBM PC, XT, AT, PS/2 or compatible with 512K RAM
Software: DOS 3.1 or higher; MS-DOS Extensions
CD-ROM Drive: any IBM-compatible

ARRANGEMENT AND CONTROL
Record fields: author, descriptor, journal name, publication year, title
Searchable: all

SEARCH SOFTWARE AND CAPABILITIES
Software: Dataware CD-Answer
Capabilities: Keyword, Boolean, novice search mode, field searching, proximity searching, truncation, nesting, index searching, search saving, sorting, printing, downloading

PRINT/ONLINE/OTHER MEDIA COUNTERPARTS
Print: *Environmental Periodicals Bibliography*
Online: Environmental Bibliography — DIALOG

NETWORK LICENSING ARRANGEMENTS
Contact vendor

TITLE ERIC

PUBLISHER Producer: Educational Resources Information Center, ORI, Inc.
Vendors: DIALOG, OCLC, SilverPlatter

SCOPE AND CONTENT

Bibliographic database sponsored by the U.S. Department of Education, consisting of the Resources in Education (RIE) file and the Current Index to Journals in Education (CIJE) file as prepared by the Information Systems Unit of ORI. Abstracts of articles published in over 700 journals and other important education literature. Coverage is back to 1966. DIALOG, OCLC, and SilverPlatter versions of ERIC are updated quarterly. (Publisher's brochure)

ERIC is the most important index to materials in the field of education. The CIJE portion covers the largest number of education journals of any index available on CD-ROM. The RIE portion covers a broad array of ephemeral material, including dissertations, government documents, conference papers, curriculum guides, technical reports, and more, available on microfiche at many academic libraries. The date coverage is about twenty-five years. Informative abstracts also increase research value. Becki Whitaker, information retrieval specialist at the Indiana Cooperative Library Services Authority, points out, ERIC, of course, is part of a "core of databases that have been online for almost twenty years and now find themselves on CD-ROM." Pat Riesenman, reference librarian at Indiana University, noted that ERIC on SilverPlatter is, for them, "second most heavily used, also one of the best-constructed databases."

The interfaces are roughly equivalent in their capabilities, as are the searchable fields. OCLC separates their version into RIE and CIJE, making comprehensive searching of a time period more difficult, but this is the major difference. The Philbin and Ryan article, cited below, describes each version briefly and compares their features in a chart.

Reese and Steffey (article cited below) compared the three versions of ERIC over three years ago; some characteristics of the databases have changed since then. Their conclusions still generally hold up, though. They found that, "All three companies offer a good product with the capability of searching ERIC a bit differently. OCLC's unique use of windows makes it special. The ability to use an expert as well as novice mode with DIALOG Ondisc expands the possibilities for experienced searchers. SilverPlatter's customized formats, while they require some getting used to, do allow for a great deal of flexibility in displaying or printing results."

They conclude "As far as overall characteristics, we like DIALOG Ondisc best. It is a flexible and powerful system for searching ERIC, both for the novice and the experienced searcher. The capability of updating a search online is convenient and readily available. The Ondisc thesaurus also enables users to easily choose related terms for a comprehensive search."

Jean Reese concluded in another comparison article, "All three systems offer sophisticated searching of the ERIC database. Depending on your individual preferences for menu- or command-driven systems, you may like one over the other. If you are not interested in using the DIALOG command language, either SilverPlatter or OCLC provides a full range of searching capabilities. My one concern with OCLC is its indexing procedures and output order. DIALOG offers powerful options for expansion of searches, and while it works in a different way, is easy to learn."

Another early look at the DIALOG Ondisc version is described by Mary Kay Duggan. She worked with this version with a more sophisticated audience, library school students at Berkeley. She concluded, "DIALOG Ondisc will keep its command language users and heavy users of online searching will welcome the CD-ROM as a training tool. Berkeley's students have come to take for granted the efficient color screen designs and the speed of function key access to printing, downloading, sorting, and thesaurus browsing of terms and cross references. But I predict defections of new users to software with fewer menus to step through and with the simultaneity of windows, hopefully in combination with the full sophistication formerly available through command language."

Nancy B. Crane also took an early look at ERIC versions, providing an extensive evaluation of the DIALOG version, and briefer comparisons to the SilverPlatter and OCLC versions. She finds that "The Easy Menu Search mode of DIALOG Ondisc is an exceedingly sophisticated system, but one which an end-user can employ effectively with little or no training." She concludes, "DIALOG's OnDisc ERIC, even with its yearly licensing arrangement, should be considered a strong contender for the market of potential CD-ROM ERIC buyers. SilverPlatter's ERIC is less than one-half the cost of Ondisc for continuation (for the full service), but does little more than translate extant online search software for use with an optical database."

She continues, "At the University of Vermont, we have found that SilverPlatter's search system cannot be searched without some training. DIALOG Ondisc's Easy Menu Search can be more easily used by someone with no search training at all....What's more, OnDisc provides parallel search systems for novice and trained searchers. That novice system, unlike many CD-ROM services, has most of the power of the system designed for trained users, and in several instances...actually exceeds its power." She finds that "DIALOG Ondisc is a product that fully exploits the potential of optical technology, so has a good chance of providing SilverPlatter with some serious competition. It will have a lot of appeal for those institutions willing to pay the price."

Pamela McLaughlin evaluated all three versions of ERIC and noted features of each. She pointed out that DIALOG's version has a thesaurus, allows sorting of records, and provides for online updating. OCLC's version allows a lot of customization, has a help menu interface, has a complementary database in the Education Library, and sorts records according to relevance. SilverPlatter's version has extensive instructional information and also has a number of complementary databases available.

Sarah Gerrard evaluates the DIALOG Ondisc version of ERIC and finds that "A great deal of thought has been put into this very sophisticated piece of software. The Easy Mode is easy....This package provides a good teaching and learning medium for the novice and casual, less experienced searcher to interrogate this database. It is compatible with the way an inexperienced searcher would think. The design takes into account that the novice or casual user is task-oriented and allows for serendipity....the user can gradually progress in improving searching skills whilst achieving results as he goes along."

She continues, "Because the command mode emulates the DIALOG online mode, this again provides a good teaching and learning medium especially as the user can save a search strategy into the type-ahead buffer of the online mode. Access to the thesaurus is impressive and a lot easier to use than the hard copy. Retrieval power is also impressive on this disc and the facility for updating a search is apparently easy to carry out." Out of five stars, she gives DIALOG Ondisc ERIC three stars for customer support, four for documentation, and five for ease of use, getting started, and retrieval power.

In looking at several different CD-ROM interfaces, Paul Kahn studied DIALOG's ERIC, and found, "...the good news about this product is the optional Easy Menu interface, a simple and powerful tool for discovering information in ERIC....One of the great strengths of the menu interface is the way it displays aspects of the structure of ERIC to the user. This is in marked contrast to...the SilverPlatter interface...which do[es] not reconfigure...from database to database."

Lucie Olson also reviewed DIALOG ERIC and found, "New users will enjoy the Easy Menu Search method, and experienced users will find it a welcome innovation. Help screens are available to assist the new user, and the need to understand Boolean logic is reduced by the use of terms such as 'limit,' 'modify,' and 'exclude' in the 'Modifying Existing Search' menu. However, some practice, depending on the searcher's level of sophistication, will still be required to master the easy menu search."

She concludes, "For the experienced searcher, DIALOG Ondisc offers a fast and easy substitute to expensive online searching. Being able to update the search online using DIALOGLINK provides a valuable extra. The new user obtains a quick introduction to the ERIC database, conducts a reasonably well-constructed search, and leaves with a satisfying number of relevant hits."

Carolyn Pope evaluated ERIC from OCLC in a college library. She concluded, "The evaluation project for OCLC's ERIC on CD-ROM ran smoothly, and was virtually problem-free, apart from one or two very minor difficulties with installation of new software editions....help from OCLC Europe...by phone was prompt, friendly and efficient....contact was easily maintained. This state of affairs happily continues now that the library subscribes to ERIC on CD-ROM."

She continues, "Initially, despite publicity, take-up was slow, but after two weeks it took off with momentum, and since then ERIC on CD-ROM has received a great deal of use....comment was favourable....As a social science discipline Education benefits enormously from the good browsing facilities provided by ERIC on CD-ROM, and readers found the comprehension of the learning process involved educationally valuable."

Monical and Rible also evaluated the OCLC version of ERIC, and they conclude, "Our choice of the OCLC Search CD450 ERIC database has been a good one. Although OCLC needs to increase the retrieval speed (the method the system uses to find matching entries also is cumbersome) and, whenever users switch databases from RIE to CIJE and vice versa, the search software must be reactivated, we're confident that OCLC is committed to continuing to upgrade this product and decrease search time. [Version 3.0 of the Search CD450 software...does indeed improve search speed and provide a quicker transition from one database to another.]"

"Even with these shortcomings, the user really does benefit from the OCLC ERIC Search CD450. When compared with the time needed for manual searching of several years of ERIC, going from index to abstract and back, there is no comparison to the time saved by having computerized access. The cost has been well worth the increased accessibility to our collection and has provided our patrons with an improved means of researching education-related materials. The Search CD450 ERIC database is overwhelmingly accepted by students and faculty alike."

Jean Reese, in the January 1989 issue of *Laserdisk Professional*, evaluated the latest versions of DIALOG, OCLC, and SilverPlatter software as used with ERIC. She concluded, "DIALOG has made a real effort to enhance its product. Changing formats, sort/transfer and printing with the use of function keys makes the processes easier and more efficient. The ability to print one record at a time is a great change and most welcome. The few problems I have with printing can be smoothed over with sufficient instructions to patrons. Perhaps a change here and there in the wording would help. The addition of Related Terms to the Subject Headings search option makes that feature more powerful. DIALOG has done its homework and I believe they have an improved product as a result."

"SilverPlatter has responded to user comments by incorporating major enhancements. Searching is more convenient and powerful with the added features. SilverPlatter is the first company to incorporate a tutorial into their software. I believe this is a real indication that they listen and react to their customers' needs. They have shown a responsiveness and willingness to make their system as user friendly as possible."

"OCLC listened to its users and made substantial changes to upgrade the effectiveness of its product. Search CD450 had many good features in the old version, but the two areas of no double-posting and not displaying current records first made the system less appealing. With these taken care of the new version is a well-designed and user-friendly product."

"ERIC is undoubtably one of the most heavily used CD-ROM reference tools. With three companies in the market, the user population has a variety of choices. Because of the competition, each company has made meaningful changes and enhancements to its product. Each has spent time listening to customers and indeed, soliciting suggestions for improvement."

"Depending on your preference for a menu or command-driven system, windows, or need for a tutorial, there are three first-rate products from which to choose."

Rosemary L. Meszaros reviewed ERIC on SilverPlatter and found, "Without adequate preparation beforehand, either through the...tutorials or the user's manual, the frustration factor may be high for the first-time user who is not computer-literate. The librarian should be prepared to be asked for assistance. Because the manual is lengthy and the tutorials can take up to twenty minutes or more to complete, some provision for patron training or some condensed, 'cheat sheet' documentation is in order."

Van Auker, Frost, and Klingberg also reviewed ERIC on SilverPlatter in an early version. They concluded, "Using SilverPlatter ERIC directly with end-users made clear its shortcomings: documentation that lacked sufficient detail, awkward transitions between the three modes (Find, Show, and Print), and lack of vendor-supplied training/point-of-use aids. We had not considered CD-ROM products in order to acquire yet another reference tool requiring extensive instruction for effective use. We had hoped for the opposite: more power with less one-on-one time required. It was probably unrealistic to expect a computer-based index to teach Boolean logic and explain the structure of a large database. After all, users are not expected to sit down at *Psychological Abstracts* for the first time and use it effectively without assistance."

"To be fair, the shortcomings mentioned above are not insurmountable. Once our users received some instruction, they were able to use SilverPlatter ERIC reasonably independently. Most importantly, they had immediate and unlimited access to an outstanding database and were able to develop their search skills, particularly for multifaceted questions, at their own pace."

The database's greatest research weaknesses are its concentration on United States material, although some international material is included, and the lack of quality control for the RIE portion of the database. It is still, however, essential for education research.

Editor

REVIEWS

DIALOG
CD-ROM Lab Report 1 (June 1988): 40-41.

CD-ROM Librarian 3 (March 1988): 12-14.

CD-ROM Review 3 (July 1988): 31.

Crane, Nancy B. "Optical Product Review: DIALOG's OnDisc ERIC." *CD-ROM Librarian* 2 (July/August 1987): 26-35.

Duggan, Mary Kay. "A Look at DIALOG's First CD-ROM Product." *Optical Information Systems* 7 (November/December 1987): 401-405.

Gerrard, Sarah E. "CD-ROM Review: DIALOG Ondisc ERIC." *Online Review* 12 (August 1988): 225-232.

Kahn, Paul. "Making a Difference: a Review of the User Interface Features in

Six CD-ROM Database Products." *Optical Information Systems* 8 (July/August 1988): 169-183.

McLaughlin, Pamela W. "New Access Points to ERIC: CD-ROM Versions." *Education Libraries* 12 (Fall 1987): 73-76.

Meyer, Rick R. "Customer Experience with DIALOG Ondisc: a User Survey." *Laserdisk Professional* 1 (May 1988): 62-65.

Morabito, Margaret. "DIALOG Ondisc: ERIC." *CD-ROM Review* 2 (December 1987): 14-16.

Nicholls, Paul and Susanne Holtmann. "Research Perspectives — Women's Issues Searching with DIALOG OnDisc ERIC: Natural Language and Controlled Vocabulary Strategies." *Laserdisk Professional* 2 (May 1989): 97-103.

Olson, Lucie. "Experiencing CD-ROM ERIC." *Education Libraries* 12 (Fall 1987): 77-80.

Philbin, Paul and Joe Ryan. "ERIC and Beyond: a Survey of CD-ROMs for Education Collections." *Laserdisk Professional* 1 (November 1988): 17-27.

Reese, Jean. "A Comparison and Evaluation of Three CD-ROM Products." *Optical Information Systems* 8 (May/June 1988): 123-126.

Reese, Jean. "Diskware: ERIC on Compact Disc: New Software Versions from DIALOG, OCLC & SilverPlatter." *Laserdisk Professional* 2 (January 1989): 75-80.

Reese, Jean and Ramona Steffey. "ERIC on CDROM: a Comparison of DIALOG Ondisc, OCLC's Search CD450, and SilverPlatter." *Online* 11 (September 1987): 42-45.

Schamber, Linda. *ERIC on CD-ROM: Update. ERIC Digest*, Syracuse. NY: ERIC, 1988. ED 300 031.

Sabelhaus, Linda. "CD-ROM Use in an Association Special Library: a Case Study." *Special Libraries* 79 (issue 2, 1988): 148-151.

OCLC

CD-ROM Lab Report 1 (June 1988): 42-43.

Duggan, Mary Kay. "A Look at DIALOG's First CD-ROM Product." *Optical Information Systems* 7 (November/December 1987): 401-405.

McLaughlin, Pamela W. "New Access Points to ERIC: CD-ROM Versions." *Education Libraries* 12 (Fall 1987): 73-76.

Monical, Ruth and Jim Rible. "ERIC on CD, Southern Style." *OCLC Micro* 4 (June 1988): 18-22.

Philbin, Paul and Joe Ryan. "ERIC and Beyond: a Survey of CD-ROMs for Education Collections." *Laserdisk Professional* 1 (November 1988): 17-27.

Pope, Carolyn. "An Evaluation of ERIC on CD-ROM in a College Library." *Electronic Library* 7 (April 1989): 94-97.

Reese, Jean. "A Comparison and Evaluation of Three CD-ROM Products." *Optical Information Systems* 8 (May/June 1988): 123-126.

Reese, Jean. "Diskware: ERIC on Compact Disk: New Software Versions from DIALOG, OCLC & SilverPlatter." *Laserdisk Professional* 2 (January 1989): 75-80.

Reese, Jean and Ramona Steffey. "ERIC on CDROM: a Comparison of DIALOG Ondisc, OCLC's Search CD450, and SilverPlatter." *Online* 11 (September 1987): 46-51.

Schamber, Linda. *ERIC on CD-ROM: Update. ERIC Digest*, Syracuse, NY: ERIC, 1988. ED 300 031.

SilverPlatter

Anders, Vicki and Kathy M. Jackson. "Online vs. CD-ROM—the Impact of CD-ROM Databases upon a Large Online Searching Program." *Online* 12 (November 1988): 24-32.

Bane, Robert K. and Dennis F. Tanner. "Optical Disc Technology. Databases on CD-ROM: a Tale of Two ERICs." *Technological Horizons in Education* 16 (May 1989): 51-55.

Belanger, Anne-Marie and Sandra D. Hoffman. "Factors Related to Frequency of Use of CD-ROM: a Study of ERIC in an Academic Library." *College and Research Libraries* 51 (March 1990): 153-162.

CD-ROM Lab Report 1 (June 1988): 44-45.

Duggan, Mary Kay. "A Look at DIALOG's First CD-ROM Product." *Optical Information Systems* 7 (November/December 1987): 401-405.

McLaughlin, Pamela W. "New Access Points to ERIC: CD-ROM Versions." *Education Libraries* 12 (Fall 1987): 73-76.

Morabito, Margaret. "ERIC: Educational Resources Information Center." *CD-ROM Review* 2 (June 1987): 58-61.

Meszaros, Rosemary L. "Reviews: ERIC on SilverPlatter CD-ROM." *Government Publications Review* 15 (May/June 1988): 271-272.

Philbin, Paul and Joe Ryan. "ERIC and Beyond: a Survey of CD-ROMs for Education Collections." *Laserdisk Professional* 1 (November 1988): 17-27.

Purcell, Royal. "Micros at Work: Electronic ERIC." *Small Computers in Libraries* 8 (February 1988): 18-21.

Reese, Jean. "A Comparison and Evaluation of Three CD-ROM Products." *Optical Information Systems* 8 (May/June 1988): 123-126.

Reese, Jean. "Diskware: ERIC on Compact Disk: New Software Versions from DIALOG, OCLC & SilverPlatter." *Laserdisk Professional* 2 (January 1989): 75-80.

Reese, Jean and Ramona Steffey. "ERIC on CD-ROM: a Comparison of DIALOG Ondisc, OCLC's Search CD450, and SilverPlatter." *Online* 11 (September 1987): 46.

Schamber, Linda. *ERIC on CD-ROM: Update. ERIC Digest.* Syracuse, NY: ERIC, 1988. ED 300 031.

Scott, R. Neil and Edward M. Wolpert. "ERIC and Other Education Databases: an Overview for Users." *Educational Technology* 30 (August 1990): 26-32.

Stewart, Linda and Jan Olsen, "Compact Disc Databases: Are They Good for Users?" *Online* 12 (May 1988): 48-52.

Van Auker, Rosalind, Stan Frost, and Susan Klingberg. "Reference Serials: Online Bibliographic Searching." *Reference Services Review* 15 (Winter 1987): 89-94.

EQUIPMENT AND SOFTWARE REQUIREMENTS

DIALOG
Computer: IBM PC, XT, AT, PS/2, or compatible, 512K RAM minimum, 640K RAM recommended
Software: DOS 3.1 or higher, MS-DOS Extensions
CD-ROM Drive: any IBM-compatible

OCLC
Computer: IBM PC or compatible with hard disk and 640K RAM; Macintosh
Software: DOS 3.2 or higher, MS-DOS Extensions
CD-ROM Drive: any IBM-compatible, Apple

SilverPlatter
Computer: IBM PC XT, AT, PS/2, or 100 percent compatible with hard disk, 640K RAM; Macintosh Plus, SE, or II
Software: DOS 2.1 or higher, may use MS-DOS Extensions
CD-ROM Drive: Toshiba, Hitachi, Philips, Sony, DEC, or Apple

PRICE *DIALOG* annual price, current plus nine years backfile: $795, renewal $750; complete file: $1,295, renewal $750

OCLC annual price: $425, $350 for OCLC members, for current disc. ERIC retrospective files, three discs, going back to 1967 for *Resources in Education* and 1969 for *Current Index to Journals in Education*, one-time fee: $900, $750 for OCLC members.

SilverPlatter annual price: $650, for current disc with quarterly updates. Current disc with annual updates: $390. Complete starter set, with current disc with quarterly updates and archival disc set, first year: $1,200, subsequent years: $650. Archival disc set, one-time purchase: $900. Multiple orders for quarterly subscriptions only — current disc with quarterly updates: $250, starter set — $750.

ARRANGEMENT AND CONTROL

DIALOG
Record fields: abstract, author, availability, clearinghouse code, clearinghouse number, contract/grant number, corporate source, country of publication, descriptors, document type, government level, identifiers, journal announcement, journal name, language, note, number of pages, project number, publication year, report number, source information, sponsoring agency, tar-

get audience, title
Searchable: all but number of pages

OCLC
Record fields: abstract, actual pages in document, author, availability in paper/fiche or not from EDRS, CIJE/RIE accession number, clearinghouse accession number, contract number, EDRS price, geographic source, grant number, identifiers, institution name, language, major descriptors, minor descriptors, notes, number of fiche cards required, pagination, project number, publication type, publication type code, report number, reprint available from, RIE/CIJE issue number, source, sponsoring agency, target audience, title, year of publication,
Searchable: all but EDRS price, pagination, actual pages in document, number of fiche cards required, availability in paper/fiche or not from EDRS, RIE/CIJE issue number, reprint available from, source (journal citation subfield)

SilverPlatter
Record fields: abstract, accession number, author, availability, clearinghouse, clearinghouse number, contract/grant number, corporate source, country of publication, descriptors, document type, document type number, government level, identifiers, issue, language, level of availability, note, pagination, price, publication year, report number, source file, sponsoring agency, target audience, title
Searchable: all

SEARCH SOFTWARE AND CAPABILITIES

DIALOG
Software: DIALOG Ondisc
Capabilities: keyword, Boolean, search statement retention and back referencing, field searching, field limiting, proximity searching, printing, downloading, index searching, novice mode, varied display formats, nesting, truncation, search saving, online updating, thesaurus, sorting

OCLC
Software: Search CD450
Capabilities: keyword, Boolean, search statement retention and back referencing, field searching, field limiting, proximity searching, printing, downloading, index searching, truncation, nesting, varied display formats

SilverPlatter
Software: SilverPlatter
Capabilities: keyword, Boolean, search statement retention and back referencing, field searching, field limiting, proximity searching, printing, downloading, index searching, truncation, search saving, nesting, varied display formats

PRINT/ONLINE/OTHER MEDIA COUNTERPARTS
Print: *Resources in Education, Current Index to Journals in Education*
Online: ERIC — DIALOG, BRS, EPIC, ORBIT

NETWORK LICENSING ARRANGEMENTS

DIALOG
$475 more for current file on two to ten workstations; $825 more for complete file on two to ten workstations

OCLC
No additional charge

SilverPlatter
No additional charge

TITLE ESSAY AND GENERAL LITERATURE INDEX

PUBLISHER Producer: H.W. Wilson Co.
Vendor: H.W. Wilson Co.

SCOPE AND CONTENT
This subject-author index provides access to essays and articles in English-language essay collections and anthologies, emphasizing the humanities and social sciences. A broad range of subject areas is covered, from history, economics, and political science, to religion, film and drama. Literature is given special attention. Over 19,579 significant American essays that appeared in 1,593 volumes are included. Updated annually, coverage is 1985 to date. (Publisher's brochure)

Essay and General Literature Index is unique in its coverage of essays and articles within books; nothing else provides such comprehensive access to this form of material. The disc is broadly based in its coverage, indexes a material format hard to find elsewhere, has a good-sized backfile, and uses the Wilsondisc interface, which makes it accessible for research. On the down side, the coverage is not international and abstracts are not available. The benefits of the disc can be quite rewarding, however, for researchers in the humanities and social sciences.

Editor

EQUIPMENT AND SOFTWARE REQUIREMENTS
Computer: IBM PC, XT, AT, 386, PS/2, or compatible with hard disk with 1 megabyte of space available and 640K RAM, Hercules graphics or better, modem for online updating
Software: DOS 3.1 or higher, MS-DOS Extensions
CD-ROM Drive: any IBM-compatible

PRICE Annual price: $695

ARRANGEMENT AND CONTROL
Record fields: author, title, publication date, publisher, subject headings, special features
Searchable: all

SEARCH SOFTWARE AND CAPABILITIES
Software: Wilsondisc
Capabilities: keyword, Boolean, search statement retention and back referencing, field searching, proximity searching, printing, downloading, truncation, thesaurus, online updating, novice search mode, search saving, automatic singular and plural, nesting, local holdings display

PRINT/ONLINE/OTHER MEDIA COUNTERPARTS
Print: *Essay and General Literature Index*
Online: Essay and General Literature Index — BRS, Wilsonline

NETWORK LICENSING ARRANGEMENTS
No additional charge for inbuilding access; contact Wilson for remote access charges.

TITLE EXCERPTA MEDICA CD: ANESTHESIOLOGY

PUBLISHER Producer: Elsevier Science Publishers
Vendor: SilverPlatter

SCOPE AND CONTENT

Excerpta Medica CD: Anesthesiology covers both the clinical and experimental aspects of anesthesiology including: resuscitation and intensive care medicine, pharmacology of anesthetic agents, spinal, epidural, and caudal anesthesia, and acupuncture (when used as an anesthetic procedure). Over 3,500 journals are surveyed. It is updated quarterly, coverage is back to 1980. (Publisher's brochure)

The Excerpta Medica abstract journals are known for their thorough international coverage of medical topics. For institutions with an interest in anesthesiology research, this subset of the Excerpta Medica database provides an invaluable subject focus. It is, as mentioned, international in coverage, covers a good-sized length of time, and utilizes the useful SilverPlatter interface. Its only drawbacks are the inclusion of just periodical literature and the lack of the excellent Excerpta Medica abstracts, but it is, nonetheless, a database worthy of consideration for subscription by any medical research institution.

Mark Stover commented in his review, "Excerpta Medica CD: Psychiatry (hereafter Psychiatry), one of the first databases published in the Excerpta Medica series, may be a good choice for those researching psychiatry and the medical aspects of psychology, including topics such as addiction, suicide, sexual behavior, alcoholism, and the clinical use of psychomimetic and psychotropic drugs. Experimental psychology and normal psychology are not within the scope of Psychiatry unless they relate to a psychiatric disorder. This series uses the SilverPlatter software interface, which is well-known for its ease-of-use and powerful capabilities."

He found, "A comparison of searches done in both PsycLIT and Psychiatry shows a large overlap exists between the two databases in one direction: most of the records found in Psychiatry are also found in PsycLIT but not vice versa. This means Psychiatry should not be thought of as a replacement for PsycLIT. A similar comparison between Psychiatry and MEDLINE shows a significant overlap exists between these two databases as well." He concludes, "...if a library is primarily interested in psychiatry and the medical aspects of psychology, the Excerpta Medica Psychiatry database on CD certainly presents the most affordable alternative."

Editor

REVIEWS

Stover, Mark. "CD-ROM in Brief: Excerpta Medica CD: Psychiatry." *CD-ROM Professional* 4 (March 1991): 86.

EQUIPMENT AND SOFTWARE REQUIREMENTS
Computer: IBM PC XT, AT, PS/2, or 100 percent compatible with hard disk, 640K RAM; Macintosh Plus, SE or II
Software: DOS 2.1 or higher, may use MS-DOS Extensions
CD-ROM Drive: Toshiba, Hitachi, Philips, Sony, DEC, or Apple

PRICE Annual price: $995

ARRANGEMENT AND CONTROL
Record fields: accession number, address of author, author, CAS registry number, CODEN, country of publication, descriptors, EMTags, EMTags codes, ISSN, language, publication type, publication year, source, title
Searchable: all

SEARCH SOFTWARE AND CAPABILITIES
Software: SilverPlatter
Capabilities: keyword, Boolean, search statement retention and back referencing, field searching, field limiting, proximity searching, printing, downloading, index searching, truncation, search saving, nesting, varied display formats

PRINT/ONLINE/OTHER MEDIA COUNTERPARTS
Print: *Excerpta Medica Abstract Journal — Anesthesiology*
Online: Embase — DIALOG, BRS, Data-Star, DIMDI, Japan Information Center of Science and Technology

NETWORK LICENSING ARRANGEMENTS
$1,495 for multiusers

TITLE EXCERPTA MEDICA CD: CARDIOLOGY

PUBLISHER Producer: Elsevier Science Publishers
Vendor: SilverPlatter

SCOPE AND CONTENT
Includes over 270,000 abstracts and citations selected and indexed by Excerpta Medica. Information covered includes cardiology, cardiovascular diseases, and cardiovascular surgery. Also included are diagnosis, treatment, epidemiology, and prevention as well as all aspects of individual cardiovascular dis-

eases and disorders. Over 3,500 journals are surveyed; updated quarterly, coverage is back to 1981. (Publisher's brochure)

Excerpta Medica abstract journals are known the world over for their excellent international medical coverage and the quality of their abstracts. Any institution with a research interest in cardiology should consider this CD-ROM for its collection. The size of the backfile, the focus on one area of medicine, the excellent Excerpta Medica abstracts, the international coverage, and the SilverPlatter interface all make this ideal for research purposes. The drawback is the focus on periodical literature.

Editor

EQUIPMENT AND SOFTWARE REQUIREMENTS
Computer: IBM PC XT, AT, PS/2, or 100 percent compatible with hard disk, 640K RAM; Macintosh Plus, SE, or II
Software: DOS 2.1 or higher, may use MS-DOS Extensions
CD-ROM Drive: Toshiba, Hitachi, Philips, Sony, DEC, or Apple

PRICE Annual price: $995

ARRANGEMENT AND CONTROL
Record fields: abstract, accession number, address of author, author, CAS registry number, CODEN, country of publication, descriptors, EMTags, EMTags codes, ISSN, language, publication type, publication year, source, title
Searchable: all

SEARCH SOFTWARE AND CAPABILITIES
Software: SilverPlatter
Capabilities: keyword, Boolean, search statement retention and back referencing, field searching, field limiting, proximity searching, printing, downloading, index searching, truncation, search saving, nesting, varied display formats

PRINT/ONLINE/OTHER MEDIA COUNTERPARTS
Print: *Excerpta Medica Abstract Journal — Cardiology*
Online: Embase — DIALOG, BRS, Data-Star, DIMDI, Japan Information Center of Science and Technology

NETWORK LICENSING ARRANGEMENTS
$1,495 for multiusers

TITLE EXCERPTA MEDICA CD: DRUGS AND PHARMACOLOGY

PUBLISHER Producer: Elsevier Science Publishers
Vendor: SilverPlatter

SCOPE AND CONTENT
Drugs and Pharmacology contains more than 900,000 citations and abstracts spanning five discs. It provides comprehensive coverage of drugs and pharmacology literature, including the effects and use of all drugs and potential drugs, and the clinical and experimental aspects of pharmacokinetics and pharmacodynamics. The side effects and adverse effects of drugs are also covered. Drugs are mentioned by trade name. Over 3,500 journals are surveyed; updated quarterly, coverage goes back to 1980. (Publisher's brochure)

Elsevier Science Publishers are especially known for their coverage of the drug and pharmacology field, among their other excellent abstracting journals. The presence of lengthy abstracts, the international coverage, the long backfile, and the focus on one broad topic area make this highly valuable for pharmacological research. The SilverPlatter search interface is quite useful for research purposes. The only weakness is the focus exclusively on periodical literature.

Henry Saxe, in evaluating Excerpta Medica: Drugs and Pharmacology, felt that, "This product, designed for medical and health science libraries, should appeal to clinical researchers, medical students, pharmacy and pharmacology students and researchers, other health sciences students, and medical and health science librarians."

He concludes, "On a scale of 1 (hardest) to 5 (easiest), Drugs & Pharmacology deserves a 5 for ease of installation and use. Learning to use this database was simple and quick. Installation was easy and required no special computer knowledge or expertise. Even if this is your first CD-ROM installation, careful reading of the manual and following the instructions should provide a relatively easy and trouble-free experience. The users' manual is well written and put together and rates a 4.5. A 5 rating was only withheld because of the reluctance to give any manual a perfect mark, but this manual is as close as I have found. Overall, this is a highly satisfactory product."

Editor

REVIEWS
Saxe, Henry. "Optical Product Review: Excerpta Medica CD: Drugs and

Pharmacology," *CD-ROM Librarian* 6 (January 1991): 37-39.

EQUIPMENT AND SOFTWARE REQUIREMENTS
Computer: IBM PC XT, AT, PS/2, or 100 percent compatible with hard disk, 640K RAM; Macintosh Plus, SE, or II
Software: DOS 2.1 or higher, may use MS-DOS Extensions
CD-ROM Drive: Toshiba, Hitachi, Philips, Sony, DEC, or Apple

PRICE Annual price: $3,495

ARRANGEMENT AND CONTROL
Record fields: abstract, accession number, address of author, author, CAS registry number, CODEN, country of publication, descriptors, EMTags, EM-Tags codes, ISSN, language, publication type, publication year, source, title
Searchable: all

SEARCH SOFTWARE AND CAPABILITIES
Software: SilverPlatter
Capabilities: keyword, Boolean, search statement retention and back referencing, field searching, field limiting, proximity searching, printing, downloading, index searching, truncation, search saving, nesting, varied display formats

PRINT/ONLINE/OTHER MEDIA COUNTERPARTS
Print: *Excerpta Medica Abstract Journal — Drugs and Pharmacology*
Online: Embase — DIALOG, BRS, Data-Star, DIMDI, Japan Information Center of Science and Technology

NETWORK LICENSING ARRANGEMENTS
$5,245 for multiusers

TITLE EXCERPTA MEDICA CD: GASTROENTEROLOGY

PUBLISHER Producer: Elsevier Science Publishers
Vendor: SilverPlatter

SCOPE AND CONTENT
This title will span two discs with its 195,000 abstracts and citations. All aspects of gastroenterology are covered, including digestive system diseases and disorders, diseases and disorders of the mouth, pharynx, the hepatobiliary

system, exocrine pancreas, peritoneum, mesentery and omentum. Over 3,500 journals are surveyed; updated quarterly with coverage going back to 1981. (Publisher's brochure)

Excerpta Medica abstract journals are known for the quality of their international medical literature coverage. This CD-ROM focuses fairly narrowly on gastroenterology, but this will aid researchers in this area to do their research more quickly and completely. The presence of useful abstracts, the international coverage, the lengthy backfile, and the highly capable SilverPlatter interface make this an excellent research tool. The sole weakness is the focus on periodical literature.

Editor

EQUIPMENT AND SOFTWARE REQUIREMENTS
Computer: IBM PC XT, AT, PS/2, or 100 percent compatible with hard disk, 640K RAM; Macintosh Plus, SE, or II
Software: DOS 2.1 or higher, may use MS-DOS Extensions
CD-ROM Drive: Toshiba, Hitachi, Philips, Sony, DEC, or Apple

PRICE Annual price: $995

ARRANGEMENT AND CONTROL
Record fields: abstract, accession number, address of author, author, CAS registry number, CODEN, country of publication, descriptors, EMTags, EMTags codes, ISSN, language, publication type, publication year, source, title
Searchable: all

SEARCH SOFTWARE AND CAPABILITIES
Software: SilverPlatter
Capabilities: keyword, Boolean, search statement retention and back referencing, field searching, field limiting, proximity searching, printing, downloading, index searching, truncation, search saving, nesting, varied display formats

PRINT/ONLINE/OTHER MEDIA COUNTERPARTS
Print: *Excerpta Medica Abstract Journal — Gastroenterology*
Online: Embase — DIALOG, BRS, Data-Star, DIMDI, Japan Information Center of Science and Technology

NETWORK LICENSING ARRANGEMENTS
$1,495 for multiusers

TITLE EXCERPTA MEDICA CD: IMMUNOLOGY AND AIDS

PUBLISHER Producer: Elsevier Science Publishers
Vendor: SilverPlatter

SCOPE AND CONTENT
This two-disc set includes 260,000 records, with 7,000 records added per update. The scope of this set includes all aspects of clinical and experimental immunology as well as immunity, autoimmunity, hypersensitivity, histocompatibility, and all aspects of the immune system. There is extensive coverage of cancer immunology, immunotherapy, immunopharmacology, and immunological aspects of transplantation, paraproteinemia, and the lymphoreticular system. Information on AIDS is also well covered. Over 3,500 journals are surveyed; updated quarterly, coverage is back to 1980. (Publisher's brochure)

The vital and timely topics of immunology and AIDS are covered well by this database, which is based on one of the world-renowned Excerpta Medica abstract journals. The international coverage, the focus on one topic area, the lengthy backfile, and the capabilities of the SilverPlatter interface make this excellent for research. The only weaknesses of this database are the lack of abstracts and the focus on journal literature.

Editor

EQUIPMENT AND SOFTWARE REQUIREMENTS
Computer: IBM PC XT, AT, PS/2, or 100 percent compatible with hard disk, 640K RAM; Macintosh Plus, SE, or II
Software: DOS 2.1 or higher, may use MS-DOS Extensions
CD-ROM Drive: Toshiba, Hitachi, Philips, Sony, DEC, or Apple

PRICE Annual price: $1,145

ARRANGEMENT AND CONTROL
Record fields: accession number, address of author, author, CAS registry number, CODEN, country of publication, descriptors, EMTags, EMTags codes, ISSN, language, publication type, publication year, source, title
Searchable: all

SEARCH SOFTWARE AND CAPABILITIES
Software: SilverPlatter
Capabilities: keyword, Boolean, search statement retention and back referencing, field searching, field limiting, proximity searching, printing, down-

loading, index searching, truncation, search saving, nesting, varied display formats

PRINT/ONLINE/OTHER MEDIA COUNTERPARTS
Print: *Excerpta Medica Abstract Journal — Immunology and AIDS*
Online: Embase — DIALOG, BRS, Data-Star, DIMDI, Japan Information Center of Science and Technology

NETWORK LICENSING ARRANGEMENTS
$1,720 for multiusers

TITLE EXCERPTA MEDICA CD: NEUROSCIENCES

PUBLISHER Producer: Elsevier Science Publishers
Vendor: SilverPlatter

SCOPE AND CONTENT
This title spans two discs and includes more than 325,000 citations. The product covers a range of neurosciences and is especially strong in neurology and neurosurgery, epilepsy, and neuromuscular disorders. Nonclinical articles on neurophysiology and animal models for human neuropharmacology are also covered. Over 3,500 journals are surveyed; updated quarterly, coverage is back to 1980. (Publisher's brochure)

The Excerpta Medica abstracting journals are known in all medical institutions for their extensive international coverage of topics. This CD-ROM focuses on neurology and other neurosciences, a vitally important area of medicine. The international coverage, the focus on one topic, the lengthy backfile, and the SilverPlatter searching capabilities make this a useful research CD-ROM for any institution with an interest in medicine and psychology. The only weaknesses are the focus on journal literature and the failure to provide abstracts.

Editor

EQUIPMENT AND SOFTWARE REQUIREMENTS
Computer: IBM PC XT, AT, PS/2, or 100 percent compatible with hard disk, 640K RAM; Macintosh Plus, SE, or II
Software: DOS 2.1 or higher, may use MS-DOS Extensions
CD-ROM Drive: Toshiba, Hitachi, Philips, Sony, DEC, or Apple

PRICE Annual price: $1,145

ARRANGEMENT AND CONTROL

Record fields: accession number, address of author, author, CAS registry number, CODEN, country of publication, descriptors, EMTags, EMTags codes, ISSN, language, publication type, publication year, source, title
Searchable: all

SEARCH SOFTWARE AND CAPABILITIES

Software: SilverPlatter
Capabilities: keyword, Boolean, search statement retention and back referencing, field searching, field limiting, proximity searching, printing, downloading, index searching, truncation, search saving, nesting, varied display formats

PRINT/ONLINE/OTHER MEDIA COUNTERPARTS

Print: *Excerpta Medica Abstract Journal — Neurosciences*
Online: Embase — DIALOG, BRS, Data-Star, DIMDI, Japan Information Center of Science and Technology

NETWORK LICENSING ARRANGEMENTS

$1,720 for multiusers

TITLE EXCERPTA MEDICA CD: OBSTETRICS & GYNECOLOGY

PUBLISHER Producer: Elsevier Science Publishers
Vendor: SilverPlatter

SCOPE AND CONTENT

Excerpta Medica CD: Obstetrics & Gynecology encompasses human obstetrics and gynecology, including endocrinology and menstrual cycle, infertility, prenatal diagnosis and fetal monitoring, anticonception, breast cancer diagnosis, sterilization, psychosexual problems, and neonatal care of normal children. Over 3,500 journals are surveyed; updated quarterly, coverage is back to 1980. (Publisher's brochure)

As mentioned about the other Excerpta Medica "extracted" databases published by SilverPlatter, Obstetrics & Gynecology should provide any medical institution with an invaluable subject-focused collection of information. This especially vital topic is probably the concern of almost any general medical institution, and this database provides good abstracts of international periodical literature in the area. The backfile is over ten years long, and the SilverPlatter interface is quite useful for research purposes. The only drawbacks with some of these databases is their coverage of only periodical literature and the lack of abstracts, but it still certainly provides the bulk of the important medical information.

Editor

EQUIPMENT AND SOFTWARE REQUIREMENTS
Computer: IBM PC XT, AT, PS/2, or 100 percent compatible with hard disk, 640K RAM; Macintosh Plus, SE, or II
Software: DOS 2.1 or higher, may use MS-DOS Extensions
CD-ROM Drive: Toshiba, Hitachi, Philips, Sony, DEC, or Apple

PRICE Annual price: $995

ARRANGEMENT AND CONTROL
Record fields: accession number, address of author, author, CAS registry number, CODEN, country of publication, descriptors, EMTags, EMTags codes, ISSN, language, publication type, publication year, source, title
Searchable: all

SEARCH SOFTWARE AND CAPABILITIES
Software: SilverPlatter
Capabilities: keyword, Boolean, search statement retention and back referencing, field searching, field limiting, proximity searching, printing, downloading, index searching, truncation, search saving, nesting, varied display formats

PRINT/ONLINE/OTHER MEDIA COUNTERPARTS
Print: *Excerpta Medica Abstract Journal — Obstetrics & Gynecology*
Online: Embase — DIALOG, BRS, Data-Star, DIMDI, Japan Information Center of Science and Technology

NETWORK LICENSING ARRANGEMENTS
$1,495 for multiusers

TITLE EXCERPTA MEDICA CD: PATHOLOGY

PUBLISHER Producer: Elsevier Science Publishers
Vendor: SilverPlatter

SCOPE AND CONTENT
Excerpta Medica CD: Pathology includes general pathology and organ pathology, pathophysiology and pathological anatomy, as well as laboratory methods and techniques used in pathology. General pathology topics range from cellular pathology; fetal and neonatal pathology, including congenital disorders; injury (both chemical and physical); inflammation and infection; immunopathology; collagen diseases; and cancer pathology. Over 3,500 journals are surveyed; updated quarterly, coverage is back to 1980. (Publisher's brochure)

The Excerpta Medica Pathology CD-ROM, just as with the other Excerpta Medica CDs, draws from an excellent international source of medical research information. This CD-ROM provides a useful subject focus in a necessary medical area; it covers international information well, and with a more than ten-year backfile. The SilverPlatter interface is quite suitable for research purposes. Although the coverage is limited to periodicals and abstracts are not provided, nonperiodical literature does not matter as much in medicine, and this would be a useful acquisition for any medical research institution.

Editor

EQUIPMENT AND SOFTWARE REQUIREMENTS
Computer: IBM PC XT, AT, PS/2, or 100 percent compatible with hard disk, 640K RAM; Macintosh Plus, SE, or II
Software: DOS 2.1 or higher, may use MS-DOS Extensions
CD-ROM Drive: Toshiba, Hitachi, Philips, Sony, DEC, or Apple

PRICE Annual price: $995

ARRANGEMENT AND CONTROL
Record fields: accession number, address of author, author, CAS registry number, CODEN, country of publication, descriptors, EMTags, EMTags codes, ISSN, language, publication type, publication year, source, title
Searchable: all

SEARCH SOFTWARE AND CAPABILITIES
Software: SilverPlatter
Capabilities: keyword, Boolean, search statement retention and back referencing, field searching, field limiting, proximity searching, printing, downloading, index searching, truncation, search saving, nesting, varied display formats

PRINT/ONLINE/OTHER MEDIA COUNTERPARTS
Print: *Excerpta Medica Abstract Journal — Pathology*
Online: Embase — DIALOG, BRS, Data-Star, DIMDI, Japan Information Center of Science and Technology

NETWORK LICENSING ARRANGEMENTS
$1,495 for multiusers

TITLE EXCERPTA MEDICA CD: PSYCHIATRY

PUBLISHER Producer: Elsevier Science Publishers
Vendor: SilverPlatter

SCOPE AND CONTENT
All ten years of information on the topic—over 145,000 records—fit on one disc. Approximately 7,000 records are added per update. All aspects of psychology and psychiatry are covered, including addiction, alcoholism, sexual behavior, and suicide. Mental deficiency and the clinical use or abuse of psychotropic and psychomimetic agents are also included. Over 3,500 journals are surveyed; updated annually, coverage is back to 1980. (Publisher's brochure) (See page 112 for reviews.)

The Excerpta Medica abstract journals are well-known for their thorough international coverage of most aspects of medicine. Their databases have research strengths in their international scope, their subject focus intensity, their lengthy backfiles, and the utility of the SilverPlatter interface. This one on psychiatry and psychology is no exception. As with some of the others, the main weaknesses from a research point of view are the lack of abstracts and the focus on periodical literature.

Editor

EQUIPMENT AND SOFTWARE REQUIREMENTS
Computer: IBM PC XT, AT, PS/2, or 100 percent compatible with hard disk, 640K RAM; Macintosh Plus, SE, or II
Software: DOS 2.1 or higher, may use MS-DOS Extensions
CD-ROM Drive: Toshiba, Hitachi, Philips, Sony, DEC, or Apple

PRICE Annual price: $995

ARRANGEMENT AND CONTROL
Record fields: accession number, address of author, author, CAS registry number, CODEN, country of publication, descriptors, EMTags, EMTags codes, ISSN, language, publication type, publication year, source, title
Searchable: all

SEARCH SOFTWARE AND CAPABILITIES
Software: SilverPlatter
Capabilities: keyword, Boolean, search statement retention and back referencing, field searching, field limiting, proximity searching, printing, downloading, index searching, truncation, search saving, nesting, varied display formats

PRINT/ONLINE/OTHER MEDIA COUNTERPARTS
Print: *Excerpta Medica Abstract Journal — Psychiatry*
Online: Embase — DIALOG, BRS, Data-Star, DIMDI, Japan Information Center of Science and Technology

NETWORK LICENSING ARRANGEMENTS
$1,495 for multiusers

TITLE EXCERPTA MEDICA CD: RADIOLOGY AND NUCLEAR MEDICINE

PUBLISHER Producer: Elsevier Science Publishers
Vendor: SilverPlatter

SCOPE AND CONTENT
Excerpta Medica CD: Radiology & Nuclear Medicine covers radiodiagnosis, radiotherapy and radiobiology, ultrasound diagnosis, thermography, adverse reactions to radiotherapy, and techniques and apparatus. The nuclear medicine portion includes diagnostic and therapeutic applications of radioisotopes in bio-

medicine, the radiobiology of radioisotopes, aspects of radiohygiene, new labeling techniques, and tracer applications. Over 3,500 journals are surveyed. It is updated annually, coverage is back to 1980. (Publisher's brochure)

The Excerpta Medica Radiology & Nuclear Medicine CD-ROM fills a valuable niche in the medical research area, as do the other specialized Excerpta Medica databases. It has international coverage, uses the research-capable SilverPlatter interface, and has a workable subject focus. It also has a good-sized backfile. The drawbacks, as with some other databases, are the lack of abstracts and the focus exclusively on periodicals. Any medical institution, however, could profit from in-house access to this database.

Editor

EQUIPMENT AND SOFTWARE REQUIREMENTS
Computer: IBM PC XT, AT, PS/2, or 100 percent compatible with hard disk, 640K RAM; Macintosh Plus, SE, or II
Software: DOS 2.1 or higher, may use MS-DOS Extensions
CD-ROM Drive: Toshiba, Hitachi, Philips, Sony, DEC, or Apple

PRICE Annual price: $995

ARRANGEMENT AND CONTROL
Record fields: accession number, address of author, author, CAS registry number, CODEN, country of publication, descriptors, EMTags, EMTags codes, ISSN, language, publication type, publication year, source, title
Searchable: all

SEARCH SOFTWARE AND CAPABILITIES
Software: SilverPlatter
Capabilities: keyword, Boolean, search statement retention and back referencing, field searching, field limiting, proximity searching, printing, downloading, index searching, truncation, search saving, nesting, varied display formats

PRINT/ONLINE/OTHER MEDIA COUNTERPARTS
Print: *Excerpta Medica Abstract Journal — Radiology & Nuclear Medicine*
Online: Embase — DIALOG, BRS, Data-Star, DIMDI, Japan Information Center of Science and Technology

NETWORK LICENSING ARRANGEMENTS
$1,495 for multiusers

TITLE EXCERPTA MEDICA LIBRARY SERVICE

PUBLISHER Producer: Elsevier Science Publishers
Vendor: SilverPlatter

SCOPE AND CONTENT
Excerpta Medica Abstract Journals on CD-ROM contains the equivalent of the over forty Excerpta Medica abstract journals published between 1984 to 1987, inclusive. The years 1988–1989 are available exclusively to subscribers of the printed abstract journals. Approximately 150,000 abstracts are covered per year. In addition to these over forty abstract journals on CD-ROM, three other abstract journals—AIDS, Forensic Science, and Environmental Health and Pollution Control—which are not included in the print full-set subscription are included on the CD. Over 3,500 journals are abstracted. This database is updated semiannually. It is a two-disc purchase. (Publisher's brochure)

The Excerpta Medica abstract journals are well known for their thorough international coverage of most aspects of medicine. Their databases have research strengths in their international scope, their good abstracts, the great range of their coverage of all aspects of medicine, and the utility of the SilverPlatter interface. Any research institution covering the entire breadth of the medical field will find this CD-ROM version of the abstract journals invaluable. The main weaknesses from a research point of view is the focus on periodical literature and the moderate-sized backfile.

Martin Courtois, from the Science Library at Michigan State University, lists the Excerpta Medica database among his choices for research databases, commenting, "For medical libraries and university libraries that support biomedical programs, Excerpta Medica is a good complement to Medline, and will provide better coverage on drug-related and toxicology topics. EM is also very good for locating citations on health care in countries outside the U.S. Coverage on CD-ROM is only from 1984, and only subscribers to the *Excerpta Medica* abstract journals will receive the more recent years....We have this at MSU, but only because EM started sending it free to EM subscribers. EM is a major medical database, but I would recommend that libraries consider the CD-ROM only after they have Medline on CD."

Editor

EQUIPMENT AND SOFTWARE REQUIREMENTS
Computer: IBM PC XT, AT, PS/2, or 100 percent compatible with hard disk, 640K RAM; Macintosh Plus, SE, or II
Software: DOS 2.1 or higher, may use MS-DOS Extensions
CD-ROM Drive: Toshiba, Hitachi, Philips, Sony, DEC, or Apple

PRICE Annual price: $2,495; 1988–1989 disc, one-time cost: $895; 1984–1987 disc, one-time cost: $1,500; subscribers to the full-set of Excerpta Medica Abstract Journals: $495

ARRANGEMENT AND CONTROL
Record fields: abstract, accession number, address of author, author, CAS registry number, CODEN, country of publication, descriptors, EMTags, EMTags codes, ISSN, language, publication type, publication year, source, title
Searchable: all

SEARCH SOFTWARE AND CAPABILITIES
Software: SilverPlatter
Capabilities: keyword, Boolean, search statement retention and back referencing, field searching, field limiting, proximity searching, printing, downloading, index searching, truncation, search saving, nesting, varied display formats

PRINT/ONLINE/OTHER MEDIA COUNTERPARTS
Print: *Excerpta Medica Abstract Journals*
Online: Embase — DIALOG, BRS, Data-Star, DIMDI, Japan Information Center of Science and Technology

NETWORK LICENSING ARRANGEMENTS
Contact vendor

TITLE F & S INDEX

PUBLISHER Producer: Predicasts, Inc.
Vendor: SilverPlatter

SCOPE AND CONTENT

Facts and figures about companies, products, markets, and applied technology are provided in all manufacturing and service areas. Major trade and business journals, and government publications, from over 1,000 different sources are here. In addition to the one- and two-line summaries in F & S Index, the discs contain abstracts from the PROMT database and some full-text articles.

F & S Index Plus Text gives you coverage of all manufacturing and service industries and gives you coverage of important information on a wide range of topics dealing with business and applied technology, such as market size and share, new products, industry trends and forecasts, mergers and acquisitions, government policies and regulation, economic climate, consumer demographics, and more. Predicasts' product, event, and country codes can be used for retrieval. Each disc in the subscription contains one year of back data. Updating is monthly, and an annual archival disc is included at the end of each year to provide subscribers with a permanent library of business and technology information. (Publisher's brochure)

Predicasts databases are known for their intensive coverage of company information and industry news. The F & S Index on SilverPlatter is the only Predicasts information in CD-ROM format, and it forms an excellent research resource for United States and international business information. The inclusion of several formats of materials, the international scope, the provision of abstracts, excerpts, and full text, where available, the extensive Predicasts classification system for products, events, and countries, and the excellent SilverPlatter interface make this an excellent addition to the CD-ROM collection of any institution doing business research. The main drawback to the database at this time is the short backfile—only 1990. This will, of course, change with time.

Editor

REVIEWS

"Some Sensible Terms from Predicasts." *Library Monitor*, issue 22 (August 1990).

EQUIPMENT AND SOFTWARE REQUIREMENTS
Computer: IBM PC XT, AT, PS/2, or 100 percent compatible with hard disk, 640K RAM; Macintosh Plus, SE, or II
Software: DOS 2.1 or higher, may use MS-DOS Extensions
CD-ROM Drive: Toshiba, Hitachi, Philips, Sony, DEC, or Apple

PRICE Annual price, complete set: $6,000; U.S. disc only: $2,500, Europe/international disc only: $3,500; print subscribers to either index, both discs: $5,000; print subscribers to complete set, both discs: $4,000; print subscribers to U.S. index, U.S. disc: $2,000; print subscribers to either index, Europe/international disc: $3,000; print subscribers to complete set, Europe/ international disc: $2,500

ARRANGEMENT AND CONTROL
Record fields: company name, country, event name, ISSN, product name, source, text, title
Searchable: all

SEARCH SOFTWARE AND CAPABILITIES
Software: SilverPlatter
Capabilities: keyword, Boolean, search statement retention and back referencing, field searching, field limiting, proximity searching, printing, downloading, index searching, thesaurus, search saving

PRINT/ONLINE/OTHER MEDIA COUNTERPARTS
Print: *F & S Index: United States*, *F & S Index: Europe/International*
Online: PROMT — DIALOG, BRS, Data-Star, VU/Text F & S Index — DIALOG, BRS, Data-Star

NETWORK LICENSING ARRANGEMENTS
No additional charge

TITLE FOOD SCIENCE AND TECHNOLOGY ABSTRACTS

PUBLISHER Producer: International Food Information Service
Vendor: SilverPlatter

SCOPE AND CONTENT

FSTA is the Food Science and Technology Abstracts database produced by the International Food Information Service (IFIS) of the United States, the United Kingdom, the Netherlands, and the Federal Republic of Germany. FSTA covers topics, such as microbiology, toxicology and hygiene, economics and statistics, engineering, packaging, dietary foods, beverages, fruits, vegetables, nuts, sugars, cereals, fats and oils, milk and dairy products, eggs, meat, and spices and additives. It contains the most important information from 1,800 scientific journals on food science and food technology published throughout the world, as well as important information from books, proceedings, reports, pamphlets, patents, legislation, and more. The over 350,000 English-language abstracts included are prepared from work originally published in more than forty languages. Approximately 18,000 new records are added each year. Updating is annual, and coverage is back to 1969. (Publisher's brochure)

FSTA is far and away the most important food science database in the world and the only such database available on CD-ROM. It has absolutely no defects as a research database. It covers its subject field exhaustively, has abstracts, covers a variety of formats, has an extensive backfile, is international in scope, and boasts an interface quite suitable for research. Any library with a research interest in food science, home economics, nutrition, environmental health, and other related topics will find this an invaluable database.

Martin Courtois, of the Michigan State University Science Library, commented, "FSTA...covers over 1800 journals as well as patents, standards, books, conference proceedings, and dissertations. All foods and all aspects of human food commodities and processing, except the production of raw foods, are covered."

"FSTA offers worldwide coverage of the literature, and the CD-ROM version will be a great aid to researchers who want to limit their searchers to English language and/or U.S. authors. Libraries that support research programs in food science and nutrition will want FSTA and CAB Abstracts (for coverage of nutrition topics)..."

Editor

EQUIPMENT AND SOFTWARE REQUIREMENTS
Computer: IBM PC XT, AT, PS/2, or 100 percent compatible with hard disk, 640K RAM; Macintosh Plus, SE, or II
Software: DOS 2.1 or higher, may use MS-DOS Extensions
CD-ROM Drive: Toshiba, Hitachi, Philips, Sony, DEC, or Apple

PRICE Annual price: $4,750; renewal: $1,850; for print subscribers: $3,800; renewal: $1,440

ARRANGEMENT AND CONTROL
Record fields: abstract, address of author, author, corporate author, descriptors, identifiers, ISSN, ISBN, language, language of summaries, patent assignee, patent country, patent number, priority patent, publication type, publication year, publisher, source, subject code, title, update code
Searchable: all

SEARCH SOFTWARE AND CAPABILITIES
Software: SilverPlatter
Capabilities: keyword, Boolean, search statement retention and back referencing, field searching, field limiting, proximity searching, printing, downloading, index searching, truncation, search saving, nesting, varied display formats

PRINT/ONLINE/OTHER MEDIA COUNTERPARTS
Print: *Food Science and Technology Abstracts*
Online: FSTA — DIALOG, CAN/OLE, Data-Star, DIMDI, ESA/IRS, Gesellschaft fur Elektronische Medien mbH, Japan Information Center of Science and Technology, ORBIT

NETWORK LICENSING ARRANGEMENTS
Contact vendor

TITLE GEOREF

PUBLISHER Producer: American Geological Institute
Vendor: SilverPlatter

SCOPE AND CONTENT
This CD is the equivalent of the American Geological Institute's GEOREF database and the *Bibliography and Index of Geology*. GEOREF is a comprehensive resource with over 1.5 million citations, many with abstracts, covering the geology of North America from 1785 and the rest of the world from 1933. Over 4,000 journals in forty languages are scanned as well as books, maps, reports, USGS Publications, and U.S. and Canadian masters theses and doctoral dissertations. The database is updated quarterly. (Publisher's brochure)

GEOREF is the world's foremost geological database. No institution supporting geological research should be without it. Its comprehensiveness, its international coverage, its excellent archival information, its coverage of a variety of material formats, its provision of abstracts with many citations, and the SilverPlatter interface make it an excellent example of a database developed for research. The sole weakness is the fact that all of the entries do not have abstracts. It is still the most important CD-ROM to consult in this field.

Martin Courtois, science librarian at Michigan State University, comments about GEOREF, "...GEOREF is unique in that it provides a very complete backfile....More than 4,000 journals are indexed, along with conference proceedings, books, and dissertations. All aspects of geology and earth sciences are covered on a worldwide basis....GEOREF is the major database in geology, and will give the researcher much more precise access than its print equivalents."

Editor

EQUIPMENT AND SOFTWARE REQUIREMENTS
Computer: IBM PC XT, AT, PS/2, or 100 percent compatible with hard disk, 640K RAM; Macintosh Plus, SE, or II
Software: DOS 2.1 or higher, may use MS-DOS Extensions
CD-ROM Drive: Toshiba, Hitachi, Philips, Sony, DEC, or Apple

PRICE Annual price: $2,600; print subscriber: $1,950

ARRANGEMENT AND CONTROL

Record fields: abstract, accession number, author, availability, category code, CODEN, conference, country of publication, descriptors, document type, ISBN, ISSN, language, language of summary, map, map coordinates, note, organizational source, physical description, publication year, publisher, report number, source, subfile, title

Searchable: all

SEARCH SOFTWARE AND CAPABILITIES

Software: SilverPlatter

Capabilities: keyword, Boolean, search statement retention and back referencing, field searching, field limiting, proximity searching, printing, downloading, index searching, truncation, search saving, nesting, varied display formats

PRINT/ONLINE/OTHER MEDIA COUNTERPARTS

Print: *Bibliography and Index of Geology, Bibliography and Index of Micropaleontology*

Online: GEOREF — DIALOG, CAN/OLE, ORBIT, STN

Other Media: Bibliography and Index of Geology Exclusive of North America, Bibliography and Index of Geology — microfilm and microfiche

NETWORK LICENSING ARRANGEMENTS

$3,900 for multiusers; $2,925 for print subscribers

TITLE GPO MONTHLY CATALOG

PUBLISHER Producer: Government Printing Office

Vendor: Information Access Company (Government Publications Index), OCLC, SilverPlatter, H.W. Wilson (also includes Index to U.S. Government Periodicals)

SCOPE AND CONTENT

Contains citations from 1976 to present for government publications, such as books, reports, studies, serials, maps, and more from the *Monthly Catalog* published by the U.S. Government Printing Office. Included are topics like finance, business, demographics, agriculture, medicine, and public health.

Descriptors and categories set by the Library of Congress give you quick access to exactly the publications you need. Each citation in this powerful database contains all the information needed to locate the document at the library, at the nearest depository, or to order directly from the Government Printing Office. Information Access Company's version is updated monthly, OCLC's and SilverPlatter's bimonthly, and Wilson's annually. (Publisher's brochure)

For libraries who do not already have widespread access to *Monthly Catalog* in a computerized format, a CD-ROM copy is absolutely essential for research purposes. Researchers in all subject areas need to have computerized access to the listing of most materials published by the government. The breadth of subject access and the uniquely indepth coverage of one essential material format, government documents, make this a necessity for a research CD-ROM collection. The database's weaknesses are its lack of abstracts and its (understandable) focus on the United States.

Most of the interfaces have similar capabilities, except for the Information Access Company version, which is limited in its searching ability, unless it is mounted on a system using Infotrac 2000 software. (If it is not on Infotrac 2000 software, it only has simple keyword and Boolean "anding" capabilities for searching.) The Wilsondisc version may have an advantage in its inclusion of the Index to U.S. Government Periodicals along with GPO, and in its ability to access the GPO online database for only the cost of telecommunication.

An early article, by Peter Hernon, compared the Information Access Company version of GPO Monthly Catalog to several other technical services-oriented versions of it, and provided a comparative chart.

An article, cited below, from *Choice* reviewed three cataloging-oriented versions of GPO Monthly Catalog and the SilverPlatter and Wilson versions. About SilverPlatter, it notes, "The searching options of SilverPlatter are the most sophisticated," but "Novice searchers will have the most trouble with SilverPlatter." It rates the SilverPlatter version fourth of the five products reviewed.

Wilson is a "badly outrun" fifth. Wilson and GPO make "an unhappy union." About Wilson, the review continues, "To its credit, the Wilson CD includes the Index to U.S. Government Periodicals (IGP), but its claim to provide coverage through 12/31/88 on the reviewed disc is erroneous. IGP documentation and sample searches clearly show that IGP has fallen a year behind schedule; there were no citations on the disc more current than October 1987. Efforts to tailor the Wilson system to the MoCat database are perfunctory; for example, the online help screens for viewing a citation give a sample citation from Applied Science and Technology Index. This explanation of a citation to the magazine *Offshore* tells readers little about how to read a government documents citation." Although this review is almost two years old, it provides areas to inquire into, when considering the Wilson database.

McClamroch and Williamson find SilverPlatter's version of GPO to be "a powerful retrieval product." They conclude, "If...your clientele is generally more knowledgeable about online searching or using CD-ROM indexes, GPO on SilverPlatter offers a very powerful retrieval system."

Dena Adams also reviewed GPO on SilverPlatter and found, "SilverPlatter offers the high recall and flexibility of free-text searching, yet the search guides...are system-generic and at times cumbersome. Search features include a history of search sets, which can be useful in refining a search, and the 'lateral' search function. Despite these considerable advantages, the system is less user friendly...and would likely require more staff time to assist users with the complicated operations."

Editor

REVIEWS

Information Access Company
Hernon, Peter. "Comparison of Services for the Monthly Catalog of United States Government Publications." *Government Information Quarterly* 4 (issue 1, 1987): 101-106.

SilverPlatter
Adams, Dena. "Reviews: GPO on SilverPlatter (CD-ROM)." *Government Information Quarterly* 6 (issue 3, 1989): 325-327.

"Government Information," *Preview* 1 (December 1989): 10.

"GPO on SilverPlatter (CD-ROM)," *Preview* 2 (September 1989): 10.

McClamroch, Jo and Edgar Williamson. "Auto-Graphics vs. SilverPlatter: the Monthly Catalog on CD-ROM." *Library Hi Tech News* (September 1989): 1-6.

Plum, Terry and Hans Raum. "Monthly Catalog on CD-ROM." *Choice* 27 (September 1989): 59-60.

Serials Review 15 (1989): 63-70.

Wilson
Plum, Terry and Hans Raum. "Monthly Catalog on CD-ROM." *Choice* 27 (September 1989): 59-60.

EQUIPMENT AND SOFTWARE REQUIREMENTS

Information Access Company
Computer: IBM PC, XT, AT, or compatible with 640K RAM
Software: DOS 3.3 or higher, MS-DOS Extensions
CD-ROM Drive: any IBM-compatible

OCLC
Computer: IBM PC or compatible with hard disk and 640K RAM; Macintosh
Software: DOS 3.2 or higher, MS-DOS Extensions
CD-ROM Drive: any IBM-compatible, Apple

SilverPlatter
Computer: IBM PC XT, AT, PS/2, or 100 percent compatible with hard disk, 640K RAM; Macintosh Plus, SE, or II
Software: DOS 2.1 or higher, may use MS-DOS Extensions
CD-ROM Drive: Toshiba, Hitachi, Philips, Sony, DEC, or Apple

Wilson
Computer: IBM PC, XT, AT, 386, PS/2, or compatible with hard disk with 1MB of space available and 640K RAM, Hercules graphics or better, modem for online updating
Software: DOS 3.1 or higher, MS-DOS Extensions
CD-ROM Drive: Hitachi, Phillips, Sony

PRICE *Information Access Company* annual price: $2,500, including hardware; *OCLC* annual price: $350, $300 for OCLC members; *SilverPlatter* annual price: $600; *Wilson* annual price: $995

ARRANGEMENT AND CONTROL

Information Access Company
Record fields: author, citation, SuDocs number, title

OCLC
Record fields: actions, added entry, added entry — series, augmented title, author, bibliographic note, bibliographic history note, biographical note, cita-

tion note, coded mathematical map data, CODEN, conference name, contents note, contents type, corporate author, country of publication, credits note, cumulative index/finding aids note, current frequency, data on capture session, date of publication, DDC class number, dissertation note, edition statement, editor note, file characteristics, former frequency, former OCLC record number, former titles or variations, frequency, funding note, general note, government document classification number, government document number, host item entry, imprint, intended audience note, ISBN, ISSN, item number, key title, language, language of summary, LC card number, LC class number, linking entry complexity note, local subjects, locally assigned DDC class number, locally assigned LC-type class number, main series entry, map data, musical presentation area, NLC class number, nonspecific relationship entry, numbering peculiarities note, numerical designation, OCLC record number, original version note, performer note, photoreproduction note, physical description, place of publication, preceding entry, price, publication type, related computer files note, romanized title, series, short title, source of data file data, standard technical report number, stock number, subjects, subseries, succeeding entry, summary note, supplement note, supplement/special series entry, technical details, technical report number, title, translation of title, type of report note, uniform title, USGPO Monthly Catalog entry number, variant access title, varying forms of name, varying forms of title, with note
Searchable: all but physical description, current frequency, frequency, former frequency, price, numerical designation, bibliographic note, bibliographic history note, citation note, type of report note, numbering peculiarities note, intended audience note, supplement note, photoreproduction note, cumulative index/finding aids note, linking entry complexity note

SilverPlatter
Record fields: accession number, author, corporate author, descriptors, item number, notes, OCLC number, other titles, physical description, publication type, publication year, report number, series, source, SuDocs number, title, update code
Searchable: all

Wilson
Record fields: accession number, author, date of entry, Dewey Decimal Number, fiction indicator, government document number, journal source, language, LC card number, physical description, publisher, record type, subject descriptor, title, title remainder, year of publication
Searchable: all

SEARCH SOFTWARE AND CAPABILITIES

Information Access Company
Software: Information Access Company
Capabilities: keyword, Boolean "anding," printing, thesaurus, downloading, local holdings indication

OCLC
Software: Search CD450
Capabilities: keyword, Boolean, search statement retention and back referencing, field searching, field limiting, proximity searching, printing, downloading, index searching, truncation, nesting, varied display formats

SilverPlatter
Software: SilverPlatter
Capabilities: keyword, Boolean, search statement retention and back referencing, field searching, field limiting, proximity searching, printing, downloading, index searching, truncation, search saving, varied display formats, nesting

Wilson
Software: Wilsondisc
Capabilities: keyword, Boolean, search statement retention and back referencing, field searching, proximity searching, printing, downloading, truncation, thesaurus, online updating, novice search mode, search saving, automatic singular and plural, nesting, local holdings display

PRINT/ONLINE/OTHER MEDIA COUNTERPARTS

Print: *Monthly Catalog of United States Government Publications*
Online: GPO Monthly Catalog — DIALOG, BRS, Wilsonline, EPIC

NETWORK LICENSING ARRANGEMENTS

OCLC: No additional charge

SilverPlatter: No additional charge

Wilson: No additional charge for inbuilding access; contact Wilson for remote access charges.

TITLE HEALTH REFERENCE CENTER

PUBLISHER Producer: Information Access Company
Vendor: Information Access Company

SCOPE AND CONTENT

Health Reference Center includes an index to over 130 core publications on health, fitness, nutrition, and medicine. Publications covered include professional journals, consumer-oriented magazines and newsletters. It includes health-related articles from approximately 3,000 other magazines and newspapers. Provides article summaries of professional medical journals, specially written in lay language. Also includes the full text of approximately eighty of the core health and medical publications and selected full text from the remaining general interest magazines and professional journals. Article references are integrated with the text of leading medical and drug reference books; a medical dictionary and a proprietary tutorial database of background information on 300 diseases and medical conditions. Approximately 450 pamphlets are currently included, with the number expected to climb to 800. Index coverage begins in 1987, full text in 1989. Updating is done monthly. (Publisher's brochure)

The Health Reference Center represents the kind of value that can be added to information when it is put in CD-ROM format. Any researcher looking into medical and health-related topics, but wanting to cover not only the clinical literature, has no other choice than to use this comprehensive database. The combination of article citations, summaries and full text with material from reference books and a medical dictionary make this an invaluable and unique research source. Those in nonmedical areas researching medical topics and those wanting to trace coverage of health, medicine and nutrition in popular literature will find this a vital database.

Kaya and Yang, cited below, find the Health Reference Center provides "...particularly good sources for information on alternative health programs/approaches. Patrons can easily find citations to herbal and folk medicines, and diets, which are not easily accessible in traditional medical sources." They find the database to be "...user-friendly and [a] convenient end-user system...the browsing capability of the CD-ROM...is very useful and patrons can use it to expand their searches. In most cases, cross references are also very helpful." They conclude that the database "...meets the stated purpose for which it was designed...has more to offer users....We recommend the quality..." of the product.

In reviewing the Health Index, of which Health Reference Center is an expanded version, Lynne Fox notes that, "Health Index will offer a wide selection of materials not available in other databases when the index achieves its projected plan of covering the most recent four years. IAC has also included many valuable consumer health periodicals not readily available elsewhere..." She concludes that Health Index is "...a natural choice for public libraries. Medium to large libraries in academic settings with health programs or strong undergraduate interest in health issues should also benefit from a subscription. Even medical libraries with a large general public clientele could find advantages in a subscription. In fact, any library faced with the dilemma of providing accurate, easily accessed, non-technical medical information...is likely to find Health Index a valuable reference tool."

Cecil Chase mentions the Health Index Plus (a variation on the Health Reference Center containing less material) in a description of CD-ROMs at Oregon Institute of Technology. The article notes, "Health Index Plus from Information Access has been especially popular because of its unusual indexing policy. It does full indexing of certain periodicals which relate primarily to health, such as *Prevention*, and it does partial indexing—health articles only—of a great many more titles which may have some health-focused articles. These titles range from *Better Homes and Gardens*, and *FDA Consumer* to the *Washington Post*....This makes it very useful to every level of inquirer, from advanced nursing students to patients needing amplification of their doctor's explanation."

The database does have weaknesses: right now, the backfile is rather small, the emphasis is on the United States, and the Infotrac searching capabilities are limited. The recent addition of simple keyword and Boolean capability do make it at least minimally acceptable for research, however.

Editor

REVIEWS

Chase, Cecil L. "CD-ROMs at the Oregon Institute of Technology." *CD-ROM Librarian* 5 (December 1990): 21-22.

Fox, Lynne M. "CD-ROM in Brief: Health Index." *Laserdisk Professional* 2 (September 1989): 79-81.

Kaya, Kathryn K. and Andrea M. Yang. "Consumer Health Information from Information Access Company." *Database* 14 (February 1991): 54-56.

Preview 2 (issue 2, 1989): 29.

EQUIPMENT AND SOFTWARE REQUIREMENTS
Computer: IBM PC, XT, AT, or compatible with 640K RAM
Software: DOS 3.3 or higher, MS-DOS Extensions
CD-ROM Drive: any IBM-compatible

PRICE Annual price, with hardware: $11,800; without hardware: $9,800

ARRANGEMENT AND CONTROL
Searchable: subject headings, title, author

SEARCH SOFTWARE AND CAPABILITIES
Software: Information Access Company
Capabilities: keyword, Boolean "anding," printing, thesaurus, downloading, local holdings indication

PRINT/ONLINE/OTHER MEDIA COUNTERPARTS
Online: Health Periodicals Index — DIALOG

NETWORK LICENSING ARRANGEMENTS
Contact vendor

TITLE HEALTHPLAN-CD

PUBLISHER Producer: National Library of Medicine, American Hospital Association, National Health Planning Information Center
Vendor: Cambridge Scientific Abstracts, CD Plus, SilverPlatter

SCOPE AND CONTENT
HealthPLAN-CD is a bibliographic file covering the nonclinical aspects of health care delivery, including, but not limited to, all aspects of administration and planning of health care facilities, health insurance and financial management, licensure and accreditation, personnel management, staff, planning, quality assurance, health maintenance organizations (HMOs) and related topics. The file, which contains data dating from 1975, includes over 420,000 citations supplied by the National Library of Medicine (NLM), the American Hospital Association, and the National Health Planning Information Center (NHPIC). It also includes the entire *Hospital Literature Index.* Compact

Cambridge and SilverPlatter versions are updated quarterly. CD Plus is updated monthly. (Publisher's brochure)

In evaluating SilverPlatter's version of the Health Planning database, James Harrington states, "Overall I like this product. The indexing is consistent with other medical products (i.e., Medline). An experienced searcher will like the flexibility offered for performing a search. It has a superb manual, and SilverPlatter provides excellent customer service." (This article is cited below.)

The Health Planning and Administration database is the only extensive collection of material in machine-readable form that focuses on the "business" of health—hospital management, insurance, health care personnel, and more. Hospitals and other institutions focusing on health administration should have this highly useful database. Its lengthy backfile, the presence of abstracts, the useful subject research focus, and the SilverPlatter or Cambridge information retrieval interface all make it very suitable for research in its topic areas. Its drawbacks for research are the U.S. focus and the limitation to periodical literature only. It is still vitally important in the subject area it covers.

Editor

REVIEWS

SilverPlatter
Harrington, James. "Optical Product Review: HealthPLAN." *CD-ROM Librarian* 5 (October 1990): 19-21.

EQUIPMENT AND SOFTWARE REQUIREMENTS

Cambridge
Computer: IBM PC, XT, AT, PS/2, or 100 percent compatible with hard disk, 640K RAM
Software: DOS 3.1 or higher
CD-ROM Drive: any IBM-compatible

CD Plus
Computer: IBM PC XT, AT, PS/2, or 100 percent compatible with hard disk,

640K RAM
Software: DOS 3.1 or higher, MS-DOS Extensions
CD-ROM Drive: any IBM-compatible

SilverPlatter
Computer: IBM PC XT, AT, PS/2 or 100 percent compatible with hard disk, 640K RAM; Macintosh Plus, SE, or II
Software: DOS 2.1 or higher, may use MS-DOS Extensions
CD-ROM Drive: Toshiba, Hitachi, Philips, Sony, DEC, or Apple

PRICE *Cambridge* price: $795. Renewal: $695; *CD Plus* annual price: $1,995; CD Plus Medline subscribers: $1,495; *SilverPlatter* annual price: $850

ARRANGEMENT AND CONTROL

Cambridge
Record fields: abstract, author, author affiliation, corporate entry, entry month, ID number, ISSN, journal code, journal subset, language, major subject headings, MeSH word, minor subject headings, new material, notes, number of references, original title, personal name as subject, publication type, publication year, secondary source identifier, source, special list indicator, supporting agency, title, title continuation, unique identifier,
Searchable: all but corporate entry, number of references, original title, supporting agency, title continuation

CD Plus
Record fields: abstract, accession number, address of author, author, contract or grant numbers, country of publication, ISSN, language, major MeSH headings, Medical Subject Headings, original title, personal name, publication year, source, subset, title, update code
Searchable: all

SilverPlatter
Record fields: abstract, accession number, address of author, author, contract or grant numbers, country of publication, ISSN, language, major MeSH headings, Medical Subject Headings, original title, personal name, publication year, source, subset, title, update code
Searchable: all

SEARCH SOFTWARE AND CAPABILITIES

Cambridge
Software: Cambridge Scientific Abstracts
Capabilities: keyword, field searching, printing, downloading, thesaurus, online updating

CD Plus
Software: CD Plus
Capabilities: keyword, Boolean, novice mode, search statement retention and back referencing, field searching, proximity searching, printing, downloading, term explosion, field limiting, truncation, search saving, local holdings display, thesaurus, current awareness searches, automatic cross referencing, related record searching, varied display formats

SilverPlatter
Software: SilverPlatter
Capabilities: keyword, Boolean, search statement retention and back referencing, field searching, field limiting, proximity searching, printing, downloading, index searching, truncation, search saving, varied display formats, nesting

PRINT/ONLINE/OTHER MEDIA COUNTERPARTS
Print: *Hospital Literature Index*
Online: Health Planning and Administration — DIALOG, BRS, MEDLARS, DIMDI

NETWORK LICENSING ARRANGEMENTS

Cambridge: No additional charge

CD Plus: Networkable only on CD PLUS PLUSNET. PLUSNET1 serves up to four users at $35,000 plus. PLUSNET2 serves up to twenty users at $81,000; it includes dial access

SilverPlatter: No additional charge

TITLE HUMANITIES INDEX

PUBLISHER Producer: H.W. Wilson Co.
Vendor: H.W. Wilson Co.

SCOPE AND CONTENT

Humanities Index provides thorough, accurate indexing of 345 English-language periodicals. Students, teachers, researchers, and librarians rely on Humanities Index for easy access to timely information. Coverage is back to February 1984; updating is quarterly.

Humanities Index encompasses an eclectic range of subject matter, indicating the best contemporary scholarship on the best ideas of the past millennium. From Shakespeare to Schopenhauer, from Malthus to Miro, from choreography to hagiography, Humanities Index has it covered. Among the disciplines included are: archaeology and classical studies, art and photography, folklore, history, journalism and communications, language and literature, literary and political criticism, music and performing arts, philosophy, and religion and theology. Humanities Index also offers numerous listings for newly published works of fiction, drama, and poetry, and contains listings of citations to reviews of significant new books in the humanities.

The nearly 350 publications indexed by Humanities Index include some of our best-known scholarly journals—*Partisan Review*, *Artforum*, *PMLA*, *The Times Literary Supplement*—as well as numerous lesser-known but equally important smaller specialized magazines, such as *James Joyce Quarterly*, *Romance Philology*, and *Environmental Ethics*. Professional librarians with backgrounds in the humanities thoroughly and accurately index these journals, insuring efficient searches and more complete utilization of your periodical collection. (Publisher's brochure)

Since there are so few humanities databases on CD-ROM, and none focusing on the broad range of the humanities, Humanities Index is a valuable guide for the researcher. Its broad, otherwise inaccessible, subject coverage, the decent-sized backfile and the capabilities of the Wilson interface make it quite suitable for research. Its limitations must be realized: it covers periodicals only, not on an extensive international basis, and it provides no abstracts. It can still serve researchers as a valuable guidepost into the humanities literature, although, and is worthy of consideration by any institution supporting humanities research.

Pat Riesenman, reference librarian at Indiana University, calls Humanities Index "somewhat useful...I am not a fan of the WILSON system—I especially loathe WILSEARCH, which I feel often confuses users—people need to know more than they really know to use it adequately and they therefore get unsatisfactory results."

John Jaffe, in his library's evaluation of Humanities Index, found that, "The WILSONDISC system appeals to the trained searcher who can gather a great body of relevant material by using Boolean free text searching. Students were thwarted by Boolean, however....Faculty members appreciated the ability to access the WILSONDISC online sources directly from the same terminal used to search the CD-ROM databases; however, in practice they actually used other terminals to search DIALOG sources online when they sought more information....Students were discouraged from searching the WILSONLINE databases by the training that online access demands....For most undergraduate research projects, however, the maximum three-month lag in currency on the WILSONDISC system was not a factor in the value of the search results."

Paul Nicholls, cited below, gives Humanities Index three stars, out of a possible four, for data quality and search power, and four stars for ease of use.

Editor

REVIEWS

Jaffe, John G. "For Undergraduates: InfoTrac MAGAZINE INDEX Plus or WILSONDISC with Reader's Guide and Humanities Index?" *American Libraries* 19 (issue 9, 1988): 759-761.

Nicholls, Paul T. *CD-ROM Collection Builder's Toolkit: the Complete Handbook of Tools for Evaluating CD-ROMS.* Weston, CT: Pemberton Press, 1990.

EQUIPMENT AND SOFTWARE REQUIREMENTS

Computer: IBM PC, XT, AT, 386, PS/2, or compatible with hard disk with 1MB of space available and 640K RAM, Hercules graphics or better, modem for online updating
Software: DOS 3.1 or higher, MS-DOS Extensions
CD-ROM Drive: any IBM-compatible

PRICE Annual price: $1,295

ARRANGEMENT AND CONTROL

Record fields: author, title, journal title, citation, publication date, subject headings, special features
Searchable: all but citation

SEARCH SOFTWARE AND CAPABILITIES

Software: Wilsondisc

Capabilities: Keyword, Boolean, search statement retention and back referencing, field searching, proximity searching, printing, downloading, truncation, thesaurus, online updating, novice search mode, search saving, automatic singular and plural, nesting, local holdings display.

PRINT/ONLINE/OTHER MEDIA COUNTERPARTS
Print: *Humanities Index*
Online: Humanities Index — BRS, Wilsonline

NETWORK LICENSING ARRANGEMENTS
No additional charge for in-building access; contact Wilson for remote access charges.

TITLE ICONDA

PUBLISHER Producer: International Council for Building Research, Studies, and Documentation
Vendor: SilverPlatter

SCOPE AND CONTENT
ICONDA is the international construction database from the International Council for Building Research, Studies, and Documentation (CIB). Information is contributed to the database by professional organizations in fourteen countries. The database provides bibliographic references with abstracts to articles published worldwide in more than 800 journals and series, books, conference proceedings, reports, and other nonconventional literature. Topics covered include: all aspects of building construction, civil engineering, architecture, and town planning. Coverage is from 1976 to the present, with over a quarter of a million records. The database is updated semiannually. (Publisher's brochure)

For its breadth of coverage in construction, its international focus, the provision of abstracts, the size of its backfile and the coverage of a variety of material formats, ICONDA should be in any research institution dealing with construction, civil engineering, and architecture. The SilverPlatter search interface is entirely suitable for research purposes. For any institution dealing in these subject areas, as a research database, ICONDA has no weaknesses.

Editor

EQUIPMENT AND SOFTWARE REQUIREMENTS
Computer: IBM PC XT, AT, PS/2, or 100 percent compatible with hard disk, 640K RAM
Software: DOS 2.1 or higher, may use MS-DOS Extensions
CD-ROM Drive: Toshiba, Hitachi, Philips, Sony, DEC

PRICE Annual price: $950

ARRANGEMENT AND CONTROL
Record fields: abstract, accession number, added link, author, author address, availability, beginning page, CODEN, conference details, control number, corporate author, date, descriptors, document number, edition, end page, ISSN, language, language of summary, notes, original title, pagination, parallel title, physical description, physical edition, price, publication type, publication year, publisher, record identifier, related publications, series, source, title
Searchable: all

SEARCH SOFTWARE AND CAPABILITIES
Software: SilverPlatter
Capabilities: keyword, Boolean, search statement retention and back referencing, field searching, field limiting, proximity searching, printing, downloading, index searching, truncation, search saving, nesting, varied display formats

PRINT/ONLINE/OTHER MEDIA COUNTERPARTS
Online: ICONDA — ORBIT, STN

NETWORK LICENSING ARRANGEMENTS
Contact vendor

TITLE INDEX TO INTERNATIONAL ECONOMICS, DEVELOPMENT AND FINANCE

PUBLISHER Producer: Joint Bank-Fund Library
Vendor: Chadwyck-Healey

SCOPE AND CONTENT
The Joint Bank-Fund Library, chartered to serve the specialized information needs of the World Bank Group and the International Monetary Fund, is the

center of a network of special libraries in the Bank and the Fund. The "bibliography" portion of the Joint Bank-Fund Library's online catalog consists of an index to 1,050 current periodical titles and 700 research paper series. Public access to the library and its resources is exceedingly limited.

The Index to International Economic Development and Finance now makes this bibliographic resource available to the researcher seeking current information on international development, global economic trends, privatization, monetary policy, interest rates, debt forgiveness and rescheduling, and aid to developed or developing nations, as well as many other of today's emerging international economic topics. It will be updated and cumulated quarterly. Over 140,000 records are included in the first release.

The software used to access the data is very easy to use, permitting searching by region, country, subject, keyword, date of publication, author, title, and language (for records entered since 1987). The 4,350 assigned descriptors in the database permit access at a most specific level. It is the most tailored and subject-specific database for analysis of international economics and trade available.

Joint Bank-Fund Library staff reviews periodicals and research papers from all corners of the world to bring together an international bibliographic resource tailored to meet the needs of the World Bank Group and International Monetary Fund staff. The focus of the database is articles and papers of direct relevance to the work of the Bank and the Fund. The emphasis is on substantive articles of lasting interest—analysis, research and commentary—rather than news briefs and announcements. Most important, many of the journal titles and research papers series covered, particularly those from developing countries, are not electronically indexed elsewhere.

Roughly one-third of the records contain brief annotations that are fully searchable by keyword throughout the database. Approximately 75 percent of the material is in English, 20 percent in French, Spanish, or German, and the remainder in other languages. As an added feature, records entered since 1987 may be retrieved by language as well. The Index to International Economics, Development and Finance, representing the wide variety of source materials required by World Bank Group members, makes this information available to library patrons everywhere. The database is updated quarterly. (Publisher's brochure)

This impressive economic database makes available indexing to materials not accessible previously in electronic form—this is almost enough in and of itself to recommend it to economic researchers. In addition, the database provides exemplary international coverage of a variety of formats of materials. The backfile is lengthy, and annotations are provided for some of the materials. The research capabilities of the searching interface are also quite useful.

The drawbacks of the database are the two-thirds of the database that is without abstracts, and the fact that much of the material may be difficult to access, once a citation is obtained. This is an incredibly useful source for all interested in economic research, however, and it is definitely worthy of consideration for economic research institutions. (Publisher's brochure)

EQUIPMENT AND SOFTWARE REQUIREMENTS
Computer: IBM PC, XT, AT, PS/2, or compatible with hard disk with 2MB available, and 640K RAM
Software: DOS 3.1 or higher, MS-DOS Extensions
CD-ROM Drive: any IBM-compatible

PRICE Annual price: $1,500

ARRANGEMENT AND CONTROL
Record fields: author, city of publication, country of publication, date of issue, language, source title, terms, title, vol/issue/pps
Searchable: all but source title and vol/issue/pps

SEARCH SOFTWARE AND CAPABILITIES
Software: Chadwyck-Healey
Capabilities: keyword, Boolean, search statement retention and back referencing, field searching, field limiting, printing, downloading, index searching, truncation, varied display formats, nesting, thesaurus

PRINT/ONLINE/OTHER MEDIA COUNTERPARTS
None

NETWORK LICENSING ARRANGEMENTS
No additional charge for multiusers

TITLE INDEX TO LEGAL PERIODICALS

PUBLISHER Producer: H.W. Wilson Co.
Vendor: H.W. Wilson Co.

SCOPE AND CONTENT
Index to Legal Periodicals provides thorough, reliable indexing of articles in over 550 important legal journals, yearbooks, institutes, bar association organs, university publications and law reviews, and government publications originating in the United States, Puerto Rico, Great Britain, Ireland, Canada, Australia, and New Zealand. The disc's coverage is back to August 1981; updating is quarterly.

Compiled by professional indexers who are members of the bar in their respective states, Index to Legal Periodicals provides easy access to information as varied and wide-ranging as the law itself. Subject areas covered include administrative law, antitrust law, appellate procedure, arbitration, banking law, bankruptcy, business law, civil and criminal procedure, commercial arbitration, conflict of laws, constitutional law, contracts, copyright, corporations, courts, discrimination, domestic relations, entertainment law, environmental law, evidence, fair employment practices, family law, federal rules of procedure, food, drug, and cosmetic law, industrial arbitration, inheritance, insurance, international law, international trade, judicial systems, juries, labor law, landlord-tenant law, legal aid, legislation, liability, licensing, lobbying, maritime law, minorities, municipal law, negligence, non-profit corporations, occupational safety and health, partnerships, personal injuries, pleading, pre-trial procedures, probate law and practice, products liability, public utilities, real property, securities, taxation, torts, and trade regulation. (Publisher's brochure)

Since there is only one other CD-ROM database focusing on the legal periodicals area (see Legaltrac), Index to Legal Periodicals provides an alternative for the legal researcher. For its international coverage, inclusion of some variety of material formats, long backfile, and highly research-capable Wilsondisc interface, this CD-ROM database deserves serious consideration for any institution supporting law, political science, public affairs, and other related areas. It does not include abstracts, but this is its only major drawback. Ripy (cited below) notes among its pluses that it "covers nearly ten years worth of law review and journal articles. Provides two search options end-users can learn quickly. Excellent research tool for locating legal journal citations by subject or title approach. Provides for online updates and Boolean search logic. Publisher permits use in a network environment." Its minus is "search documentation specific to the Index to Legal Periodicals is not provided." Otherwise, it does a very good job of supporting research needs.

Cary Griffith, in surveying legal CD-ROMS noted, "The CD-ROM version of the ILP offers several interesting search and update features. Researchers have a great deal of flexibility in performing searches on the CD-ROM ILP....the ILP CD-ROM product will probably be of primary interest to law libraries and, possibly, large law offices."

Laura Peritore compared Index to Legal Periodicals and Legaltrac, and concluded, "WILSONDISC's Browse and LEGALTRAC offer the most accessibility to an untrained searcher. WILSONDISC's Wilsearch offers more and is still accessible to the average library user, and results in more citations than does a Browse search. Wilsonline is for the librarian/online searcher." There is "...some [Boolean] on Wilsearch, and extensive Boolean capabilities on Wilsonline. It is very easy to update searches run in WILSONDISC's Browse and Wilsearch to within the last few days by going online. This is not an option on LEGALTRAC, nor can searches be saved on LEGALTRAC."

"The advantages and disadvantages of both systems and the different results obtained by the same or similar searches may lead to the conclusion that both are needed for thorough coverage. Or, at least, if only one is purchased, the buyer can be assured that the one selected may not be all things to all users but is simply the one best suited to a particular library's needs."

Editor

REVIEWS

Griffith, Cary. "Legal Information on CD-ROM: a Survey." *CD-ROM Professional* 3 (issue 3, 1990): 80-85.

Peritore, Laura. "LEGALTRAC and WILSONDISC: a Comparison." *Legal Reference Services Quarterly* 8 (issue 3-4, 1988): 233-244.

Ripy, Minnie Sue. "CD-ROM Title Reviews: Legal Issues — Index to Legal Periodicals." *CD-ROM EndUser* 2 (October 1990): 50-51.

EQUIPMENT AND SOFTWARE REQUIREMENTS

Computer: IBM PC, XT, AT, 386, PS/2, or compatible with hard disk with 1MB of space available and 640K RAM, Hercules graphics or better, modem for online updating

Software: DOS 3.1 or higher, MS-DOS Extensions

CD-ROM Drive: any IBM-compatible

PRICE Annual price: $1,495

ARRANGEMENT AND CONTROL
Record fields: author, title, journal title, citation, publication date, subject headings, special features
Searchable: all but citation

SEARCH SOFTWARE AND CAPABILITIES
Software: Wilsondisc
Capabilities: keyword, Boolean, search statement retention and back referencing, field searching, proximity searching, printing, downloading, truncation, thesaurus, online updating, novice search mode, search saving, automatic singular and plural, nesting, local holdings display

PRINT/ONLINE/OTHER MEDIA COUNTERPARTS
Print: *Index to Legal Periodicals*
Online: Index to Legal Periodicals — BRS, LEXIS, Westlaw, Wilsonline

NETWORK LICENSING ARRANGEMENTS
No additional charge for inbuilding access; contact Wilson for remote access charges.

TITLE INSPEC ONDISC

PUBLISHER Producer: Institution of Electrical Engineers
Vendor: UMI/Data Courier

SCOPE AND CONTENT
Since it first went online in 1969, INSPEC has become the database researchers turn to for information about physics, electrical engineering and electronics, computers/computer science, and information technology. Now, twenty years and 3.75 million records later, this definitive reference source from the Institution of Electrical Engineers has become UMI's latest ProQuest database—INSPEC Ondisc.

INSPEC Ondisc provides abstracts and indexing to over 1,000 conference proceedings, books and reports and approximately 4,200 technical journals, 750 of which are indexed cover to cover. Scientists, engineers and other researchers can use this comprehensive database to find authoritative information about lasers, semiconductors and superconductors, astronomy/astrophysics, and geophysics; optical and optoelectronic devices, power generation, signal processing, and biomedical engineering; artificial intelligence, computer aided analysis and design, peripheral equipment and networking, and materials handling; information technology as applied to business, banking, insurance, office automation, marketing and retailing; and much more.

The INSPEC Ondisc database is a three-disc set that covers 1989, 1990, and 1991. The 1991 disc is updated quarterly. Each disc contains about 250,000 records. INSPEC Ondisc also features enhanced search capabilities that include a dedicated thesaurus, "bound phrase" searching, pull-down menus, and context-sensitive help screens. Two three-year subsets are also available in CD-ROM format; INSPEC Physics and INSPEC Electronics/Computer Science. (Publisher's brochure)

Long an unparalleled example of what an online database can be, INSPEC finally has come to CD-ROM. This database is the most essential source of information for researchers in physics, electronics, and computer science, and one of the most important for those in information science and technology and computers in general. As Becki Whitaker, Information Retrieval Specialist at the Indiana Cooperative Library Services Authority, points out, INSPEC is part of a "core of databases that have been online for almost twenty years and now find themselves on CD-ROM."

Covering a great array of sources in a variety of formats, INSPEC provides excellent international coverage. Its abstracts are exemplary, and the UMI/Data Courier search interface has proven to be sophisticated enough for researchers, yet simple enough for end-users. In addition new searching capabilities are provided geared toward INSPEC.

The backfile is comparatively short in time, but this matters less in these particular subject fields, and a great amount of literature is still covered. UMI/Data Courier software has proven to be rather slow with some of its databases, but this is the only drawback to this database. The software has been modified to accommodate special aspects of INSPEC, so it remains to be seen how well it will process. Although the interface appears more complicated than the past UMI/Data Courier search software, it allows much more sophistication, and increases the research accessibility of the database. INSPEC simply must be considered for acquisition by any research institution in technology and applied sciences.

Editor

EQUIPMENT AND SOFTWARE REQUIREMENTS

Computer: IBM PC or compatible with hard disk and 640K RAM
Software: DOS 3.2 or higher, MS-DOS Extensions
CD-ROM Drive: any IBM-compatible

PRICE Annual price: $7,500; print subscribers to all three abstract journals: $3,500; physics subset: $4,500; print subscribers to *Physics Abstracts*: $4,500; electronics/computers subset: $4,500; print subscribers to *Electrical Engineering* and *Computer and Control Abstracts*: $2,100

ARRANGEMENT AND CONTROL

Record fields: abstract, abstract number, accession number, affiliation, authors, chemical index, classification codes, CODEN, conference location, conference sponsors, conference title, conference year, corporate source, country of publication, date, document type, free terms, ISBN, ISSN, journal, language, numerical index, place of publication, publishers, report/contract number, thesaurus terms, title, translated item CODEN, translated item country of publication, translated item date, translated item ISSN, translated item title, treatment
Searchable: all but volume, issue number, pages

SEARCH SOFTWARE AND CAPABILITIES

Software: UMI/Data Courier
Capabilities: keyword, Boolean, search statement retention and back referencing, field searching, proximity searching, printing, downloading, index searching, truncation, automatic searching of singular and plural, nesting, varied display formats, library holdings display, thesaurus, automatic American/British spelling searching

PRINT/ONLINE/OTHER MEDIA COUNTERPARTS

Print: *Physics Abstracts*, *Electrical Engineering Abstracts*, *Computer and Control Abstracts*
Online: INSPEC — DIALOG, BRS, CAN/OLE, CEDOCAR, Data-Star, ESA/IRS, Japan Information Center of Science and Technology, ORBIT, STN

NETWORK LICENSING ARRANGEMENTS

Contact vendor

TITLE LASERGENE SYSTEM 2000

PUBLISHER Producer: DNASTAR
Vendor: DNASTAR

SCOPE AND CONTENT
Molecular biology software for DNA and protein analysis. Includes databases of GenBank and NBRF-PIR from National Biomedical Research Foundation, Vectors, AIDS (HIV), Berlin RNA, and Brookhaven Protein Data Bank. Updating is quarterly. The time span covered is 1965 to date. (*CD-ROMs in Print*, Meckler Publications, 1991)

Lasergene provides highly focused, international coverage of a variety of formats of material. As Martin Courtois, science librarian at Michigan State University, points out, "This is expensive...and specialized (molecular biology), but provides access to information that is not available in an up-to-date or easily searchable print form, nor is it available through the major online vendors."

"This CD includes three databases: (1) GenBank contains citations to journal articles and technical reports, as well as data on DNA and RNA sequences; (2) PIR Protein Sequence Database contains descriptions of protein sequences of over 1.7 million amino acids isolated or inferred from the gene sequences—citations to literature are provided with the descriptions; (3) VectorBank contains the nucleic acid sequences of 136 frequently used cloning vectors and restriction maps."

"Scientists who need to do sequence searches may have already discovered other ways to access these databases, but for libraries that need to provide this information, Lasergene provides a unique source."

Editor

EQUIPMENT AND SOFTWARE REQUIREMENTS
Computer: IBM PC, XT, AT, or compatible with hard disk and 512K RAM, and CGA, EGA, VGA or Hercules graphics card; Macintosh with 2MB memory
Software: DOS 3.2 or higher, MS-DOS Extensions
CD-ROM Drive: any IBM or Apple compatible

PRICE Annual price: $8,900

ARRANGEMENT AND CONTROL
Record fields: bibliographic data, function of protein, how sequence was experimentally determined, sequence annotations, sequence features of biological interest, source organism, starting point of sequence, taxonomy, unambiguously determined residues within the sequence

SEARCH SOFTWARE AND CAPABILITIES
Software: GENEMAN

PRINT/ONLINE/OTHER MEDIA COUNTERPARTS
Print: *NBRF Atlas of Protein Sequence and Structure*
Online: GenBank — BIONET PIR Protein Sequence Database — BIONET

NETWORK LICENSING ARRANGEMENTS
Additional $350 to $1,000 for multiusers

TITLE LATBOOK

PUBLISHER Producer: Fernando Garcia Cambeiro
Vendor: Fernando Garcia Cambeiro

SCOPE AND CONTENT
The first phase of LatBook covers original works by regional authors (excluding translations). Latin America now has at its disposal its bibliographic database in CD-ROM format. It is the only database of its kind, prepared by more than twenty-five library professionals, who process books from Argentina, Bolivia, Brazil, Colombia, Chile, Ecuador, El Salvador, Guatemala, Mexico, Paraguay, Peru, Uruguay, Venezuela, and the Dominican Republic, with plans to incorporate other countries of Central America and the Caribbean in the future.

This is the only database of its kind prepared by an *ad hoc* team of information specialists, analysts, and linguists. It is the only database of its kind that includes books immediately after their publication, giving a more complete coverage of new publications from the region. It offers a choice of several information display formats, such as MARC, "detailed," "full," purchase order, fax, etc.

The first commercial edition includes 35,000 items, and will incorporate more than 40,000 titles each year. New editions will be published in January,

May, and September of each year. All information consulted can be stored on hard disk and printed quickly. It is easy to use; with only a few keystrokes all information is within reach.

It is designed for the bibliographic needs of libraries, book stores, scientific and cultural institutions, the communications media, and others interested in Latin America through its books. It saves time and improves service. With LatBook, hours spent consulting bibliographies became a thing of the past. Both simple and complex searches can be realized in seconds.

Each book represents a professional effort for every Latin American country, by expert librarians, making LatBook a database of the highest quality, superior to others in its field worldwide. (Publisher's brochure, provided by Glenn F. Read, Jr., Librarian for Latin American Studies, Indiana University)

LatBook is one of the few databases that provides any kind of access to the bibliography of Latin America. It should be invaluable for any research institutions interested in Latin America. The search capabilities are acceptable for research purposes, and the international scope, abstracts, and focused, specialized nature of the subject coverage make this worthy of consideration for appropriate organizations. Although it focuses on one type of material, and does not yet have much of a backfile, this database is of interest because of its rare coverage.

Editor

EQUIPMENT AND SOFTWARE REQUIREMENTS
Computer: IBM PC, XT, AT, or compatible with 512K RAM

ARRANGEMENT AND CONTROL
Record fields: author, author's sex, government or private publication, title, translation, language, monographic series, series number, publisher, city of publication, country of publication, edition date, descriptors, subjects, LatBook code, abstract, ISBN, availability, date of publication, library codes, pagination, size of publication, binding, price, edition statement
Searchable: all but pagination, size of publication, binding, price, edition statement

SEARCH SOFTWARE AND CAPABILITIES
Software: LatBook
Capabilities: keyword, Boolean, proximity searching, field searching, trunca-

tion, varied display formats, thesaurus, printing, downloading, thesaurus and menus in Spanish and English

PRINT/ONLINE/OTHER MEDIA COUNTERPARTS
Print: None
Online: None

NETWORK LICENSING ARRANGEMENTS
Contact vendor

TITLE LATIN AMERICANA

PUBLISHER Producer: National University of Mexico
Vendor: Multiconsult SC

SCOPE AND CONTENT
This bibliography includes more than 165,000 articles on the life sciences, science and technology, library sciences, social sciences, economics and humanities from Latin American and foreign journals, reports and books, published between 1978 and 1987. Most of the documents cited are in the collection of the CICH library at the National University of Mexico. The database is updated annually.

The Latin American Bibliography has no equivalent in any other country. Latin American information published in journals has been scattered throughout a wide range of databases. The Latin American Bibliography is a single database specialized on Latin America (as seen by Latin Americans as well as non-Latin Americans), that also includes the output of Latin American authors published in national journals and in journals from abroad. The user may access information from hot superconductors to the movies of Juan Orol, from brain transplants to marine flora as well as television, just citing a few available subjects. The Latin American Bibliography includes six databases.

CLASE covers 1978-1987, containing 62,700 records, updated quarterly. The database is multidisciplinary in social sciences and humanities, from Latin American periodicals and reports. All documents are in the CICH library of the National University of Mexico.

PERIODICA covers 1979-1987, containing 54,100 records, updated quarterly. The database is multidisciplinary in science and technology, from Latin

American periodicals and reports. All documents are in the CICH library of the National University of Mexico.

BIBLAT covers 1978-1987, containing 52,200 records, updated semiannually. The database is multidisciplinary in social sciences, economics, humanities, science and technology, from non-Latin American journals. Documents are available through most document procurement centers including CICH Library. The content includes information from and about Latin America and includes all fields of knowledge.

MEXINV covers 1978-1987, containing 30,000 records, updated semiannually. The database covers science, technology, social sciences, economics and humanities, from national and international journals and reports. Most documents are found in the CICH library of the National University of Mexico. The content is papers by Mexican authors. It is a subset of CLASE, PERIODICA, and BIBLAT.

DESA covers 1985, containing 500 records, updated irregularly. The database is multidisciplinary in science, technology, and the humanities, from journal articles, books, and reports. All documents are found in the CICH library of the National University of Mexico. The coverage is of natural and industrial disasters.

INFOBILA is a bibliographic database on Latin American research and development in library and information sciences, from Latin American journal articles, books, and reports. Availability is from the CUIB library of the National University of Mexico. The content is library and information science research and development in Latin America. (Publisher's brochure, provided by Glenn F. Read, Jr., Librarian for Latin American Studies, Indiana University)

Suitable for indepth research because of its unique focus of subject coverage, Latin Americana covers a variety of material formats and a reasonable length of time. It also has foreign coverage and provides an excellent perspective on any topic dealing with Latin America. It does not have abstracts, but otherwise it supports research in a specialized way.

Editor

EQUIPMENT AND SOFTWARE REQUIREMENTS
Computer: IBM PC, XT, AT, or compatible with 20MB hard disk and 512K RAM

PRICE Annual price: $995

NETWORK LICENSING ARRANGEMENTS
Contact vendor.

TITLE LEGALTRAC

PUBLISHER Producer: Information Access Company
Vendor: Information Access Company

SCOPE AND CONTENT
An index to over 800 legal publications. Sources include all major law reviews, seven legal newspapers, law specialty publications, and bar association journals. The database is sponsored by the American Association of Law Libraries. The disc's coverage begins in 1980. The database is updated monthly. (Publisher's brochure)

Legaltrac has the most extensive coverage of law journals available on a CD-ROM database. For legal researchers needing to access the periodical literature, this database is highly suitable. The number of publications covered and the broad access to legal subjects make it invaluable in the legal research area.

Strengths mentioned by four users in "Your DISCussions" (cited below) include its user-friendliness, ease of author searching, and its coverage of the legal literature. Drawbacks include the lack of keyword searching and the occasional confusion from maneuvering around the subject heading guide. This kind of problem should now be lessened because of Infotrac's slightly expanded search capabilities.

The database's weaknesses also include the lack of an international focus, the limiting to periodical formats, and the minimal nature of the Infotrac searching capabilities. With the recent addition of keyword and simple Boolean powers, though, the interface is at least acceptable for research purposes.

Paul Nicholls, in his book cited below, gives Legaltrac three out of a possible four stars overall. He gives data quality three stars, search power one star (this was before the new version was available), and ease of use four stars.

L. Scott Rawnsley took an early look at Legaltrac, and remarked that "...it did bring a new, exciting way to do a tedious old chore....our users...say that a

Legaltrac search takes one-third the time of a search of printed indexes." He comments, "If successful results are the best measure of a system's worth, Legaltrac gets high marks from our users. Eighty-four percent indicated they found information on the subject of their query." He concludes, "...my favorite statistic is this: 88 percent of our users would wait for a tied-up Legaltrac terminal to be free rather than use a printed index; 30 percent would wait longer than fifteen minutes."

Cary Griffith surveyed legal CD-ROMs, and commented, "This CD-ROM version appears to be easier to use than the online LRI, and also has additional search features; most notably the ability to browse an automated thesaurus to locate the most precise indexing term....The primary use of IAC's LegalTrac will probably be in law libraries and some other large organizations (e.g., very large law firms)."

Laura Peritore compared Legaltrac and Wilsondisc; among her conclusions were, "LEGALTRAC's Legal Resources Index is a larger database than WILSONDISC's Index to Legal Periodicals. WILSONDISC's Browse and LEGALTRAC offer the most accessibility to an untrained searcher....LEGALTRAC uses L.C. subject headings while WILSONDISC uses the I.L.P. thesaurus. Some users may be more familiar with L.C. subject headings....Using L.C. subject headings also permits searching non-legal terms that might not be in the I.L.P. thesaurus."

"The advantages and disadvantages of both systems and the different results obtained by the same or similar searches may lead to the conclusion that both are needed for thorough coverage. Or, at least, if only one is purchased, the buyer can be assured that the one selected may not be all things to all users but is simply the one best suited to a particular library's needs."

Editor

REVIEWS

Griffith, Cary. "Legal Information on CD-ROM: a Survey." *CD-ROM Professional* 3 (May 1990): 80-85.

Nicholls, Paul T. *CD-ROM Collection Builder's Toolkit: the Complete Handbook of Tools for Evaluating CD-ROMS.* Weston, CT: Pemberton Press, 1990.

Peritore, Laura. "LEGALTRAC and WILSONDISC: a Comparison." *Legal Reference Services Quarterly* 8 (issue 3-4, 1988): 233-244.

Rawnsley, L. Scott. "A Laserdisk for Law Students—IAC's Legaltrac Database." *Database* 9 (December 1986): 25-30.

"Your DISCussions: LegalTrac." *CD-ROM EndUser* 2 (October 1990): 52.

EQUIPMENT AND SOFTWARE REQUIREMENTS
Computer: IBM PC, XT, AT, or compatible with 640K RAM
Software: DOS 3.3 or higher, MS-DOS Extensions
CD-ROM Drive: any IBM-compatible

PRICE Annual price, with hardware: $4,500; without hardware: $3,500; for two stations, with hardware: $8,500, for three stations: $9,500; for four stations: $10,50, for two to four stations, without hardware: $6,500

ARRANGEMENT AND CONTROL
Record fields: abstract, author, citation, title
Searchable: Subject headings, title, author

SEARCH SOFTWARE AND CAPABILITIES
Software: Information Access Company
Capabilities: keyword, Boolean "anding," printing, thesaurus, downloading, local holdings indication

PRINT/ONLINE/OTHER MEDIA COUNTERPARTS
Print: *Current Law Index*
Online: Legal Resources Index — DIALOG, BRS, LEXIS, Westlaw
Other Media: Current Law Index — microfilm

NETWORK LICENSING ARRANGEMENTS
Contact vendor

TITLE LIBRARY LITERATURE

PUBLISHER Producer: H.W. Wilson Co.
Vendor: H.W. Wilson Co.

SCOPE AND CONTENT
Library Literature is an index to 226 journals and more than 600 monographs per year. This index includes also English- and foreign-language library periodicals, selected state journals, library school theses, conference proceedings,

films, filmstrips, pamphlets, and more. It provides complete bibliographic data; updated quarterly, coverage is back to December 1984.

Library Literature offers easy access to a broad spectrum of information crucial to the operation of university, public, special, school and professional libraries. Library Literature provides thorough coverage of topics such as automation, CD-ROMs, cataloging, censorship, circulation procedures, classification, copyright legislation, education for librarianship, employment opportunities for librarians, government funding, information brokers, library associations, library schools, national and international libraries, online searching, personnel management, preservation of materials, public relations, rare book librarianship, standardization of bibliographic records, and trends in publishing. (Publisher's brochure)

Library Literature is one of the two CD-ROM databases that focus on library bibliographic indexing (see LISA), and it is essential to any library supporting library and information science research because of its particular focus. It provides access to United States as well as foreign literature, and it covers a variety of material formats. It has a good-sized backfile, and the research capabilities of the Wilsondisc interface. The main thing that it lacks is abstracts to go with the citations. It is still invaluable for library research.

Editor

REVIEWS

Weiss, C.M. "WILSONDISC." *Library Resources & Technical Services* 32 (April 1988): 185-187.

EQUIPMENT AND SOFTWARE REQUIREMENTS

Computer: IBM PC, XT, AT, 386, PS/2, or compatible with hard disk with 1MB of space available and 640K RAM, Hercules graphics or better, modem for online updating
Software: DOS 3.1 or higher, MS-DOS Extensions
CD-ROM Drive: any IBM-compatible

PRICE Annual price: $1,095

ARRANGEMENT AND CONTROL

Record fields: author, title, journal title, citation, publication date, subject headings, special features
Searchable: all but citation

SEARCH SOFTWARE AND CAPABILITIES
Software: Wilsondisc
Capabilities: keyword, Boolean, search statement retention and back referencing, field searching, proximity searching, printing, downloading, truncation, thesaurus, online updating, novice search mode, search saving, automatic singular and plural, nesting, local holdings display

PRINT/ONLINE/OTHER MEDIA COUNTERPARTS
Print: *Library Literature*
Online: Library Literature — BRS, Wilsonline

NETWORK LICENSING ARRANGEMENTS
No additional charge for inbuilding access; contact Wilson for remote access charges.

TITLE LIFE SCIENCES COLLECTION ON CD-ROM

PUBLISHER Producer: Cambridge Scientific Abstracts
Vendor: Cambridge Scientific Abstracts

SCOPE AND CONTENT
The Life Sciences Collection contains abstracts from more than 5,000 journals, books, monographs, conference papers, U.S. patents, and other sources—covering nineteen different fields across the scope of the life sciences. Subject categories include: animal behavior, biochemistry (with three subcategories: amino acids, peptides, and proteins; biological membranes; and nucleic acids), biotechnology, calcified tissue, chemoreception, ecology, entomology, genetics, human genome, immunology, marine biotechnology, microbiology (with three subcategories: algology, mycology, and protozoology; bacteriology; and industrial and applied microbiology), neurosciences (incorporating endocrinology), oncogenes and growth factors, toxicology, and virology and AIDS. Backfiles available to 1982; database updating is quarterly. (Publisher's brochure)

As pointed out by David Allen, Life Sciences Collection is a "large collection of records from nineteen abstracts journals published by Cambridge Scientific Abstracts. Encompasses biological, medical, and agricultural sciences. Very efficient and powerful proprietary search software used with other CSA CD-ROM products." This breadth of subject coverage, the backfile availability, the variety of formats covered, the interface searching capabilities, and the provision of abstracts make this database highly suitable for life sciences research. The only minus cited by Allen was a "confusing installation procedure not properly updated to accommodate latest hardware developments," something he found in all of the CSA databases. Once installed, however, this database should be quite useful for researchers.

Colborne and Nicholls looking at Life Sciences Collection before Biological Abstracts was available on disc, noted, "Along with the Science Citation Index, this database offers the most comprehensive coverage of the life sciences available on CD-ROM. It has several advantages over SCI, however. The most important is that it is dedicated to the life sciences, so all articles cited are relevant to at least one of these disciplines. Abstracts are included, and it offers controlled vocabulary searching as well as the option of using the command mode. Finally it is made more manageable by having fewer disks, thus alleviating the number of times searches must be repeated." They conclude, "Compact Cambridge Life Sciences Collection and Science Citation Index offer the most comprehensive global coverage of all areas comprising the life sciences."

In looking at medically related databases other than Medline, Fryer, Baratz, and Helenius found about Life Sciences Collection, in the area of ease of use, "Dot level commands include a help option and the menu search mode needs little explanation. Screen color and highlighting is excellent." They conclude, "The Life Sciences Collection from Compact Cambridge will be useful to researchers in biology, biochemistry, and medicine. Students will enjoy the menu mode, while sophisticated users will appreciate the flexibility and efficiency of command level searching. The Life Sciences Collection should find a home in both medical and science libraries."

Constance Miller, in reviewing Life Sciences Collection, concluded, "The compact disc version of the Life Sciences Collection is a worthwhile investment. For a reasonable price...users can perform an unlimited number of searches on a diverse and comprehensive biological database. Even the menu-driven novice search mode allows for complex searches....While some screens lack sufficient instructions, printed help is relatively clear and comprehensive....The availability of a compact disc version of the Life Sciences Collection will bring many users in contact with a variety of valuable biological abstracting sources that they would have been unlikely to search either in print or online format."

Martin Courtois, science librarian at Michigan State University, also likes Life Sciences Collection, commenting, "While Biological Abstracts is the most comprehensive database in the life sciences, the Life Sciences Collection on CD is still a viable choice. Backfile coverage extends to 1982, whereas BA covers only to 1989. The journals indexed in BA but not in Life Sciences tend to be lesser known foreign publications, and as a result Life Sciences still provides a valuable resource for life science researchers."

Editor

REVIEWS

Allen, David P. "CD-ROM Title Reviews: Life Sciences Collection." *CD-ROM EndUser* (July 1990): 60-61.

Colborne, David and Paul Nicholls. "Biology on Disc: CD-ROM Databases for the Non-Medical Academic Life Sciences Collection." *Laserdisk Professional* 3 (January 1990): 91-96.

Fryer, R.K., N. Baratz, and M. Helenius. "Beyond Medline: a Review of Ten Non-Medline CD-ROM Databases for the Health Sciences." *Laserdisk Professional* 2 (May 1989): 27-39.

Miller, Constance R. "Compact Cambridge Life Sciences Collection." *CD-ROM Librarian* 3 (April 1988): 22-24.

EQUIPMENT AND SOFTWARE REQUIREMENTS

Computer: IBM PC, XT, AT, PS/2, or 100 percent compatible with hard disk, 640k RAM
Software: DOS 3.1 or higher; MS-DOS Extensions
CD-ROM Drive: any IBM-compatible

PRICE Annual price, current year plus backfiles to 1982: $4,995; current year plus backfiles to 1986: $3,395; current year plus backfiles to 1989: $1,895; renewal for any of the above: $1,395

ARRANGEMENT AND CONTROL

Record fields: title, original title, author, author affiliation, corporate entity, source, editor, number, note, language, abstract language, abstract, publication year, descriptors, classification code, subfile, environmental regime, conference name, conference location, conference date, new material
Searchable: all

SEARCH SOFTWARE AND CAPABILITIES

Software: Cambridge Scientific Abstracts

Capabilities: keyword, Boolean, field searching, printing, downloading, field limiting, index searching, search statement retention and back referencing, proximity searching, varied display formats, search saving, truncation, nesting

PRINT/ONLINE/OTHER MEDIA COUNTERPARTS
Print: *Animal Behavior Abstracts, Cambridge Scientific Biochemistry Abstracts, Biotechnology Research Abstracts, Calcified Tissue Abstracts, Chemoreception A, Ecology Abstracts, Endocrinology Abstracts, Genetics Abstracts, Immunology Abstracts, Marine Biotechnology Abstracts, Microbiology Abstracts, CSA Neurosciences Abstracts, Oncogenes and Growth Factors Abstracts, Toxicology Abstracts, Virology and AIDS Abstracts*
Online: Life Sciences Collection — DIALOG

NETWORK LICENSING ARRANGEMENTS
No additional charge

TITLE LISA

PUBLISHER Producer: Library Association Publishing, Ltd.
Vendor: SilverPlatter

SCOPE AND CONTENT
Abstracts of the world's literature in librarianship, information science, and related disciplines as compiled by the Library Association Publishing, Ltd. Coverage includes references on library management and materials, as well as new technologies in such areas as teleconferencing, videotext, databases, online systems, telecommunications, and electronic publishing. The 550 periodicals covered are from 100 countries and are published in over thirty languages. It covers the complete database from 1969; updating is quarterly. (Publisher's brochure)

Royal Purcell describes something of the content of LISA, noting that LISA "...covers the international library periodical domain....LISA reflects the more recent impact of information science during the twentieth century....LISA also supplies an 'abstract' summary of each article....For the convenience of the reader confronted with a huge amount of professional literature, the 'abstract' summaries condense essential data into one or more paragraphs."

An article by N. L. Moore, cited below, describes in detail, searching LISA on SilverPlatter. Nargis Husain, a producer of LISA, talks about its potential for use in developing countries. The Terbille review, cited below, reports that "It is relatively easy to learn the basic features of the SilverPlatter Information Retrieval System (SPIRS) and the particulars of Library Information Science Abstracts (LISA) using the Introduction and Guide options on the menu of the title screen." He also points out that the language composition of the database is 65 percent English, 9.6 percent German, 5.9 percent Russian, 3.5 percent French, 0.8 percent Italian, and 0.5 percent Spanish; the rest is in other European languages. This makes for a truly international scope.

Terbille concludes, "In sum, despite a few flaws, SilverPlatter's software may be recommended for most users and uses, though it could be improved by providing computerized access to the classification code scheme. The underlying database provides valuable and unparalleled coverage of international library literature, but it could use some cleaning up."

LISA is the foremost international database in library and information science. Its international coverage is a particular strength, as is its extensive backfile. The presence of lengthy abstracts is also a great asset. It is essential to any library where librarianship itself is a topic of research. The SilverPlatter search interface is eminently suitable for research purposes, providing excellent access to the data. The only weakness of LISA is that it is a periodical source only.

Editor

REVIEWS

CD-ROM Librarian 3 (issue 9, 1988): 15.

Electronic & Optical Publishing Review 8 (June 1988): 84-86.

Hartley, R.J. "LISA on CD-ROM: an Evaluation." *Online Review* 13 (February 1989): 53-56.

Husain, Nargis. "CD-ROM: an Appropriate Technology for Developing Countries — LISA's Role in Indian Libraries." *Herald of Library Science* 27 (January/April 1988): 55-61.

Moore, Nicholas L. "LISA: On-line and CD-ROM Developments." *International Forum on Information & Documentation* 14 (April 1989): 24-30.

Moore, Nicholas Lister. "CD-ROM as a Practical Medium for a Small Publishing Company: LISA's 'Seedy' Adventure." *Laserdisk Professional* 1 (November 1988): 53-58.

Moore, N. L. "Searching LISA on the SilverPlatter CD-ROM System." *Program* 22 (January 1988): 72-76.

Purcell, Royal. "Getting to Know LISA and Other Thoughts on Abstracting." *Library Software Review* (November/December 1990): 357-362.

Terbille, Charles. "Optical Product Review: LISA on CD-ROM." *CD-ROM Librarian* 5 (September 1990): 26-28.

Urbanski, Verna. "Resources & Technical Services News: CD-ROM Takes Center Stage." *Library Resources & Technical Services* 32 (issue 1, 1988): 15.

EQUIPMENT AND SOFTWARE REQUIREMENTS
Computer: IBM PC XT, AT, PS/2, or 100 percent compatible with hard disk, 640K RAM; Macintosh Plus, SE, or II
Software: DOS 2.1 or higher, may use MS-DOS Extensions
CD-ROM Drive: Toshiba, Hitachi, Philips, Sony, DEC, or Apple

PRICE Annual price: $995; with subscription to other SilverPlatter databases: $750

ARRANGEMENT AND CONTROL
Record fields: abstract, abstract number, author, classification codes, composite works, date added, descriptors, editor, feature headings, language, original title, publication year, source, title
Searchable: all

SEARCH SOFTWARE AND CAPABILITIES
Software: SilverPlatter
Capabilities: keyword, Boolean, search statement retention and back referencing, field searching, field limiting, proximity searching, printing, downloading, index searching, truncation, search saving, nesting, varied display formats

PRINT/ONLINE/OTHER MEDIA COUNTERPARTS
Print: *Library and Information Science Abstracts*
Online: LISA — DIALOG, BRS, ORBIT

NETWORK LICENSING ARRANGEMENTS
No additional charge

TITLE MATHSCI DISC

PUBLISHER Producer: American Mathematical Society
Vendor: SilverPlatter

SCOPE AND CONTENT

MathSci Disc is the newest product in the Society's commitment to furthering mathematical knowledge and communication through effective research tools. The MathSci Disc contains all the reviews and abstracts from *Mathematical Reviews* 1981 to the present, plus 70,000 bibliographic records from the current awareness journal, *Current Mathematical Publications.* This title offers access to nearly half a million records. MathSci Disc covers the literature of mathematics and related fields, such as statistics, computer science, and engineering. The database is updated semiannually. (Publisher's brochure)

In the Murdock review, cited below, it is noted that "MathSci Disc is a most welcome and useful tool to have in a university library supporting graduate programs in mathematical sciences....MathSci Disc first appeared in April 1989, and since then, patrons from mathematics, statistics and other departments have logged many hours on it." Murdock also notes, "Suggestions for improvements are: to produce a backfile disc, to update more frequently than semiannually, to add...additional statistics records, and to include an online version of the hierarchical AMS classification system."

Lepkowski's review (cited below) notes problems with SilverPlatter's rendition of mathematical symbols included in reviews, and remarks that, in order to show these symbols accurately, "...the user must download search results from SilverPlatter's MathSci Disc for editing with the American Mathematical Society's own TEX software which many mathematicians use in the preparation of their own publications."

Lepkowski concludes, about MathSci, "Mathematicians will like it a lot because it enables them to search their central bibliographic resource much more easily, and over the long term they could simply accustom themselves to downloading search results and using them on their own equipment....The mathematicians who participated in the evaluation fairly drooled at the prospect of having this database for regular use....Well-endowed libraries with large mathematics research facilities to support may find MathSci Disc a popular addition to the library's resources....Even in such settings, however, one needs to ask the question whether there are enough potential users to make the investment worthwhile....MathSci Disc from SilverPlatter seems most plausible as a database used on the individual level, incorporated into a mathematician's personal workstation, with TEX and a laser printer close at hand, rather than as a stand-alone end-user library tool."

MathSci Disc is the most comprehensive source of mathematics literature indexing available on CD-ROM. Its special strength is its status as a reviewing tool, not just an abstracting tool. Its international coverage, its subject scope, the presence of reviews and abstracts, the variety of formats covered, and the size of the backfile make it an excellent database for research, which any library with math research interests should consider. Taken along with the useful SilverPlatter searching interface, it has no major weaknesses as a research tool.

Editor

REVIEWS

Lepkowski, Frank J. "Optical Product Review: MathSci Disc: a CD-ROM Mathematics Index." *CD-ROM Librarian* 5 (September 1990): 28-30.

Murdock, Martha. "Mathematics Made Easier on Disc." *CD-ROM EndUser* 1 (February 1990): 54.

EQUIPMENT AND SOFTWARE REQUIREMENTS

Computer: IBM PC XT, AT, PS/2, or 100 percent compatible with hard disk, 640K RAM; Macintosh Plus, SE, or II
Software: DOS 2.1 or higher, may use MS-DOS Extensions
CD-ROM Drive: Toshiba, Hitachi, Philips, Sony, DEC, or Apple

PRICE Annual price: $4,324; 20 percent discount for AMS members: $3,459; discount for *Mathematical Reviews* subscribers, or for additional Math Sci subscription: $2,162; 52 percent discount for AMS members with MR subscription or additional Math Sci: $1,986; 90 percent discount for individual at institution with Math Sci subscription: $432

ARRANGEMENT AND CONTROL

Record fields: abstract, accession number, author, CODEN, collection title, contributors, cross reference paper, Current Math Publications volume/issue, document type, editor, institution, ISSN/ISBN, language, language of summary, major descriptors, math reviews issue, math reviews number, math reviews number cross reference, minor descriptors, notes, original journal title, primary subject codes, publication year, publisher, review from, review length, review-non-personal, review type, reviewer, secondary subject codes,

series, subfile, title, translated journal title
Searchable: all

SEARCH SOFTWARE AND CAPABILITIES
Software: SilverPlatter
Capabilities: keyword, Boolean, search statement retention and back referencing, field searching, field limiting, proximity searching, printing, downloading, index searching, truncation, search saving, nesting, varied display formats

PRINT/ONLINE/OTHER MEDIA COUNTERPARTS
Print: *Mathematical Reviews, Current Mathematical Publications, Current Index to Statistics, Index to Statistics and Probability, ACM Guide to Computing Literature, Computing Reviews*
Online: MathSci Online — DIALOG, BRS, ESA/IRS

NETWORK LICENSING ARRANGEMENTS
$6,486 for multiusers; $3,243 for print subscribers

TITLE MEDLINE

PUBLISHER Producer: National Library of Medicine
Vendor: Aries Systems Corporation, Cambridge Scientific Abstracts, CD Plus, DIALOG, EBSCO, SilverPlatter

SCOPE AND CONTENTS
A comprehensive biomedical library from NLM. References and abstracts from about 3,200 journals published in over seventy countries. Search *Index Medicus*, *Index to Dental Literature*, and *International Nursing Index.* MEDLINE covers clinical medicine, experimental medicine, anatomy, communication disorders, dentistry, hospital literature, microbiology, nursing, paramedical professions, parasitology, pathology, pharmacology, physiology, population and reproductive biology, psychiatry, psychology, toxicology, and veterinary medicine. Backfiles available to 1966 for Cambridge Scientific Abstracts, EBSCO, and SilverPlatter. Coverage back four years plus current year for DIALOG. Coverage back nine years plus current year for Aries. All versions are updated monthly, although Cambridge and Aries have a quarterly option. (Publisher's brochure)

MEDLINE is the essential biomedical database. In CD-ROM form, it is available going back for twenty-five years. It covers the broadest array of medical journals, and is international in scope. No medically related search can be credibly done without using MEDLINE. In the words of Becki Whitaker, information retrieval specialist at the Indiana Cooperative Library Services Authority, MEDLINE is, of course, part of a "core of databases that have been online for almost twenty years and now find themselves on CD-ROM."

Its weaknesses include the fact that 40 percent of its entries do not have abstracts, and it only covers periodicals. The Cambridge, EBSCO, and SilverPlatter versions have the longest backfiles. The EBSCO version offers many interesting features, but they do not particularly increase its research ability.

The most extensive collection of evaluative information on MEDLINE is contained in *MEDLINE on CD-ROM*, cited below. Although a bit dated, it has evaluative articles on the DIALOG, SilverPlatter, Cambridge, EBSCO, and Knowledge Finder (Aries) versions of MEDLINE. Although there is no overall recommendation of a "best" version of MEDLINE, a checklist of comparative features is included. In evaluative surveys conducted throughout the book, users strongly welcomed the availability of MEDLINE in CD-ROM form, and used it extensively. Connie Miller's article in *RQ* summarizes descriptions of the products evaluated in the book, but does not give critical information.

Bakker, Bleaker, *et al.*, compare several versions of MEDLINE, including Compact Cambridge, DIALOG, EBSCO, and SilverPlatter. About the Cambridge version, they commented, "The research team found CC to be user-friendly. Its comprehensiveness makes it a useful acquisition for an academic library." They also note, "...the advantages of the DIALOG CD-ROM...include high speed, numerous options for experienced searchers (even sorting is possible), and ease of use." About EBSCO, "This CD-ROM offers perhaps too many features, and if Ebsco were to make the system less complex, it could be a good tool to search with." Concerning the SilverPlatter version, "The SilverPlatter CD-ROM is user-friendly, with a number of self-explanatory helpscreens....A major disadvantage of the system, however, is that it slows down considerably the moment truncation is applied on 'heavy terms.'" They summarize, "The SilverPlatter, DIALOG and Compact Cambridge versions appear to be most suitable for novice or infrequent users, with the DIALOG and Ebsco versions offering extra facilities for experienced searchers." They provide an extensive, detailed checklist for comparisons.

A review in *Choice* by B. Park compares the Cambridge, EBSCO, and SilverPlatter versions of MEDLINE, and notes, "...while sometimes confusing, none is difficult to use." Park concludes, "MEDLINE is an extremely large and highly structured database, best suited for faculty, graduate, and upper-division undergraduate students. Each of these CD systems provides a user-friendly environment for searching, yet each has its peculiarities. For undergraduate use, SilverPlatter seems most useful. In libraries that already have SilverPlatter products, this one will find rapid acceptance. The standardization of search software allows instructors to concentrate on the specific database rather than the mechanics of the search process....Academic libraries serving faculty, graduate, and undergraduate students will find that the straightforward, uncomplicated approach of SilverPlatter compensates for the added features of the other systems."

Morgan, Yan, Norris and Lo evaluated DIALOG and EBSCO versions of MEDLINE at a Hong Kong academic library, and concluded, "There is no doubt that DIALOG is the product of choice because it is more user-friendly. This factor is crucial in attracting users to CD-ROM." They provide detailed user reactions to EBSCO and DIALOG.

Ladner and Barnett have done a recent comparison update of available MEDLINE versions. They note that Aries Knowledge Finder "...is probably the most unique system. Experienced searchers will probably have more trouble using this product because it does not search the way we would expect. The clinician or less experienced end-user will no doubt find the product fascinating." They also note, "One of the most sophisticated and comprehensive products is CD-PLUS MEDLINE. It has a number of options that are particularly useful to searchers." In addition, "Compact Cambridge MEDLINE was the first MEDLINE on a compact disk. It offers easy-to-use menus and a dot-dot command interface. The system provides a variety of formatting and output options." They conclude, "When faced with the variety of features offered with each product, the choice of which product best suits a library's needs becomes truly difficult."

The Underhill article evaluating the CD Plus version of MEDLINE notes that its advantages over other MEDLINE versions include its automatic mapping to MEDLINE indexing terms, comparatively few discs to use, and advanced features for trained searchers. The Nesbit article about CD Plus MEDLINE noted that, after comparing different versions of MEDLINE, Nesbit's library chose CD Plus for its ability to search more than one year simultaneously, the mapping of the patron's term to the appropriate MeSH heading, its exploding of MeSH tree structures, and its useful online tutorial and user manuals. She says, "There is a high user satisfaction and self-sufficiency with CD Plus." She notes that it does not allow postqualifying of search sets and searches of the institutional affiliation field. She concludes, however, "I cannot recommend CD Plus Medline highly enough for either end-users or professional searchers."

Kesselman agrees, giving CD Plus an accolade: "I used to think that CD-ROM was yet another format libraries had to deal with. I also felt CD-ROM was limited and not appropriate for large databases, such as MEDLINE or Chemical Abstracts. Although I felt CD-ROM was a great way to introduce end-user searching at an affordable fixed cost, it did not have the power or capabilities of online. Well, a new product, CD-Plus MEDLINE, is making me eat these words. This product and some additional new trends make me feel that CD-ROM is no longer an interim technology. CD-ROM is here to stay! What makes CD-Plus MEDLINE so powerful is the hardware configuration."

Paul Kahn, in comparing CD-ROM searching interfaces and looking at Aries' Knowledge Finder software, found that "Knowledge Finder is a unique blend of several innovations in information retrieval, wedded to a wonderfully designed user interface....When used in combination with a large bibliographic database on CD-ROM, these features redefine the task of searching for information." He also finds that, "Knowledge Finder makes excellent use of the window and pull-down menu features of the standard Macintosh interface." He concludes, "Knowledge Finder illustrates what possibilities unfold once the search application makes intelligent use of a full windowing system. Being a Macintosh application, it assumes the use of a mouse and inherits (and makes very good use of) the pull-down menus, full set of fonts, multiple windows, and general point-and-click features of the Macintosh interface."

Alan Zeichick also evaluated the Aries version of MEDLINE, and said, "The program's online help is comprehensive, error codes are written in English, menus are easy to understand, and the program is fast. But that's not all. Aries Systems loaded Medline Knowledge Finder with extra features: a medical spelling dictionary, the power to add annotations to a citation before printing it, and the ability to customize virtually everything. Medline's not just for librarians anymore. The Mac version is suited to the medical secretary, busy surgeon, or researcher. It's easy to use and non-intimidating, and that should inspire better results."

Candy Schwartz took a more recent look at the Knowledge Finder interface to MEDLINE, and found, "Aries Systems Corporation's Knowledge Finder is an innovative CD-ROM product for the Macintosh....The product's innovation comes in the use of associative retrieval techniques combined with an icon-based approach, which makes searching simple—even for the unskilled user." She concludes, "MEDLINE, in its various forms, is available from many different CD-ROM suppliers, [but]....None of the other versions support the same type of searching as Knowledge Finder and few are probably as easy for a neophyte to use with as much success....in my opinion, Knowledge Finder presents a real added value in the way in which it combines ease of use with powerful retrieval and a large degree of user control over the search process."

At the University of Illinois at Chicago, an evaluation of the EBSCO version of MEDLINE was carried out by Tylman, Laird, and Vigil. They found that "...most [users] are able to find something on their topic. Further, the impression by most is that the EBSCO CD-ROM MEDLINE system is easy to use." EBSCO brought "...a very powerful and dynamic information utility that is highly valued and appreciated by patrons."

Capodagli, Mardikian, and Uva reviewed the Cambridge version of MEDLINE in its very first form. They concluded, "If success is measured by consistently high usage, then CC/MEDLINE has been an overwhelming success at SUNY HSC Library at Syracuse. Success can also be demonstrated by an increased user understanding of MEDLINE and an awareness of MeSH indexing. Requests for more CD-ROM readers and other databases on compact disc further indicate popularity. When the cost is measured against the high use of the system, the cost per search ratio reflects a good investment. CC/MEDLINE is a source which complements the printed *Index Medicus*, the online version of MEDLINE, and which has provided improved public relations in our library."

Richard Kemp looks at the Compact Cambridge version of MEDLINE. He concludes, "The Compact Cambridge-Medline product is a well-presented information tool. Its retrieval software is versatile and pleasant to use—in both the command and menu-driven modes. However, its search rates are not as fast as other packages currently available. Furthermore, the disc...inherits the traditional problems of searching online databases of this type—such as quality of the abstract, abstracters' interpretation and referencing, controlled vocabulary indexing, etc." Out of five stars, he gives it three for customer support, four for documentation, three for ease of use, four for getting started, four for presentation of display screens, and two for retrieval power.

In a more recent review of Compact Cambridge MEDLINE, David Allen finds its pluses to be that it is a "Well-known, widely used database offered by various software publishers. Efficient and powerful Cambridge Scientific proprietary search software...." Minuses are "Confusing installation process not properly updated to accommodate latest hardware developments. Limited CD-ROM player installation compatibility with poorly defined work-around."

Charlene York recently said, however, "Users will find installing Compact Cambridge Medline Version 3.1 fairly easy....It is one of the quickest systems to install." She also noted, "Compact Cambridge Medline Version 3.1 is a very powerful searching tool that the medical profession, librarians, and students will find easy to use for any of their research needs."

York concluded, "Compact Cambridge Medline offers one of the best CD-ROM versions of Medline around, and it contains all the years of the database. It is a very powerful tool that encompasses tree number and subhead searching and offers many limiting fields. The special options (e.g., macros, configuration menus) are the system's best features. Retrieving and downloading the records operate very fast considering the size of the product. The various pricing options are a bargain considering this product's quality. First-time users will find the Menu option fairly easy to use and the experienced user will enjoy the Command option."

In a look at an early SilverPlatter version of MEDLINE, Wendy Roberts found that, "End-user searching is well catered for by this system. The on-screen instructions lead the searcher from the initial screen through to the outputting of lists of references with abstracts. On-screen help is available at all points during the search process."

Paul Anacker evaluated the SilverPlatter interface for MEDLINE. He comments, "Here is a good text-based interface....Error reporting is the weakest part of this program....I like this interface. It could stand some polish, but I think most novice users could be fairly productive with it in a short time."

In a general overview of medical databases in October 1989, Donna Lee noted about Cambridge MEDLINE, "If they eliminated the need for truncation and hyphenation of MESH terms, they might have the easiest system to use. This year's newest version allows for explosions, although the process is rather convoluted." Of SilverPlatter MEDLINE, she noted, "They have also added an explosion capability since their initial offering. SilverPlatter stands out because of the shear number of databases they offer."

Of DIALOG MEDLINE, Lee pointed out, "DIALOG also allows for explosions now, though again, it's neither easy nor obvious. DIALOG's attraction is its ability to go online from the CD-ROM software and rerun a strategy that has proved to be successful in the CD files." About EBSCO's MEDLINE, she says, "EBSCO's software provides for six levels of searching ability, from novice to expert...but none of these levels is as powerful as the online interfaces librarians are accustomed to. Combining searches is especially difficult. The explode capability is in there somewhere, but is difficult to use."

Of CD-Plus MEDLINE, she comments, "...CD-Plus does not avoid the complexities of Medline to make it appear more friendly to the end-user. In both the novice and the expert level the program forces the search to use MeSH, and suggests subheadings, broader terms, and narrower terms. The explode capability is provided through a function key." In Aries MEDLINE, "Searches can be entered as actual English sentences. Relationships between the terms may be indicated. The results are ordered from most relevant to least relevant. As the searcher goes through the documents and selects the most relevant citations, the search strategy is revised and the search is repeated. Knowledge Finder uses MeSH to the fullest, but is not limited by traditional search techniques."

In comments from users ("Your DISCussions") in *CD-ROM EndUser*, about DIALOG MEDLINE, Elizabeth Jackson says, "As soon as we switch on our two drives at 8:00 A.M., they have lines of students in front of them....The new 'Save' feature makes it easier to go back to prior research, in either command or menu format. What's nice about the disc is the monthly update disc....I couldn't be more pleased with it."

A user, Jane Saltzman, also commented about EBSCO MEDLINE, "I've had the disc for a year, and I'm very pleased with it. The interface is very user-friendly. I don't have any complaints to think of." Dr. Charlie Barnett commented, "The best interface available is on Aries Systems' MEDLINE Knowledge Finder, because of its HyperCard interface; it's very simple, easy to use."

He found, however, "Silverplatter was far superior and made more sense to use....Searches are faster." Dr. John Bloor also commented about SilverPlatter; he said, "One problem: one can't search all the way back to 1966 without switching through lots of discs...I liked the interface....I'm quite happy with it."

Users also commented about CD Plus MEDLINE, Dr. John Anderson and Naomi Adelman saying, "It's nice to have the choice between menus and the command line. Novices tend to like using menus. We're very pleased that it takes so little learning time for novices; twenty to twenty-five minutes is usually all that's required to start someone working on it....Fast customer support is amazing. One quirk: it has problems finding a singular subject if the plural form is input...Less expensive networking would be highly desirable." Peri Worthington says, "We like it, but it doesn't begin to be as fast as on-line....It's very easy to use....Complaints we have heard are related to its speed and 'limit' features. We can literally set it up on a query, leave the room and do a few tasks while waiting."

Fran Brahmi and Kellie Kaneshiro evaluate CD Plus MEDLINE in detail, and conclude, "CD Plus is a quality product; it is comprehensive, well-designed, and easy to use....Product development included many trials which eventually led to its greatest strength—innovation. As a latecomer to the CD marketplace, CD Plus has benefited from other vendors' experience and is a contender for first place in the ongoing marathon of CD-ROM competition. CD Plus includes many features available from online services such as the explode, pre-explode, root, and tree commands. It forces the user to be aware of MeSH. In addition, it offers unique features such as permuted index (ptx) and scope commands. It provides for selective dissemination of information (SDIs), searching for unbound descriptors, truncation, quick explodes, and journal holdings information. CD Plus offers the appeal of an online, main-frame system without online, telecommunications, or hit charges."

Editor

REVIEWS

Aries

Backus, Joyce E. B. "MEDLINE on CD-ROM: a Checklist." *Laserdisk Professional* 2 (July 1989): 74-81.

CD-ROM Librarian 3 (May 1988): 42+.

Kahn, Paul. "Making a Difference: a Review of the User Interface Features in Six CD-ROM Databases." *Optical Information Systems* 8 (July/August 1988): 169-183.

Ladner, Betty H. and Molly C. Barnett. "Medline on CD-ROM: Comparison Update." *Laserdisk Professional* 3 (March 1990): 67-71.

Lee, Donna. "Medical Databases on CD-ROM: MLA Meets." *CD-ROM Librarian* 4 (October 1989): 11-19.

Miller, Connie. "Some Options for End-User Searching in the Health Sciences." *RQ* 28 (Spring 1989): 395-406.

Schwartz, Candy. "Knowledge Finder Version 1.5." *CD-ROM Professional* 4 (March 1991): 40-44.

Woodsmall, Rose Marie. *et al.*, eds. *MEDLINE on CD-ROM: National Library of Medicine Evaluation Forum.* Medford, NJ: Learned Information, 1989.

"Your DISCussions: MEDLINE On Disc," *CD-ROM EndUser* 2 (May 1990): 78-79.

Zeichick, Alan L. "An Apple a Day." *CD-ROM Review* 3 (May 1988): 42-44.

Cambridge

Allen, David P. "CD-ROM Title Reviews: Compact Cambridge Medline." *CD-ROM EndUser* 2 (May 1990): 86-87.

Backus, Joyce E. B. "MEDLINE on CD-ROM: a Checklist." *Laserdisk Professional* 2 (July 1989): 74-81.

Bakker, Suzanne, Ans Bleeker, Jan van der Burg, Joop Dijkman, Arjan Hogenaar, and Gijsbert van Ramshorst. "Medline on CD-ROM: a Comparison." *Online Review* 13 (February 1989): 39-50.

Bonham, Miriam D. and Laurie L. Nelson. "An Evaluation of Four End-User Systems for Searching MEDLINE." *Bulletin of the Medical Library Association* 76 (April 1988): 171-180.

Capodagli, James A., Jackie Mardikian, and Peter A. Uva. "Brief Communications: MEDLINE on Compact Disc: End-User Searching on Compact Cambridge." *Bulletin of the Medical Library Association* 76 (April 1988): 181-183.

CD-ROM Librarian 3 (July 1988): 34.

Coons, Bill. "Journal Watch." *Laserdisk Professional* 2 (November 1989): 138.

"Four Routes to Medline on CD-ROM," *Online Review* 13 (issue 4, 1989): 329.

Glitz, Beryl. "Testing the New Technology: MEDLINE on CD-ROM in an Academic Health Sciences Library." *Special Libraries* 79 (Winter 1988): 28-33.

Information Today 4 (May 1987): 3+.

Kemp, Richard. "Compact Cambridge-Medline: a Review of Medline CD-ROM." *Electronic & Optical Publishing Review* 7 (March 1987): 26-29.

Ladner, Betty H. and Molly C. Barnett. "Medline on CD-ROM: Comparison Update." *Laserdisk Professional* 3 (March 1990): 67-71.

Laserdisk Professional 1 (September 1988): 18-28.

Lee, Donna. "Medical Databases on CD-ROM: MLA Meets." *CD-ROM Librarian* 4 (October 1989): 11-19.

MD Computing 6 (issue 1, 1989): 12.

Miller, Connie. "Some Options for End-User Searching in the Health Sciences." *RQ* 28 (Spring 1989): 395-406.

Miller, David C. "Books Reviewed: Medline on CD-ROM." *CD-ROM EndUser* 1 (October 1989): 82-84.

Park, B. "Databases." *Choice* 27 (November 1989): 472-474.

Whitsed, Nicky. "MEDLINE on CD-ROM: Early Experiences in a Small University Medical Library." *CD-ROM Librarian* 4 (June 1989): 20-25.

Woodsmall, Rose Marie *et al.*, eds. *Medline on CD-ROM: National Library of Medicine Evaluation Forum.* Medford, NJ: Learned Information, 1989.

York, Charlene C. "Optical Product Review: Compact Cambridge Medline." *CD-ROM Librarian* 5 (November 1990): 37-41.

"Your DISCussions: MEDLINE On Disc," 2 *CD-ROM EndUser* (May 1990): 78-79.

CD Plus

Brahmi, F.A. and K. Kaneshiro. "CD Plus: MEDLINE on CD-ROM." *Medical Reference Services Quarterly* 9 (Spring 1990): 29-41.

Kesselman, M.A. "Online Update." *Wilson Library Bulletin* 64 (September 1989): 92-93.

Ladner, Betty H. and Molly C. Barnett, "Medline on CD-ROM: Comparison Update." *Laserdisk Professional* 3 (March 1990): 67-71.

Lee, Donna. "Medical Databases on CD-ROM: MLA Meets." *CD-ROM Librarian* 4 (October 1989): 11-19.

Nesbit, Kathryn. "CD Plus Medline." *CD-ROM Professional* 3 (May 1990): 61-65.

Underhill, Lisa. "An Easy Road to Medline." *Physicians & Computers* (June 1990).

"Your DISCussions: MEDLINE On Disc." 2 *CD-ROM EndUser* (May 1990): 78-79.

DIALOG

Backus, Joyce E. B. "MEDLINE on CD-ROM: a Checklist." *Laserdisk Professional* 2 (July 1989): 74-81.

Bakker, Suzanne, Ans Bleeker, Jan van der Burg, Joop Dijkman, Arjan Hogenaar, and Gijsbert van Ramshorst. "Medline on CD-ROM: a Comparison." *Online Review* 13 (February 1989): 39-50.

CD-ROM EndUser (March 1989): 17-19.

Coons, Bill. "Journal Watch." *Laserdisk Professional* 2 (November 1989): 138.

"Four Routes to Medline on CD-ROM," *Online Review* 13 (issue 4, 1989): 329.

Ladner, Betty H. and Molly C. Barnett. "Medline on CD-ROM: Comparison Update." *Laserdisk Professional* 3 (March 1990): 67-71.

Laserdisk Professional 1 (September 1988): 18-28.

Lee, Donna. "Medical Databases on CD-ROM: MLA Meets." *CD-ROM Librarian* 4 (October 1989): 11-19.

Meyer, Rick R. "Customer Experience with DIALOG Ondisc: a User Survey." *Laserdisk Professional* 1 (May 1988): 62-65.

Miller, Connie. "Some Options for End-User Searching in the Health Sciences." *RQ* 28 (Spring 1989): 395-406.

Morgan, V. E., Angela S. W. Yan, Carolyn Norris, and Y. C. Lo. "MEDLINE on Disc." *CD-ROM Librarian* 5 (February 1990): 8-16.

Woodsmall, Rose Marie *et al.*, eds. *Medline on CD-ROM: National Library of Medicine Evaluation Forum.* Medford, NJ: Learned Information, 1989.

"Your DISCussions: MEDLINE On Disc," 2 *CD-ROM EndUser* (May 1990): 78-79.

EBSCO

Backus, Joyce E. B. "MEDLINE on CD-ROM: a Checklist." *Laserdisk Professional* 2 (July 1989): 74-81.

Bakker, Suzanne, Ans Bleeker, Jan van der Burg, Joop Dijkman, Arjan Hogenaar, and Gijsbert van Ramshorst. "Medline on CD-ROM: a Comparison." *Online Review* 13 (February 1989): 39-50.

Coons, Bill. "Journal Watch." *Laserdisk Professional* 2 (November 1989): 138.

"Four Routes to Medline on CD-ROM," *Online Review* 13 (issue 4, 1989): 329.

Ladner, Betty H. and Molly C. Barnett. "Medline on CD-ROM: Comparison Update." *Laserdisk Professional* 3 (March 1990): 67-71.

Laserdisk Professional 1 (September 1988): 18-28.

Lee, Donna. "Medical Databases on CD-ROM: MLA Meets." *CD-ROM Librarian* 4 (October 1989): 11-19.

MD Computing 6 (issue 1, 1989): 12.

Miller, Connie. "Some Options for End-User Searching in the Health Sciences." *RQ* 28 (Spring 1989): 395-406.

Morgan, V. E., Angela S. W. Yan, Carolyn Norris, and Y. C. Lo. "MEDLINE on Disc." *CD-ROM Librarian* 5 (February 1990): 8-16.

Park, B. "Databases." *Choice* 27 (November 1989): 472-474.

Tylman, Vislava, Kimberly Laird, and Peter Vigil. "Evaluation of a CD-ROM Medline System in an Academic Health Sciences Library." *Proceedings National Online Meeting* (1989): 439-442.

Woodsmall, Rose Marie *et al.*, eds. *Medline on CD-ROM: National Library of Medicine Evaluation Forum.* Medford, NJ: Learned Information, 1989.

"Your DISCussions: MEDLINE On Disc." 2 *CD-ROM EndUser* (May 1990): 78-79.

SilverPlatter

Anacker, Paul. "Screen Test: Best Performance in a Supporting Role: the User Interface." *CD-ROM EndUser* 2 (May 1990): 72-73.

Backus, Joyce E. B. "MEDLINE on CD-ROM: a Checklist." *Laserdisk Professional* 2 (July 1989): 74-81.

Bakker, Suzanne, Ans Bleeker, Jan van der Burg, Joop Dijkman, Arjan Hogenaar, and Gijsbert van Ramshorst. "Medline on CD-ROM: a Comparison." *Online Review* 13 (issue 1, 1989): 39.

Coons, Bill. "Journal Watch." *Laserdisk Professional* 2 (November 1989): 138.

Ladner, Betty H. and Molly C. Barnett. "Medline on CD-ROM: Comparison Update." *Laserdisk Professional* 3 (March 1990): 67-71.

Laserdisk Professional 1 (September 1988): 18-28.

Lee, Donna. "Medical Databases on CD-ROM: MLA Meets." *CD-ROM Librarian* 4 (October 1989): 11-19.

Miller, Connie. "Some Options for End-User Searching in the Health Sciences." *RQ* 28 (Spring 1989): 395-406.

Park, B. "Databases." *Choice* 27 (November 1989): 472-474.

Roberts, Wendy. "Information Technology: CD-ROM Databases — Medline on SilverPlatter." *Health Libraries Review* 6 (March 1989): 52-54.

Woodsmall, Rose Marie *et al.*, eds. *Medline on CD-ROM: National Library of Medicine Evaluation Forum.* Medford, NJ: Learned Information, 1989.

"Your DISCussions: MEDLINE On Disc." 2 *CD-ROM EndUser* (May 1990): 78-79.

EQUIPMENT AND SOFTWARE REQUIREMENTS

Aries
Computer: Macintosh Plus, SE, or II with 2MB RAM
Software: Apple System Software 6.02
CD-ROM Drive: SCSI CD-ROM drive

Cambridge
Computer: IBM PC, XT, AT, PS/2, or 100 percent compatible with hard disk, 640k RAM
Software: DOS 3.1 or higher; MS-DOS Extensions
CD-ROM Drive: any IBM-compatible

CD Plus
Computer: IBM PC XT, AT, PS/2, or 100 percent compatible with hard disk, 640K RAM
Software: DOS 3.1 or higher, MS-DOS Extensions
CD-ROM Drive: any IBM-compatible

DIALOG
Computer: IBM PC, XT, AT, PS/2, or compatible, 512K RAM minimum, 640K RAM recommended
Software: DOS 3.1 or higher, MS-DOS Extensions
CD-ROM Drive: any IBM-compatible

EBSCO
Computer: IBM PC, XT, AT, PS/2, or compatible, with hard disk, 640K RAM, modem for ordering
Software: DOS 3.1 or higher, MS-DOS Extensions, Smartcom or equivalent telecommunications software for ordering
CD-ROM Drive: Amdek, Hitachi, Philips, Sony

SilverPlatter
Computer: IBM PC XT, AT, PS/2, or 100 percent compatible with hard disk, 640K RAM; Macintosh Plus, SE, or II
Software: DOS 2.1 or higher, may use MS-DOS Extensions
CD-ROM Drive: Toshiba, Hitachi, Philips, Sony, DEC, or Apple

PRICE *Aries* annual price, nine-year backfile: $2,895, monthly updating $595 additional; five-year backfile: $2,395, monthly updating $595 additional; two-year backfile: $1,795, monthly updating $595 additional

Cambridge annual price, entire file, monthly updates: $2,795. Current year plus four backfile years, monthly updates: $1,695. Current year plus nine backfile years, quarterly updates: $1,495. Current year, monthly updates: $1,250, individual backfiles: $250 per year.

CD Plus price, 1966 to date: $3,495 for the first year, $2,495 for renewals. Most recent five years disc: $1,495 annually.

DIALOG annual price: $995, for current plus one-year backfile (two discs); for current plus six-year backfile: $1,895

EBSCO annual price: $3,400, for full file 1966 to present, updated monthly. Current year annual subscription with previous year's backfile, updated monthly: $900. Backfile annual subscriptions, back through 1983: $200 per year's disc. Backfile annual subscriptions, three-year increments, from 1966 to 1982: $450 per three-years discs.

SilverPlatter annual price: Volume 1, 1966 to 1977: $1,250; Volume 2, 1978 to 1982: $750; Volume 3, 1983 to 1987: $900; Volume 4, 1988 to present: $950; Volume 3 and Volume 4: $1,495; all four volumes: $2,250; multiple order discount 50 percent

ARRANGEMENT AND CONTROL

Aries
Record fields: abstract, article source, article title, author, CAS Registry Number, citation type, comments, grant ID number, indexing check tag, ISSN, journal group, language, major topical descriptor, Medline indexing date, minor topical descriptor, named subject, NLM call number, NLM journal code, publication type, secondary source identifier, vernacular title, unique NLM identifier
Searchable: all

Cambridge
Record fields: abstract, author, author affiliation, CAS Registry Number, entry month, identifier, ISSN, journal code, language, major Medical Subject Headings, minor Medical Subject Headings, new material, personal name, source, special list indicator, subset, title, unique identifier
Searchable: all

CD Plus
Record fields: abstract, authors, journal, Medical Subject Headings, registry

numbers, title, unique identifier
Searchable: all

DIALOG
Record fields: abstract, accession number, author, call number, CAS registry number, check tag, contract/grant number, corporate source, country of publication, descriptor code, descriptors, document type, identifiers, ISSN, journal announcement, journal code, journal name, language, named person, publication year, subfile, summary language, source information, title
Searchable: all but journal volume, issue, pagination (included in source)

EBSCO
Record fields: abstract, author, author address, CAS Registry Number, entry month, ISSN, language, Medical Subject Headings, source, subset, title, unique identifier, year of publication, Z numbers
Searchable: all

SilverPlatter
Record fields: abstract, accession number, address of author, author, CAS Registry or EC number, comment, contract or grant numbers, country of publication, gene symbol, ISSN, language, major Medical Subject Headings, minor Medical Subject Headings, name of substance, original title, personal name, publication year, secondary source identifier, source, subset of MEDLINE, title, update code
Searchable: all but address of author

SEARCH SOFTWARE AND CAPABILITIES

Aries
Software: Knowledge Finder
Capabilities: keyword, Boolean, field searching, proximity searching, printing, downloading, term explosion, truncation, thesaurus, relevance ranking, varied display formats, index searching

Cambridge
Software: Cambridge Scientific Abstracts
Capabilities: keyword, Boolean, field searching, printing, downloading, field limiting, index searching, varied display formats, search saving, search statement retention and back referencing, proximity searching, truncation, nesting, thesaurus, online updating

CD Plus
Software: CD Plus
Capabilities: keyword, Boolean, novice mode, search statement retention and back referencing, field searching, proximity searching, printing, downloading, term explosion, field limiting, truncation, search saving, local holdings display, thesaurus, current awareness searches, automatic cross referencing, related record searching, varied display formats, index searching, nesting

DIALOG
Software: DIALOG Ondisc
Capabilities: keyword, Boolean, search statement retention and back referencing, field searching, field limiting, proximity searching, printing, downloading, index searching, novice mode, varied display formats, nesting, truncation, search saving, online updating, thesaurus, sorting

EBSCO
Software: Grateful Med
Capabilities: keyword, Boolean, search statement retention and back referencing, field searching, proximity searching, printing, downloading, index searching, novice mode, varied display formats, search saving, thesaurus, local holdings indication, document ordering capability, bibliography production capability, interlibrary loan request production, truncation

SilverPlatter
Software: SilverPlatter
Capabilities: keyword, Boolean, search statement retention and back referencing, field searching, field limiting, proximity searching, printing, downloading, index searching, truncation, thesaurus, search saving, nesting, varied display formats, term explosion

PRINT/ONLINE/OTHER MEDIA COUNTERPARTS

Print: *Index Medicus, International Nursing Index, Index to Dental Literature*
Online: MEDLINE — DIALOG, BRS, MEDLARS, Data-Star, PaperChase, Mead Data Central, Questel, DIMDI, Australian MEDLINE Network, Japan Information Center of Science and Technology, Karolinska Institutets Bibliotek och Informationscentral, MEDIS

NETWORK LICENSING ARRANGEMENTS

Aries: Nine-year backfile: $5,995; five-year backfile: $4,495; two-year backfile: $2,995

Cambridge: No additional charge

CD Plus: Networkable only on CD PLUS PLUSNET. PLUSNET1 serves up to four users at $35,000 plus. PLUSNET2 serves up to twenty users at $81,000. It includes dial access.

DIALOG: $497.50 more for current plus one-year file for two to ten workstations; $947.50 more for current plus four years file for two to ten workstations.

SilverPlatter: No additional charge

TITLE METADEX COLLECTION

PUBLISHER Producer: Materials Information, ASM International, Institute of Metals
Vendor: DIALOG

SCOPE AND CONTENT
Three well-known databases, Metadex, Materials Business File, and Engineered Materials Abstracts, are combined to provide comprehensive coverage of: international literature on metallurgy, technical, and commercial developments in iron, steel, and nonferrous metals, world literature on polymers, ceramics and composite materials for use in the design, construction, and operation of structures, and the practices of materials science and engineering as they relate to these materials. Coverage is back to 1985, with quarterly updating.

Metadex provides comprehensive coverage of international metals literature. Informative abstracts are included for most records. Materials Business File covers technical and commercial developments in materials, including iron and steel, nonferrous metals, composites, ceramics, and plastics. Over 1,300 magazines, trade publications, news briefs and announcements are reviewed for inclusion. Engineered Materials Abstracts provides comprehensive coverage of the world's published literature concerning the science of polymers, ceramics, and composite materials intended for use in the design, construction, and operation of structures equipment and systems, and the practices of materials science and engineering as they related to these materials. Informative abstracts are included for most records.

Metadex provides comprehensive information on materials science and engineering including processes and properties; products, process development, and manufacturing; fuel, energy usage, raw materials, and recycling; plant developments and descriptions; engineering, machinery, and control and testing; environmental issues, waste treatment, and health and safety; applications, competitive materials, and substitution; management, training, regulations, and marketing; economics, statistics, resources, and reserves; and world industry news, company information, and general issues. (Publisher's brochure)

Metadex Collection includes some of the world's foremost databases focusing on engineering metals and other materials. The subscriber receives added value having three databases in one collection; this also facilitates ease of research. The range and focus of subject coverage, the international breadth, the presence of abstracts, the good-sized backfile, the coverage of a variety of material formats, and the excellent DIALOG searching interface all make this database indispensable to any institution supporting research in any area of materials engineering. This database has no major drawbacks as a research resource in its subject field.

Editor

EQUIPMENT AND SOFTWARE REQUIREMENTS
Computer: IBM PC, XT, AT, PS/2, or compatible, 512K RAM minimum, 640K RAM recommended
Software: DOS 3.1 or higher, MS-DOS Extensions
CD-ROM Drive: any IBM-compatible

PRICE Annual price: $6,950; for print subscribers to *Engineered Materials Abstract* or *Metals Abstracts*: $5,560

ARRANGEMENT AND CONTROL
Record fields: abstract, accession number, alloy class code, alloy class name, author, conference location, conference title, conference year, corporate source, descriptors, document type, element symbol, group number, identifiers, ISBN/ISSN, journal announcement, journal name, language, patent application date, patent number, periodic index term, publication year, publisher, report number, section heading, section heading code, source information, title
Searchable: all but source information

SEARCH SOFTWARE AND CAPABILITIES
Software: DIALOG Ondisc
Capabilities: keyword, Boolean, search statement retention and back refer-

encing, field searching, field limiting, proximity searching, printing, downloading, index searching, novice mode, varied display formats, nesting, truncation, search saving, online updating, thesaurus, sorting

PRINT/ONLINE/OTHER MEDIA COUNTERPARTS

Print: *Metals Abstracts, Metals Abstracts Index, Alloys Index*
Online: Metadex — CAN/OLE, CEDOCAR, Data-Star, DIALOG, ESA/IRS, FIZ Technik, ORBIT, STN. Materials Business File — CAN/OLE, CEDOCAR, Data-Star, DIALOG, ESA/IRS, ORBIT, STN Engineered Materials Abstracts — DIALOG, ESA/IRS, ORBIT, STN

NETWORK LICENSING ARRANGEMENTS

Double the single user fee (above) for two to ten workstations

---

TITLE MLA INTERNATIONAL BIBLIOGRAPHY

PUBLISHER Producer: Modern Language Association
Vendor: H.W. Wilson Co.

SCOPE AND CONTENT

Featuring a faceted indexing system that helps you to focus on the exact subject you're searching, the MLA International Bibliography database speeds retrieval of accurate information on modern languages and literatures, folklore, linguistics, literary themes and genres, and numerous related topics that cross national literatures or other classified boundaries. From reader response theory to Sudanese Arabic dialect, from the metaphysical poets to the literature of Zimbabwe, the MLA International Bibliography provides easy access to thousands of subjects.

The subject coverage includes works on literature transmitted orally, in print, or in audiovisual media and on human language, including both natural languages and invented languages that exhibit the characteristics of human language (e.g., sign language, Esperanto, computer-programming languages), are indexed. Works on subjects such as aesthetics, human behavior, communication, and information processes are included if they treat human language or literature.

Subjects covered include: African linguistics and literatures, American literature, Asiatic linguistics, Brazilian literature, Celtic literatures, Commonwealth literatures, comparative and historical linguistics, East European literatures, English literature, folklore, French literature, genres, German literature, Indo-European linguistics, international languages, Italian literature, Latin American literature, literary criticism and theory, modern Greek literature, Netherlandic literature, non-verbal communication, Oriental literatures, Portuguese literature, professional topics, Scandinavian literatures, Spanish literature, themes, theoretical and descriptive linguistics, and more.

With a master list of more than 3,000 periodicals and series indexed, the MLA International Bibliography also covers monographs, book collections, dissertation abstracts, festschriften, and a variety of other sources, for a total of nearly a quarter of a million citations dating back to 1981. A subscription to MLA International Bibliography on Wilsondisc includes unlimited searching (excluding telecommunications fees) of the online database on Wilsonline. Updating is quarterly. (Publisher's brochure)

MLA International Bibliography is without rival in its subject focus on language and literature. Although some librarians have perceived problems with its indexing, with the database in its user-friendliness, and with the Wilsondisc implementation of it, it is irreplaceable in providing research access to the material it covers. It is also unquestionably better and more accessible than the print version, and has satisfied end users in the field, as noted by McClamroch, Stein, and Williamson, cited below. As Becki Whitaker, Information Retrieval Specialist at the Indiana Cooperative Library Services Authority, points out, MLA is part of a "core of databases that have been online for almost twenty years and now find themselves on CD-ROM."

Pat Riesenman, reference librarian at Indiana University, describes MLA as "very useful—wish it were on SilverPlatter, since I don't admire the WILSON system—and also find the database structure unnecessarily complex (e.g., the three-letter 'codes' identifying the various subject elements—confusing, inconsistent, wholly useless for searching since they must be converted to two-letter codes for that purpose—the problems here are shared between MLA and Wilson). Still, it is useful, and I would welcome a backfile."

Pat Riesenman also reviewed MLA in *RQ*, and found, "Using MLA in our library from January through June 1988 was much more frustrating than using any other of ten CD-ROM products (including three other Wilson databases and three on SilverPlatter)....For all its defects, MLA on disc is extremely useful. A patron described it recently as 'a tremendous tool, enormously helpful.'"

After conducting an end-user survey, McClamroch, Stein, and Williamson found "...the survey respondents appeared to be overwhelmingly satisfied with MLA on CD-ROM....the survey results suggest that this product is easy to use for both the first-time searcher and the searcher who has made prior use of MLA on CD-ROM." The authors concluded that "...there seems to be a favorable response to MLA on CD-ROM. End-users appear to appreciate how easy it is to get a satisfactory number of citations using the compact disk index as compared to using the MLA printed index. We feel, however, that our findings may say less about the quality of this product than about the difficulty and the cost, in terms of time, of using the printed index."

Paul Kahn, in comparing different CD-ROM searching interfaces, called Wilsondisc "...the best example of the seamless integration of CD-ROM and telecommunications capabilities in a single application currently on the market." He notes, however, "With the exception of the Browse facility, the product offers the same interface options for searching information on the CD-ROM or online. This 'one size fits all' approach is convenient for the command interface, but is seriously inadequate in the case of the Wilsearch menu interface...."

He finds, "Doing a search using the Wilsearch menu is visually structured, but it is no less complex than using the Wilsonline command language. Complexity is, in fact, increased since the system performs transformations of the user's input that may or may not be helpful. Although the transformations performed and the special syntax required is documented in the help files, they are not explained in the menu interface itself." He notes, "The part of the interface that does not use commands is Wilsearch. Once users have selected Wilsearch, they are presented with a full screen form in which to fill in search terms. The problem here is that the form itself does not really tell users what to do or what the results of an action will be....Users will not necessarily get the desired result by typing what they have in mind....As a result, the syntax of filling in this form is just as complex as any command interface."

Kahn notes that, "In MLA, there is simply no support in the Wilsearch form for the complex subject descriptors....Unfortunately, much of the database structure is simply unavailable to the user."

Norman Desmarais, in his thorough review of MLA, found some problems with ease of retrieval with the Wilsondisc and Wilsonline modes of searching, in addition to questions of authority control and spelling accuracy. He concluded, however, "Despite its shortcomings, many users will probably find searching the MLA on CD-ROM preferable to the paper edition because of its multi-year access and the relatively quick response time. The printed edition presents its own peculiar obstacles to information retrieval, not the least of which is the division into five volumes. The CD-ROM version has demonstrated some significant modifications in its very brief existence. Future updates can be expected to continue this trend."

Borgstrom, Holtzclaw, and Leiding reviewed MLA Bibliography on CD-ROM recently, and they summarized their feelings at the beginning of their article. "The Modern Language Association International Bibliography has long served as the research tool of choice for scholars of modern languages, literature, linguistics, and folklore. The CD-ROM version offers enhanced speed, flexibility, and ease of use, significantly simplifying the research process for the humanities scholar. Libraries that serve these patrons would be well-advised to consider purchasing this valuable resource," they find.

In particular, they feel, "The availability of clear online Help is a real strength of the database. The presence of screen prompts throughout facilitates efficient searching. The directions for the search request menu in WILSEARCH are clear and helpful. When available, the ability to also access the online version in order to retrieve the most recent citations is particularly useful."

They conclude, "The CD-ROM version of the MLA International Bibliography is successful in that it leads to substantially reduced search time and greater flexibility than the print version through additional access points. Intended for a fairly narrow scholarly market, the CD-ROM is appropriate for use only in settings which serve these users, most likely in an academic environment. The CD-ROM version preserves the bibliography's basic form and function while expediting the subject search process, thus making it a valuable tool for humanities scholars and the libraries that serve them."

Philbin, Ryan, and Ryan state that, "We feel that MLA is a product of great potential with incomplete implementation. Libraries should wait until the following minimum improvements are made before purchasing: Complete documentation is provided....Resolution of the problems in the BROWSE search mode....The WILSEARCH menu should be redesigned to accurately reflect the available search options in MLA."

They conclude, "Larger issues which will not go away include: It is the reviewers impression that at best MLA has only a partially developed authority control. It is obscured in the paper version, apparent in the online version, and frightening in the WILSONDISC implementation. Users who value Wilson's craftsman-like approach to indexing will shudder when they closely scrutinize WILSONDISC's MLA's BROWSE mode."

"A major asset of the Wilson products is the uniform 'look and feel.' While MLA may always stretch the users sense of this, if Wilson and MLA make the changes suggested here they will be in the ballpark."

S. Lehmann, in the *Choice* review, expresses some problems with MLA Bibliography on CD-ROM. It is concluded, "Given these problems, the thinness of the database, and the inconsistency of indexing, fruitful searches will usually...search in free text or invoke the 'neighbor' command, which displays an alphabetic array of terms and phrases, permitting variants and inconsistencies to be spotted. Unlike Wilson's own databases, MLA does not provide the 'expand' (online thesaurus) option....This is a rich database that offers considerable convenience to scholars and upper-division and graduate students, but to take full advantage of it, Wilson needs to rethink the design developed for their own indexes. Wilson user support is helpful, but improvement in documentation is not too much to expect. For the moment, MLA/Wilson resembles a Porsche engine in a Yugo body."

Paul Nicholls, in his book, cited below, gave MLA Bibliography three stars out of a possible four. He gave it two stars for data quality, three for search power, and four for ease of use.

For its international coverage, its indexing of a variety of material formats, its good-sized backfile, its unique subject coverage, and the basic capabilities the Wilsondisc interface provides, MLA International Bibliography is vital to the research collections of institutions supporting study of literature, language, linguistics, folklore, and related areas. It does not have abstracts, and indexing and the interface could be improved, but this is still unquestionably an important research database on CD-ROM.

Editor

REVIEWS

Borgstrom, Amy, John Holtzclaw, and Reba Leiding, "Wilsondisc's MLA on CD-ROM." *CD-ROM Professional* 3 (September 1990): 64-68.

Desmarais, Norman. "MLA Bibliography on CD-ROM: a User's Perspective." *Optical Information Systems* 9 (May/June 1989): 138-143.

Feustle, Jr., Joseph A. "Electronic Databases: a Brief Survey." *Hispania* 71 (September 1988): 724-28.

Kahn, Paul. "Making a Difference: a Review of the User Interface Features in

Six CD-ROM Database Products." *Optical Information Systems* 8 (July/August 1988): 169-183.

Lehmann, S. "Databases: MLA International Bibliography." *Choice* 26 (September 1988): 94.

McClamroch, Jo, Linda Lawrence Stein, and Edgar Williamson, "MLA on CD-ROM: End Users Respond." 19 *Reference Services Review* (Spring 1991): 81-86.

Nicholls, Paul T. *CD-ROM Collection Builder's Toolkit: the Complete Handbook of Tools for Evaluating CD-ROMs.* Weston, CT: Pemberton Press, 1990.

Philbin, Paul, Bonnie Ryan, and Joe Ryan, "WILSONDISC: Modern Language Association Bibliography." *CD-ROM Librarian* 3 (June 1988): 26-32.

Riesenman, C. Patricia. "MLA International Bibliography (CD-ROM)." *RQ* 28 (Winter 1988): 258-260.

EQUIPMENT AND SOFTWARE REQUIREMENTS
Computer: IBM PC, XT, AT, 386, PS/2, or compatible with hard disk with 1MB of space available and 640K RAM, Hercules graphics or better, modem for online updating
Software: DOS 3.1 or higher, MS-DOS Extensions
CD-ROM Drive: any IBM-compatible

PRICE Annual price: $1,495; 10 percent discount for two to four copies: $1,345; 15 percent discount for five to nine copies: $1,270; 20 percent discount for ten or more copies: $1,195

ARRANGEMENT AND CONTROL
Record fields: accession number, descriptor element, language code, personal name main author, record type, sequence number, source, title
Searchable: all

SEARCH SOFTWARE AND CAPABILITIES
Software: Wilsondisc
Capabilities: keyword, Boolean, search statement retention and back referencing, field searching, proximity searching, printing, downloading, truncation, thesaurus, online updating, novice search mode, search saving, automatic singular and plural, nesting, local holdings display

PRINT/ONLINE/OTHER MEDIA COUNTERPARTS
Print: *MLA International Bibliography*
Online: MLA International Bibliography — DIALOG, Wilsonline

NETWORK LICENSING ARRANGEMENTS
No additional charge for inbuilding access; contact Wilson for remote access charges.

TITLE MOVE: SAE MOBILITY ENGINEERING TECHNOLOGY ON CD-ROM

PUBLISHER Producer: SAE International
Vendor: SAE International

SCOPE AND CONTENT
SAE technical papers and books are recognized throughout the automotive and aerospace industries for their long-term reference value. In the past, searching for technical mobility information often meant hours of tedious research. Sometimes, this involved hundreds and hundreds of dollars of on-line database search charges. Now, access mobility research information immediately on CD-ROM.

CD-ROM brings you the power of online searching with the convenience and cost-effectiveness of using a PC. MOVE, SAE Mobility Engineering Technology on CD-ROM, combines advanced search and retrieval software with the latest CD-ROM data storage technology to provide a fast, efficient, and productive mobility research service—that resides on your personal computer!

MOVE enables you to quickly and efficiently access bibliographic information on every technical paper published by SAE. This includes information on over 37,000 technical papers from 1906-1990! (Abstracts are included for all papers published since 1967.) In addition, MOVE contains abstracts and bibliographic information for every SAE book published from 1965-1990. This includes information on over 700 conference proceedings, special publications, Advances in Engineering series books, Progress in Technology series books, and authored books. MOVE also identifies any technical paper included in a volume of the prestigious SAE Transactions.

A powerful, easy-to-use system, MOVE helps you navigate through this collection of mobility technology with on-screen instructions, offering on-line context-sensitive help whenever you need it. With MOVE, you'll be able to easily retrieve documents written on a certain subject, by a particular author or organization, or during a particular time period. MOVE is updated annually. (Publisher's brochure)

SAE technical information is highly cited and respected in the field of mobility and transportation engineering. The MOVE CD-ROM database gathers, and makes more easily accessible, indexing and abstracting of their vast array of publications. Any institution interested in engineering in the covered areas should consider this CD-ROM.

Although by its nature limited to one society's publications, these publications are so important in their field and cover such a broad scope, that the utility of the database in its field is great. Of course, the institution should hold many of SAE's publications in order to make their use of the database practicable. The search software MOVE uses provides research capabilities, abstracts are included for most of the database, and the backfile is quite lengthy. This database should definitely promote research in the fields it covers.

Editor

EQUIPMENT AND SOFTWARE REQUIREMENTS
Computer: IBM PC, XT, AT, PS/2, or compatible with hard disk and 640K RAM
Software: DOS 3.1 or higher, MS-DOS Extensions 2.0 or higher
CD-ROM Drive: any IBM-compatible

PRICE Annual price: $1,495; standing order customers of all SAE Technical Papers: $750

ARRANGEMENT AND CONTROL
Record fields: abstract, author, author affiliation, document number, organization, publication year, subject terms, title
Searchable: all but author affiliation

SEARCH SOFTWARE AND CAPABILITIES
Software: SAE
Capabilities: keyword, Boolean, search set retention and back referencing, field searching, proximity searching, truncation, printing, downloading, automatic cross referencing, related record searching, varied display formats

PRINT/ONLINE/OTHER MEDIA COUNTERPARTS
Print: *SAE Technical Literature Abstracts*
Online: SAE Global Mobility Database — ESA/IRS, ORBIT

NETWORK LICENSING ARRANGEMENTS
$4,500 for multiusers; $3,000 for standing order subscribers of SAE technical papers

---

TITLE MUSE

PUBLISHER Producer: International Repertory of Music Literature
Vendor: NISC—National Information Services Corporation

SCOPE AND CONTENT
Muse (MUsic SEarch) is the CD-ROM counterpart of *RILM Abstracts of Music Literature* and contains 100,000 abstracts from over 300 journals and all significant literature on music history, theory, analysis, performance, instruments, voice, liturgy acoustics, psychology, ethnomusicology, and related disciplines. Coverage is 1970-1984 and is updated annually.

RILM Abstracts is the world's most complete continuously updated bibliography of music literature, providing general readers and scholars with easy access to all significant music literature. RILM offers broad insight into the international music scene, covering books, journals, newsletters, conference proceedings, catalogs, dissertations, and reports of governments and of international bodies. Scholarship from all countries—in Europe, the Americas, Africa, Asia, and Australia—is fully documented in RILM.

RILM Abstracts has distinguished itself from other music bibliographies in three important ways. First, its coverage of writings on music is international, thorough, and complete. Second, it contains thousands of abstracts of the source material, proving to be on its own a vast source of information about music. Third, its indexing provides access to the material through a virtually unlimited number of ways. RILM is the standard bibliography of music literature: all major libraries and almost every specialized music library own the printed volumes of RILM. Many libraries and individuals also access the RILM material through computer links to the database distributor DIALOG.

The breadth of the subject matter contained in RILM makes its database a prime candidate to distribute on CD-ROM. Providing far more than mere bibliographic data on music, the CD-ROM gives users instant access to disciplines related to music, ranging from dance to archaeology, from religion to linguistics.

NISC's disc contains the complete text of all the issues and cumulative annual indexes of the printed *RILM Abstracts*. In addition to the ease of searching the CD-ROM medium with the powerful NISC software, the data itself has been improved in a number of ways. Numerous typing and printing errors have been corrected, and some groups of data have been standardized in their format. Abbreviations for many bibliographic details, such as the name of the journal, are spelled out.

Advantages over RILM's online file are considerable: Numerous abstracts lost in uploading the database to the online service have been restored; titles of items not in English are presented in their original language; diacritics and cross-references are all visible; all codes and abbreviations have been spelled out and standardized across all records in the database. NISC also created separate indexes for authors of reviews, authors of all other items, and an exhaustive index of all proper names found anywhere in the records. A reliable means of searching by the year of publication and ISBN is finally also available. (Publisher's brochure)

Although it is a very slowly updated file, RILM Abstracts is still a major resource in the area of music research, and it provides coverage of the musical field found in no other CD-ROM database. Its coverage of a variety of material formats, its intensive scope in music, its international breadth, the provision of abstracts, and the long, although out of date, time period covered make it an excellent research tool for any institution interested in music. Its primary weakness is the time gap.

Editor

EQUIPMENT AND SOFTWARE REQUIREMENTS
Computer: IBM PC, XT, AT, PS/2, or compatible with 512K RAM
Software: DOS 3.1 or higher, MS-DOS Extensions
CD-ROM Drive: any IBM-compatible

PRICE Annual price: $995

ARRANGEMENT AND CONTROL
Record fields: abstract, abstract number, author, corporate source, descriptor, document type, journal announcement, journal name, language, publication

year, publisher, section heading, section heading code, special feature, source information, title
Searchable: all

SEARCH SOFTWARE AND CAPABILITIES
Software: Dataware
Capabilities: keyword, Boolean, novice search mode, field searching, proximity searching, truncation, nesting, index searching, search saving, sorting, printing, downloading

PRINT/ONLINE/OTHER MEDIA COUNTERPARTS
Print: *RILM Abstracts*
Online: Music Literature International (RILM) — DIALOG

NETWORK LICENSING ARRANGEMENTS
Contact vendor

TITLE MUSIC INDEX

PUBLISHER Producer: Harmonie Park Press
Vendor: Chadwyck-Healey

SCOPE AND CONTENT
The Music Index on CD-ROM consolidates approximately 200,000 citations from eight annual cumulations, is more current by five years than RILM Abstracts, complements monthly publication of *The Music Index*, and permits searching by name, event, musical category, musical instrument, musical group, historical period, theme and specific subject.

The Music Index is the single most current and most heavily used index to music periodical literature. The only other major bibliographic project for musical literature—RILM Abstracts—is published much more slowly, the most recent issue covering materials from 1983.

The Music Index on CD-ROM joins this respected reference product to high-volume information retrieval technology. The Music Index on CD-ROM provides the researcher with access to all kinds of periodical literature data in musicology, ethnography, and historiography. Subjects include personalities, groups, types and forms of music, the history of music, and musical instruments from the earliest recorders to computer-enhanced synthesizers. The

Music Index on CD-ROM also indexes book reviews, reviews of recordings and performances, as well as first performances and obituaries. (Publisher's brochure)

As recently announced in *Advanced Technology/Libraries*, "The Music Index on CD-ROM contains information on music periodical literature from over 350 journals published in twenty countries. Citations include illustrations, biographies, portraits, and other important bibliographical information. The initial disc will cover material from 1981 to 1988 and will be updated annually."

The Music Index is a widely respected research tool in a field where the literature is not that well-covered. The other major database in this area (see RILM Abstracts) does have abstracts and Music Index does not, but Music Index covers 1981 to 1988, as opposed to 1970 to 1984.

Music Index is international in scope, although it covers only periodical literature. The Chadwyck-Healey interface is fairly well-proven for bibliographic databases without abstracts. It can be clumsy for complicated searches, but it is user-friendly and does provide the necessary research capabilities. Any institution supporting music research should investigate this CD-ROM database.

Editor

REVIEWS
Advanced Technology/Libraries 20 (March 1991): 5.

EQUIPMENT AND SOFTWARE REQUIREMENTS
Computer: IBM PC, XT, AT, PS/2, or compatible with hard disk and 640K RAM
Software: DOS 3.1 or higher, MS-DOS Extensions
CD-ROM Drive: any IBM-compatible

PRICE Annual price: $1,250

ARRANGEMENT AND CONTROL
Record fields: author, date, description, periodical source, subject, title
Searchable: all

SEARCH SOFTWARE AND CAPABILITIES
Software: Chadwyck-Healey
Capabilities: keyword, Boolean, search statement retention and back refer-

encing, field searching, field limiting, printing, downloading, index searching, truncation, varied display formats, nesting, thesaurus, menus and help messages in German, English, or French

PRINT/ONLINE/OTHER MEDIA COUNTERPARTS
Print: *Music Index*

NETWORK LICENSING ARRANGEMENTS
No additional charge for multiusers

TITLE NEWSPAPER ABSTRACTS ONDISC

PUBLISHER Producer: University Microfilms International/Data Courier
Vendor: UMI/Data Courier

SCOPE AND CONTENT
Whether researchers are looking for one story, tracking a series of articles, or just trying to see who did what, when it happened, where, and why, Newspaper Abstracts Ondisc is the source to turn to.

It's the most convenient access to articles from some of the most respected newspapers in the country, all indexed virtually cover to cover. Newspapers included are *The Atlanta Constitution* (with selected articles from *The Atlanta Journal*), *The Boston Globe*, *The Chicago Tribune*, *The Christian Science Monitor*, *Los Angeles Times*, *The New York Times*, *Wall Street Journal*, and *The Washington Post.*

You can subscribe to the entire set, or select *The New York Times* plus the newspapers your users turn to most often. Choose national coverage alone, add your own regional newspaper, or select the balance that access to all regional newspapers can provide. And with papers such as *The New York Times* and *The Wall Street Journal*, Newspaper Abstracts Ondisc is not only a great source for general news, but also an excellent reference for timely coverage of the world of business. No matter which papers you select, each record in the database provides all of the information users need to decide whether an article is relevant to their research.

All indexing is fully cross-referenced, and abstracts are prepared with the express approval of the newspaper's editorial staff.

Your subscription to the database is updated monthly. Most subscriptions include indexing from 1985 forward (1987 plus for *The New York Times*, 1989 plus for *The Washington Post*). (Publisher's brochure)

Although newspapers may not be the first source one thinks of in the context of research, they can be the place to look for unique information in the areas of business coverage, arts reviews, local news, and local/regional views of national and international events. This kind of information could well be useful to researchers in political science, history, sociology, criminology, public affairs, the humanities, business, and more.

Alexa Jaffurs finds in her comparison of Newspaper Abstracts Ondisc, Newsbank Electronic Index, and National Newspaper Index, "Perhaps the Cadillac of the newspaper databases, UMI's Newspaper Abstracts Ondisc combines powerful free-text searching capabilities with extensive indexing." She does feel, though, "While someone unfamiliar with the program could probably manage a simple search, the more refined elements of the program will be lost to them. If the system is purchased, some type of instruction should be planned to teach users the full range of search capabilities."

She concludes, "Of the three products, UMI's Newspaper Abstracts Ondisc offers the most extensive search capabilities and indexing. Where the institution has made a commitment to training end-users to really use the full capabilities of computer searching, UMI's system should be considered."

S. Leach's review is less enthusiastic, noting, "Although UMI stresses its commitment to quality indexing and strict editorial control, there are many inconsistencies." It concludes, "NA will be best used as an access source to the microfilm versions of these papers, and as a source for free-text retrieval for such information as product and company names."

Booklist compares Newspaper Abstracts and National Newspaper Index. It concludes, "Newspaper Abstracts Ondisc has the advantage of more powerful searching capabilities. It also has brief abstracts, and libraries can select the newspapers for which they want indexing. However, while searching the basic system is easy, using all the options offered for access is more complicated. Librarians will have to offer training if users are to get the full benefit of many special functions."

Cheryl LaGuardia agrees, noting, "...a basic problem in NAO is that search screens are too subtle; they lack explicit, readily available instructions to get searchers started." She does feel, though, that "The NAO database's scope is most impressive....Given the papers indexed, this is an invaluable multidisciplinary database." She concludes, "In sum, Newspaper Abstracts Ondisc provides adequate, timely access to valuable sources. The new monthly updates are an especially strong point in its favor. It is not transparent to use and users will require some instruction to search it effectively, but with a few adjustments (mostly in screen design) a revised version could be an ideal CD-ROM tool. In its present incarnation, it is recommended for general-purpose use in libraries with readily available patron instruction."

Jewell and Pearson in their review conclude, "We have identified a number of causes for concern about NAO, but would like to emphasize that we consider it to be a very good product that is mostly in need of fine-tuning. For example, we feel that several search procedures could be made clearer (at minimal cost) by changing a few screens."

"A more difficult area for UMI to address is the way in which cross references are integrated into the system. Users do understand cross reference lists at the beginning of subject heading entries, but may not realize that the NAO system allows for modification by searching a word or phrase directly from the abstract. While the 'Subjects' field can be helpful, it is not as useful as a cross reference system based on hierarchical relationships among terms. The complete absence of 'see references' is a definite drawback."

Of course, due to its scope, Newspaper Abstracts Ondisc only covers one format of material, but it has a decent-sized backfile, provides abstracts, has international information, and uses the user-friendly and research-capable UMI interface. Although this interface can be clumsy and slow for executing complicated searches, it does provide research capabilities. The subscriber can even choose which newspapers to index. This is probably the one newspaper database to choose in supporting research needs.

Editor

REVIEWS

"Featured Reviews: National Newspaper Index on CD-ROM and Newspaper Abstracts Ondisc," *Booklist* 86 (issue 3, 1989): 382-386.

Jaffurs, Alexa. "Newspapers on CD-ROM: Timely Access to Current Events." *Laserdisk Professional* 2 (May 1989): 19-26.

Jewell, Timothy D. and Glenda J. Pearson. "Optical Product Review: Newspaper Abstracts Ondisc and its Competitors." *CD-ROM Librarian* 3 (September 1988): 22-28.

LaGuardia, Cheryl. "Newspaper Abstracts Ondisc." *RQ* 29 (Spring 1990): 425-426.

Leach, S. "Newspaper Abstracts." *Choice* 26 (October 1988): 299-300.

EQUIPMENT AND SOFTWARE REQUIREMENTS
Computer: IBM PC or compatible with hard disk and 640K RAM
Software: DOS 3.2 or higher, MS-DOS Extensions
CD-ROM Drive: any IBM-compatible

PRICE Annual price, complete set: $2,950; annual price, automatically including *NYT* ($1,500): *AC*, *BG*, *CT*, *LAT*, *WP*: $350 each; *CSM*: $150; *WSJ*: $795

ARRANGEMENT AND CONTROL
Record fields: abstract, article headline, article length, article location, company names, publication date, publication name, special feature, subject headings
Searchable: all

SEARCH SOFTWARE AND CAPABILITIES
Software: UMI/Data Courier
Capabilities: keyword, Boolean, search statement retention and back referencing, field searching, proximity searching, printing, downloading, index searching, truncation, automatic searching of singular and plural, nesting, varied display formats, library holdings display

PRINT/ONLINE/OTHER MEDIA COUNTERPARTS
Online: Newspaper Abstracts — DIALOG Courier Plus — DIALOG

NETWORK LICENSING ARRANGEMENTS
Additional $100 per node/terminal

TITLE NTIS

PUBLISHER Producer: National Technical Information Service
Vendor: DIALOG, OCLC, SilverPlatter

SCOPE AND CONTENT
Indexes U.S. government-sponsored research, development and engineering reports and analyses prepared by federal agencies, their contractors and grant-

ees. It contains abstracts of unclassified, publicly available reports, software packages and data files from 300 government agencies, including NASA, DOD, DOE, EPA, DOT, Department of Commerce and some state and local government agencies. NTIS is the central source for the public sale of U.S. government-sponsored research, development and engineering reports. Nearly 2 million titles are included.

The database covers a wide variety of topics in engineering, mathematics, physical, biological and social sciences, and business, including aerodynamics, astrophysics, biomedical technology, combustion, energy, information science, NASA earth resources survey program, oceanography, propulsion and fuels, and health planning. DIALOG coverage goes back to 1980. OCLC and SilverPlatter coverage go back to 1983. Updating for all versions is quarterly. (Publisher's brochure)

This database is especially essential for large research-oriented libraries covering technical subject areas, especially if they receive many of the government technical reports covered. NTIS covers a much wider array of subject information than just technology; any area the U.S. government may have done work in is worth checking, and these reports are not cited consistently in most other subject databases. Informative abstracts are included with most citations. The database is an excellent source of vital primary research.

NTIS' "weakness" is that most libraries do not own a substantial number of the technical reports cited. Note that the DIALOG version goes back three years farther than the SilverPlatter.

Martin Courtois, of the Science Library at Michigan State University, notes that, "Few libraries will have a large collection of the technical reports contained in this database, and most users would be frustrated with the time delay in ordering publications from NTIS. The sheer size of its print counterpart *Government Reports Announcements and Index* and the difficulty in locating incomplete citations in the print index, however, make the CD-ROM version a valuable finding tool for libraries with large NTIS collections."

Colborne and Nicholls note also that "DIALOG offers fuller coverage than the other products." They emphasize the DIALOG Ondisc version as being more user-friendly. They point out, in evaluating NTIS as a life sciences research tool, "NTIS would be valuable for the collection which had a combination of information needs in the life sciences and the engineering sciences."

Joseph Clark describes NTIS' coverage of world technology in his article, cited below, and how CD-ROMs expand that access. Alan S. King reviews NTIS in the DIALOG version and finds, "The retrieval software developed by DIALOG for its OnDisc products is easy to use and offers something for every level of user....End-users will find an intelligent system of menus and prompts to guide them to the information they need. Staff and patron responses to the system at my library have all been favorable. DIALOG's NTIS is a first-rate product."

King concludes, "DIALOG's NTIS OnDisc is a valuable product for most any academic or research library. Despite its few flaws, DIALOG has created a product that is doing much to shrink the gap between the online and ondisc environments."

Editor

REVIEWS

Clark, Joseph E. "NTIS: a Key Partner in Unlocking the World's Technology." *Information Services & Use* 9 (issue 5, 1990): 289-294.

DIALOG

Colborne, David and Paul Nicholls, "Biology on Disk: CD-ROM Databases for the Non-Medical Academic Life Sciences Collection." *Laserdisk Professional* 3 (January 1990): 91-96.

King, Alan S. "CD-ROM in Brief: NTIS." *Laserdisk Professional* 2 (March 1989): 81-83.

Meyer, Rick R. "Customer Experience with DIALOG Ondisc: a User Survey." *Laserdisk Professional* 1 (May 1988): 62-65.

EQUIPMENT AND SOFTWARE REQUIREMENTS

DIALOG

Computer: IBM PC, XT, AT, PS/2, or compatible, 512K RAM minimum, 640K RAM recommended
Software: DOS 3.1 or higher, MS-DOS Extensions
CD-ROM Drive: any IBM-compatible

OCLC

Computer: IBM PC or compatible with hard disk and 640K RAM; Macintosh
Software: DOS 3.2 or higher, MS-DOS Extensions
CD-ROM Drive: Any IBM-compatible, Apple

SilverPlatter
Computer: IBM PC XT, AT, PS/2, or 100 percent compatible with hard disk, 640K RAM; Macintosh Plus, SE, or II
Software: DOS 2.1 or higher, may use MS-DOS Extensions
CD-ROM Drive: Toshiba, Hitachi, Philips, Sony, DEC, or Apple

PRICE *DIALOG* annual price: $3,600, for full coverage to 1980; for current year plus four year backfile: $2,350; *OCLC* price: $2,295, $1,995 for OCLC members; annual renewal fee: $1,995, $1,795 for OCLC members; *SilverPlatter* annual price: $2,500

ARRANGEMENT AND CONTROL

DIALOG
Record fields: abstract, author, CAS registry number, contract number, corporate source, country of publication, descriptors, document type, identifiers, journal announcement, language, note, NTIS accession number, publication year, report number, section heading, section heading code, source information, sponsoring information, title
Searchable: all but source information

OCLC
Record fields: abstract, accession number, announcement journal volume and issue codes, author, availability note, contract or grant numbers, corporate source, country of publication code, identifiers, item description, language, major descriptors, minor descriptors, monitoring agencies, NTIS price, number of issues in set, pagination, primary description (set), project numbers, report date, report numbers, subject category codes, supplementary notes, table of contents, task numbers, title, title annotation, title note
Searchable: all but NTIS price, item description, announcement journal volume and issue codes, pagination, number of issues in set

SilverPlatter
Record fields: abstract, accession number, agency source code, author, country of intellectual origin, corporate author code, corporate source, descriptors, identifiers, language, major descriptors, notes, price code, publication year, report date/pagination, report number, subject categories, subject category codes, title, update code
Searchable: all

SEARCH SOFTWARE AND CAPABILITIES

DIALOG
Software: DIALOG Ondisc
Capabilities: keyword, Boolean, search statement retention and back referencing, field searching, field limiting, proximity searching, printing, downloading, index searching, novice mode, varied display formats, nesting, truncation, search saving, online updating, thesaurus, sorting

OCLC
Software: Search CD450
Capabilities: keyword, Boolean, search statement retention and back referencing, field searching, field limiting, proximity searching, printing, downloading, index searching, truncation, nesting, varied display formats

SilverPlatter
Software: SilverPlatter
Capabilities: keyword, Boolean, search statement retention and back referencing, field searching, field limiting, proximity searching, printing, downloading, index searching, truncation, search saving, nesting, varied display formats

PRINT/ONLINE/OTHER MEDIA COUNTERPARTS
Print: *Government Reports Announcements and Index*
Online: NTIS — DIALOG, BRS, CAN/OLE, Data-Star, ESA/IRS, ORBIT, STN

NETWORK LICENSING ARRANGEMENTS
Contact vendor

TITLE NURSING AND ALLIED HEALTH (CINAHL) – CD

PUBLISHER Producer: CINAHL
Vendor: Cambridge Scientific Abstracts, CD Plus, SilverPlatter

SCOPE AND CONTENT
Nursing and Allied Health (CINAHL) – CD is the *Cumulative Index to Nursing and Allied Health Literature*. It provides access to virtually all English language nursing journals, publications of the American Nurses' Association, the National League for Nursing, and primary journals in more than a dozen

allied health disciplines. It also includes selected articles from approximately 3,200 biomedical journals indexed in *Index Medicus*; from approximately twenty journals in the field of health sciences librarianship; and from educational, behavioral sciences, management, and popular literature. Coverage is from 1983 to the present. Updating for the SilverPlatter version is bimonthly. (Publisher's brochure)

Nursing and Allied Health's focus on nursing is unmatched by any other database. It is absolutely essential for research in any field of nursing or allied health. Its coverage of more than just journals, its comprehensiveness in its subject fields, the presence of abstracts on some of the records, the good-sized backfile, and its international focus make it necessary for any institution doing research in areas of nursing, health administration, allied health areas, and other related topics. The interfaces available are highly suitable for research purposes. The only weakness of the database is that abstracts are not available for a majority of the records.

Steven Schmidt, in a recent evaluation of CINAHL–CD on SilverPlatter, remarked, "Since the early 1960s, the *Cumulative Index to Nursing and Allied Health Literature*, commonly known as CINAHL, has provided an important resource in the health sciences area. The CINAHL–CD equivalent continues the tradition." He notes the usefulness of the new thesaurus feature, and concludes, "All in all, CINAHL–CD offers a welcome addition to the field, giving the ease of SilverPlatter searching to a known and trusted source." Connie Miller describes CINAHL on CD as an option for end-user medical searching, but does not really evaluate it.

Robert Pringle also reviewed CINAHL on SilverPlatter, and comments, "Excellent for providing access to literature for nurses and allied health professionals, students and faculty, and health care articles more generally accessible to the lay public than is material in medical journals. The SilverPlatter software is intuitive enough to make this a good end-user program. Installation was straightforward, with useful documentation. A version of the software providing 'explosive' capability, i.e., the ability to choose a subject term from the thesaurus and all the more specific subject terms related to it in one step, is due in the fall of 1989, and is eagerly awaited by users of the product. The feature has been demonstrated and is undergoing refinement."

Editor

REVIEWS

SilverPlatter
Miller, Connie. "Some Options for End-User Searching in the Health Sciences." *RQ* 28 (Spring 1989): 395-406.

Optical Information Systems Update 8 (issue 14, 1989).

Pringle, Jr., Robert M. "CD-ROM in Brief: Nursing & Allied Health (CINAHL) on CD." *Laserdisk Professional* 3 (January 1990): 78-79.

Schmidt, Steven J. "Optical Product Review: CINAHL-CD on SilverPlatter." *CD-ROM Librarian* 6 (January 1991): 39-41.

EQUIPMENT AND SOFTWARE REQUIREMENTS

Cambridge
Computer: IBM PC, XT, AT, PS/2, or 100 percent compatible with hard disk, 640k RAM
Software: DOS 3.1 or higher; MS-DOS Extensions
CD-ROM Drive: any IBM-compatible

CD Plus
Computer: IBM PC XT, AT, PS/2, or 100 percent compatible with hard disk, 640K RAM
Software: DOS 3.1 or higher, MS-DOS Extensions
CD-ROM Drive: any IBM-compatible

SilverPlatter
Computer: IBM PC XT, AT, PS/2, or 100 percent compatible with hard disk, 640K RAM; Macintosh Plus, SE, or II
Software: DOS 2.1 or higher, may use MS-DOS Extensions
CD-ROM Drive: Toshiba, Hitachi, Philips, Sony, DEC, or Apple

PRICE *Cambridge* annual price: $950; *CD Plus* annual price: $950; *SilverPlatter* annual price: $95, 10 percent discount to Nursesearch subscribers

ARRANGEMENT AND CONTROL

Cambridge
Record fields: abstract, accession number, author, entry month, journal code, journal subset, major subject heading, minor subject heading, new material,

notes, publication type, publication year, publisher, source, title
Searchable: all but notes

CD Plus
Record fields: abstract, accession number, author, descriptors, document type, journal subsets, major descriptors, minor descriptors, publication year, serial identifier, source, subheadings, title, UMI order number, update code
Searchable: all

SilverPlatter
Record fields: abstract, accession number, author, descriptors, document type, journal subsets, major descriptors, minor descriptors, publication year, serial identifier, source, subheadings, title, UMI order number, update code
Searchable: all

SEARCH SOFTWARE AND CAPABILITIES

Cambridge
Software: Cambridge Scientific Abstracts
Capabilities: keyword, Boolean, field searching, printing,
downloading, field limiting, index searching, varied display formats, search saving, search statement retention and back referencing, proximity searching, truncation, nesting, thesaurus, online updating

CD Plus
Software: CD Plus
Capabilities: keyword, Boolean, novice mode, search statement retention and back referencing, field searching, proximity searching, printing, downloading, term explosion, field limiting, truncation, search saving, local holdings display, thesaurus, current awareness searches, automatic cross referencing, related record searching, varied display formats

SilverPlatter
Software: SilverPlatter
Capabilities: keyword, Boolean, search statement retention and back referencing, field searching, field limiting, proximity searching, printing, downloading, index searching, truncation, thesaurus, search saving, nesting, varied display formats, term explosion

PRINT/ONLINE/OTHER MEDIA COUNTERPARTS

Print: *Cumulative Index to Nursing and Allied Health Literature*
Online: Nursing and Allied Health — DIALOG, BRS

NETWORK LICENSING ARRANGEMENTS

Cambridge: No additional charge

CD Plus: Networkable only on CD PLUS PLUSNET. PLUSNET1 serves up to four users at $35,000 plus; PLUSNET2 serves up to twenty users at $81,000, includes dial access

SilverPlatter: No additional charge

TITLE ORTHOLINE

PUBLISHER Producer: National Library of Medicine
Vendor: Aries Systems Corporation

SCOPE AND CONTENTS

Easy and rapid access to the biomedical journal literature most frequently used by orthopaedists. Each disc contains up to a third of a million journal article references from the National Library of Medicine's Medline database for the current year and ten prior years. Features MeSH vocabulary and thesaurus file for a variety of flexible searching options, including cross references, subheads, and groupings of related terms.

The Ortholine Archive, which is updated annually, contains only the database for ten prior years. The current database is updated quarterly or monthly, depending on option chosen. (Publisher's brochure)

Paul Kahn, in comparing CD-ROM searching interfaces and looking at Aries' Knowledge Finder software, found that "Knowledge Finder is a unique blend of several innovations in information retrieval, wedded to a wonderfully designed user interface....When used in combination with a large bibliographic database on CD-ROM, these features redefine the task of searching for information." He also finds that "Knowledge Finder makes excellent use of the window and pull-down menu features of the standard Macintosh interface." He concludes, "Knowledge Finder illustrates what possibilities unfold once the search application makes intelligent use of a full windowing system. Being a Macintosh application, it assumes the use of a mouse and inherits (and makes very good use of) the pull-down menus, full set of fonts, multiple windows, and general point-and-click features of the Macintosh interface."

Ortholine provides a unique, subject-focused subset of Medline for those institutions in the Apple "world" desirous of providing a database that supports orthopaedics and related matters only. This presents the topic area in a manageable way for research specialists. Just as with the rest of Medline, abstracts are often provided, and coverage is international, although the focus is on periodical literature; it is usually sufficient to cover medical fields, however. This database is recommended for those institutions wanting to support research in orthopaedics in a specialized way.

Editor

REVIEWS

Kahn, Paul. "Making a Difference: a Review of the User Interface Features in Six CD-ROM Databases." *Optical Information Systems* 8 (July/August 1988): 169-183.

EQUIPMENT AND SOFTWARE REQUIREMENTS

Computer: Macintosh Plus, SE, or II with 2MB RAM
Software: Apple System Software 6.02
CD-ROM Drive: SCSI CD-ROM drive

PRICE Annual price, current: $1,695, monthly updating $595 additional; annual price, archive: $1,195

ARRANGEMENT AND CONTROL

Record fields: abstract, article source, article title, author, CAS Registry Number, citation type, comments, grant ID number, indexing check tag, ISSN, journal group, language, major topical descriptor, Medline indexing date, minor topical descriptor, named subject, NLM call number, NLM journal code, publication type, secondary source identifier, vernacular title, unique NLM identifier
Searchable: all

SEARCH SOFTWARE AND CAPABILITIES

Software: Knowledge Finder
Capabilities: keyword, Boolean, field searching, proximity searching, printing, downloading, term explosion, truncation, thesaurus, relevance ranking, varied display formats, index searching

PRINT/ONLINE/OTHER MEDIA COUNTERPARTS

Print: *Index Medicus, International Nursing Index, Index to Dental Literature*
Online: Medline — DIALOG, BRS, MEDLARS, Data-Star, PaperChase,

Mead Data Central, Questel, DIMDI, Australian Medline Network, Japan Information Center of Science and Technology, Karolinska Institutets Bibliotek och Informationscentral, MEDIS

NETWORK LICENSING ARRANGEMENTS
$1,995 – $2,995 for multiusers; contact vendor for details

TITLE OSH-ROM/MHIDAS

PUBLISHER Producer: National Institute for Occupational Safety and Health, United Kingdom Health and Safety Executive, United Nations International Labour Organisation
Vendor: SilverPlatter

SCOPE AND CONTENT
OSH-ROM is a collection of occupational health and safety information. It contains four complete bibliographic databases: NIOSHTIC, database of the National Institute for Occupational Safety and Health (U.S.A.); HSELINE, database of the Health and Safety Executive (U.K.); CISDOC, database of the International Occupational Safety and Health Information Centre of the International Labour Organisation (U.N.); and MHIDAS, the Major Hazard Incident Data Service, developed by the Major Hazards Assessment Unit of the British Health and Safety Executive. Collectively these databanks contain over 300,000 citations taken from over 500 journals and 100,000 monographs and technical reports. Updating is quarterly. (Publisher's brochure)

In considering this database, Paul Nicholls, in his book cited below, assigns it four out of a possible four stars, giving it four stars for data quality, and three stars for search power and ease of use.

Fryer, Baratz, and Helenius, in evaluating the implementation of the SilverPlatter search software with OSH-ROM, found "Despite the need to search three separate databases, the system is user-friendly. The dictionary file in each database clearly illustrates the discipline of the subject. Some fields are unique to each database; yet the same field label can mean different things in different databases. Unfortunately, there is no save capability among the three databases which makes it impossible to coordinate a final printout of citations."

They conclude, "OSH-ROM is of great importance to those involved in the health and safety of workers, occupational medicine, public health, and environmental health issues. It will have broad appeal to students, physicians, and research staff."

Dion Lindsay reviewed an early version of OSH-ROM and found, "...SilverPlatter SPIRS...software makes the system suitable for both the professional searcher and the inexperienced end user: its functions are generally clear and easy to follow and are well backed-up by help screens, on-screen guides to the databases and a user manual." He concludes, "For anyone searching health and safety databases for longer than twenty h[ours] a year, OSH-ROM is good value. In terms of accessibility for new or occasional searchers it rates above its online equivalents—and there are probably few situations where its lack of currency would necessitate use of the only slightly more up-to-date online sources."

OSH-ROM/MHIDAS is an absolutely essential database for research in any institution dealing with occupational safety and health, business, manufacturing technology, environmental health and other areas. The breadth of subject coverage, the international nature of the database, the presence of abstracts, the variety of material formats included, and the research strengths of the SilverPlatter interface all make this an excellent research database. In its subject area, this database has no major weaknesses, and should be considered by a library with the above interests.

Editor

REVIEWS

Fryer, R.K., N. Baratz, and M. Helenius. "Beyond Medline: a Review of Ten Non-Medline CD-ROM Databases for the Health Sciences." *Laserdisk Professional* 2 (issue 3, 1989): 27-39.

Lindsay, Dion. "Information Technology: CD-ROM Databases — OSH-ROM on SilverPlatter." *Health Libraries Review* 6 (March 1989): 54-55.

Nicholls, Paul T. *CD-ROM Collection Builder's Toolkit: the Complete Handbook of Tools for Evaluating CD-ROMS.* Weston, CT: Pemberton Press, 1990.

EQUIPMENT AND SOFTWARE REQUIREMENTS

Computer: IBM PC XT, AT, PS/2, or 100 percent compatible with hard disk, 640K RAM; Macintosh Plus, SE, or II

Software: DOS 2.1 or higher, may use MS-DOS Extensions

CD-ROM Drive: Toshiba, Hitachi, Philips, Sony, DEC, or Apple

PRICE Annual price: $900

ARRANGEMENT AND CONTROL

Record fields: abstract, accession number, author, CAS registry number, CODEN, convention number, descriptors, ISBN, ISSN, language, major descriptors, minor descriptors, original title, publication year, record number, report number, source, specialist category, subject category, title, Universal Decimal Code
Searchable: all

SEARCH SOFTWARE AND CAPABILITIES

Software: SilverPlatter
Capabilities: keyword, Boolean, search statement retention and back referencing, field searching, field limiting, proximity searching, printing, downloading, index searching, truncation, search saving, nesting, varied display formats

PRINT/ONLINE/OTHER MEDIA COUNTERPARTS

Print: *Safety and Health at Work-ILO-CIS Bulletin*
Online: CIS Abstracts — CCINFOline, ESA/IRS, Questel. HSELine — Data-Star, ESA/IRS, ORBIT. Occupational Safety and Health — DIALOG, CCINFOline, ORBIT.

NETWORK LICENSING ARRANGEMENTS

No additional charge

TITLE PAIS ON CD-ROM

PUBLISHER Producer: Public Affairs Information Service, Inc.
Vendor: SilverPlatter

SCOPE AND CONTENT
Worldwide information selected from a variety of authoritative sources—books, pamphlets, government publications, reports of public and private agencies, periodicals and conference proceedings are indexed. Factual and statistical information is included with surveys, demographics, and analytical works. About 900 journals are indexed.

Information for business—acquisitions and mergers, banking regulations, corporate histories, copyright issues in high technology, court decisions, insurance, multinational corporations.

Information for labor—arbitration, collective bargaining, working conditions, legislation.

Information for economists—credit, deflation, finance, gross national product, money.

Information for policy makers—public opinion, capital punishment, taxation, environment, power resources, firearms, national defense, social welfare, aging, hazardous wastes, homelessness, developing countries.

Information for medical/health planners—health maintenance organizations, AIDS, nutrition, Medicaid, ethics, genetics, malpractice, research.

PAIS on CD-ROM has information for all students, researchers, and educators in every discipline of the social sciences and law and its scope is both national and international. The disc's coverage dates back to 1972. The database is updated quarterly. (Publisher's brochure)

PAIS is a leading database in all areas relating to public affairs, from political science and sociology, to business and economics, to health care and more. It is a truly international database and tops in its field. It is an invaluable social science resource for almost any institution.

Pat Riesenman, reference librarian at Indiana University, calls PAIS "a very useful database—I am looking forward with great anticipation to its reincarnation on SilverPlatter....I would also welcome a backfile."

Its previous, awkward interface, which made it difficult to support research, has been replaced by the excellent SilverPlatter interface. It covers a variety of material formats, especially giving excellent coverage of government documents. It also has a lengthy backfile and some records have brief annotations. The only drawback is that more of the records do not have these, and they are not very lengthy. It has been reviewed extensively, but these reviews are of the previous interface. All in all, this is an essential social science research collection.

In reviewing PAIS in its original version, William Middleton pointed out, "PAIS has cumulated fourteen years of its two excellent print indexes, the *PAIS Bulletin* and *PAIS Foreign Language Index*, and combined them into one database of over 275,000 records." He finds, "The database is rich and fourteen-year cumulation [is] generous...." Any problems he had with PAIS were related to the original version of the database's retrieval software.

Debora Cheney also reviewed PAIS in its original version. She found, "Its strengths include excellent coverage of political and economic topics and the long list of English- and foreign-language periodicals and monographs it indexes, including publications from the United States government and international organizations. Its main weakness is that it lacks an abstract with each entry." She also noted other problems with the original search interface.

Philbin, Ryan, and Ryan found serious weaknesses in the original version of PAIS, too, but concluded, "...in the case of PAIS on CD-ROM, we like it, and believe it deserves to be in your library." They report, "The primary users of PAIS...are those interested in business, economic, and social conditions, public administration, and international relations." The *Choice* reviewer also found, "On the whole, PAIS on CD-ROM is a very useful product. Users learn to use it quickly and with a minimum of training by library staff."

Editor

REVIEWS

CD-ROM Lab Report 1 (June 1988): 12-13.

CD-ROM Review 3 (July 1988): 30.

Cheney, Debora. "PAIS on CD-ROM." *RQ* 27 (Summer 1988): 567-568.

Dionne, J. "Databases: PAIS on CD-ROM." *Choice* 25 (July/August 1988): 1680.

Middleton, William C. "CD-ROM in Brief: PAIS." *Laserdisk Professional* 1 (May 1988): 99-100.

Philbin, Paul, Bonnie Ryan, and Joe Ryan. "Optical Product Review: PAIS on CD-ROM." *CD-ROM Librarian* 4 (January 1989): 26-32.

EQUIPMENT AND SOFTWARE REQUIREMENTS
Computer: IBM PC XT, AT, PS/2, or 100 percent compatible with hard disk, 640K RAM
Software: DOS 2.1 or higher, may use MS-DOS Extensions
CD-ROM Drive: Toshiba, Hitachi, Philips, Sony, DEC

PRICE Annual price: $1,600; discount to print subscribers: $1,405

ARRANGEMENT AND CONTROL
Record fields: accession number, author, descriptors, ISBN, ISSN, language, Library of Congress card number, note, physical description, price, publication type, publication year, series note, source, SuDocs number, title
Searchable: all

SEARCH SOFTWARE AND CAPABILITIES
Software: SilverPlatter
Capabilities: keyword, Boolean, search statement retention and back referencing, field searching, field limiting, proximity searching, printing, downloading, index searching, thesaurus, search saving

PRINT/ONLINE/OTHER MEDIA COUNTERPARTS
Print: *PAIS Bulletin*, *PAIS Foreign Language Index*
Online: PAIS — DIALOG, BRS, Data-Star

NETWORK LICENSING ARRANGEMENTS
two to four users: $2,992.50; five to eight users: $3,990

TITLE PASCAL CD-ROM

PUBLISHER Producer: INIST-CNRS Institut de l'Information Scientifique et Technique
Vendor: INIST DIFFUSION

SCOPE AND CONTENTS
The PASCAL database is a multilingual, multidisciplinary bibliographic database covering the core of world literature in science, technology, and medicine. Online since 1973, the PASCAL database now includes over eight million references, with 450,000 references added yearly. The PASCAL CD-ROM contains one-year of database references in all the scientific areas covered. Updated semiannually, backfiles are available through 1987. (Publisher's brochure)

PASCAL is a highly renowned international scientific and technical database. It is especially suitable for institutions that need coverage of the European scientific and technical literature. It covers a variety of material formats, is international in focus, and allows coverage of a wide range of disciplines. It is an important database to consider for subscription.

Editor

EQUIPMENT AND SOFTWARE REQUIREMENTS
Computer: IBM PC/XT/AT/386, PS/2, or compatible with 640K RAM
Software: DOS 3.1 or higher, MS-DOS Extensions
CD-ROM Drive: any IBM-compatible

PRICE Annual price: $2,830 for current, one-year subscription; $1,415 each for 1987, 1988, 1989, or 1990 editions; $7,075 for 1987 through 1990 subscription

SEARCH SOFTWARE AND CAPABILITIES
Software: GTI (Jouve)

PRINT/ONLINE/OTHER MEDIA COUNTERPARTS
Print: *PASCAL*
Online: PASCAL — DIALOG, Questel, ESA/IRS

NETWORK LICENSING ARRANGEMENTS
Contact vendor

TITLE PATHLINE

PUBLISHER Producer: National Library of Medicine
Vendor: Aries Systems Corporation

SCOPE AND CONTENTS

Easy and rapid access to the biomedical journal literature most frequently used by clinical and experimental pathologists. Each disc contains up to a third of a million journal article references from about 300 journals from the National Library of Medicine's Medline database for the current year and four prior years. Features MeSH vocabulary and thesaurus file for a variety of flexible searching options, including cross references, subheads and groupings of related terms.

The Pathline Archive, which is updated annually, contains only the database for four or eight prior years. The current database is updated quarterly or monthly, depending on option chosen. (Publisher's brochure)

Paul Kahn, in comparing CD-ROM searching interfaces and looking at Aries' Knowledge Finder software, found that "Knowledge Finder is a unique blend of several innovations in information retrieval, wedded to a wonderfully designed user interface....When used in combination with a large bibliographic database on CD-ROM, these features redefine the task of searching for information." He also finds that, "Knowledge Finder makes excellent use of the window and pull-down menu features of the standard Macintosh interface." He concludes, "Knowledge Finder illustrates what possibilities unfold once the search application makes intelligent use of a full windowing system. Being a Macintosh application, it assumes the use of a mouse and inherits (and makes very good use of) the pull-down menus, full set of fonts, multiple windows, and general point-and-click features of the Macintosh interface."

Pathline is another of Aries Systems Corporation's subject focused subsets of Medline, which can be very useful for organizations wanting to have a database that focuses on pathology-related information. It is also one of the few applications tailored to the Apple "world." As with Medline itself, the coverage is international, and abstracts are included for many records. The backfile is of a very useful size for the medical field. Although the coverage is only on periodicals, this is the most useful area in the field of medicine, anyway. For institutions wanting a subject focus for research on pathology, Pathline should be very suitable.

Editor

REVIEWS

Kahn, Paul. "Making a Difference: a Review of the User Interface Features in Six CD-ROM Databases." *Optical Information Systems* 8 (July/August 1988): 169-183.

EQUIPMENT AND SOFTWARE REQUIREMENTS
Computer: Macintosh Plus, SE, or II with 2MB RAM
Software: Apple System Software 6.02
CD-ROM Drive: SCSI CD-ROM drive

PRICE Annual price, current and eight prior years: $2,095, monthly updating $595 additional; annual price, current and four prior years: $1,695, monthly updating $595 additional; annual price, archive for eight years: $1,595; annual price, archive for four years: $1,195

ARRANGEMENT AND CONTROL
Record fields: abstract, article source, article title, author, CAS Registry Number, citation type, comments, grant ID number, indexing check tag, ISSN, journal group, language, major topical descriptor, Medline indexing date, minor topical descriptor, named subject, NLM call number, NLM journal code, publication type, secondary source identifier, vernacular title, unique NLM identifier
Searchable: all

SEARCH SOFTWARE AND CAPABILITIES
Software: Knowledge Finder
Capabilities: keyword, Boolean, field searching, proximity searching, printing, downloading, term explosion, truncation, thesaurus, relevance ranking, varied display formats, index searching

PRINT/ONLINE/OTHER MEDIA COUNTERPARTS
Print: *Index Medicus*, *International Nursing Index*, *Index to Dental Literature*
Online: Medline — DIALOG, BRS, MEDLARS, Data-Star, PaperChase, Mead Data Central, Questel, DIMDI, Australian Medline Network, Japan Information Center of Science and Technology, Karolinska Institutets Bibliotek och Informationscentral, MEDIS

NETWORK LICENSING ARRANGEMENTS
$2,995 for multiusers

TITLE PHILOSOPHER'S INDEX

PUBLISHER Producer: Philosophy Documentation Center
Vendor: DIALOG

SCOPE AND CONTENT

Academic institutions with strong programs in the humanities will welcome the addition of Philosopher's Index on CD-ROM. Philosopher's Index provides indexing and abstracts from books and over 270 journals of philosophy and related interdisciplinary fields published in the U.S. and the Western World. Coverage is from 1940 to the present for the U.S. materials, and 1967 to the present for non-U.S. references. The database will be updated quarterly.

A major source of information in the area of aesthetics, epistemology, ethics, logic, and metaphysics, it is also a rich source of material on the philosophy of various disciplines such as education, history, law, religion, and science. (Publisher's brochure)

Philosopher's Index has long been a highly useful humanities research source in print and as an online database. It covers journals and books, provides an international focus, includes abstracts, has a useful research subject focus, and uses the excellent DIALOG searching interface. As a research database in its subject area, it is well nigh flawless. It also has a lengthy backfile. Any institution supporting research in general philosophy, religion, or discipline-specific philosophy in areas such as law, medicine, and science should consider acquisition of this excellent research database.

Editor

EQUIPMENT AND SOFTWARE REQUIREMENTS

Computer: IBM PC, XT, AT, PS/2, or compatible, 512K RAM minimum, 640K RAM recommended
Software: DOS 3.1 or higher, MS-DOS Extensions
CD-ROM Drive: any IBM-compatible

PRICE Initial price: $750, current, 1980 to date; complete, 1940 to date: $1,500; renewal: $495

ARRANGEMENT AND CONTROL

Record fields: abstract, author, descriptor, document type, journal announcement, journal name, language, named person, publisher, publication year, title, update
Searchable: all

SEARCH SOFTWARE AND CAPABILITIES

Software: DIALOG Ondisc
Capabilities: keyword, Boolean, search statement retention and back refer-

encing, field searching, field limiting, proximity searching, printing, downloading, index searching, novice mode, varied display formats, nesting, truncation, search saving, online updating, sorting, thesaurus

PRINT/ONLINE/OTHER MEDIA COUNTERPARTS
Print: *Philosopher's Index*
Online: Philosopher's Index — DIALOG

NETWORK LICENSING ARRANGEMENTS
Contact vendor

TITLE POLTOX I: POLLUTION AND TOXICOLOGY DATABASE ON CD-ROM

PUBLISHER Producer: Cambridge Scientific Abstracts, National Library of Medicine, International Food Information Service
Vendor: Cambridge Scientific Abstracts

SCOPE AND CONTENT
Combines seven comprehensive resources—including five available exclusively from Cambridge—to give you unprecedented access to pollution and toxicology information. Encompassing a full ten-years' worth of data (last ten years, 700,000 records in all) and updated quarterly, PolTox addresses environmental issues, public health issues, and drug and medical issues in both basic research and applied technology. You'll get fast, convenient access to information from:

Pollution Abstracts—all the environmental information you need to ensure ongoing compliance and resolve problems relating to any type of pollution.

Toxicology Abstracts—the most widely used journals in the field, covering industrial and agricultural chemicals, household products, pharmaceuticals, and other substances.

The National Library of Medicine's TOXLINE subfile, with comprehensive information on the toxicological, pharmacological, biochemical, and physiological effects of drugs and other chemicals.

Ecology Abstracts—an interdisciplinary digest of current research on how organisms of all kinds interact with their environment.

Health and Safety Science Abstracts—a comprehensive survey of timely issues in public health, safety, and risk management.

The entire toxicology section of the International Food Information Services's Food Science and Technology Abstracts, covering topics from contamination and carcinogens to waste production and management.

ASFA, Part 3: Aquatic Pollution and Environmental Quality—a new addition to the Aquatic Sciences & Fisheries Abstracts series focusing on contamination of the world's oceans, seas, lakes, and estuaries. (Publisher's brochure)

The combination of databases available on Poltox is unparalleled in the coverage of all areas relating to environmental health and the toxic effects humanity can have on the environment, and the environment can have on humanity. This database is a prime example of the excellent enhancing of information's value possible with CD-ROM. This database is invaluable to anyone dealing with pollution, occupational safety, toxicology, environmental food problems, other environmental hazards, and related areas.

The variety of material formats covered, the international focus, the lengthy backfile, the provision of abstracts, the subjects covered, and the utility of the Cambridge searching interface all make this an exemplary research database without serious drawbacks.

Editor

EQUIPMENT AND SOFTWARE REQUIREMENTS
Computer: IBM PC, XT, AT, PS/2, or 100 percent compatible with hard disk, 640k RAM
Software: DOS 3.1 or higher, MS-DOS Extensions
CD-ROM Drive: any IBM-compatible

PRICE Annual price: $1,495; 15 percent discount if POLTOX II or III purchased.

ARRANGEMENT AND CONTROL
Record fields: abstract, author, author affiliation, CAS Registry Number, CODEN, conference, corporate entry, database name, descriptors, entry month, ISBN, ISSN, language, major Medical Subject Headings, minor Medical Subject Headings, number, new material, publication type, publication year, publisher, secondary source identifier, source, subfile, supporting agency, title, unique identifier

Searchable: all

SEARCH SOFTWARE AND CAPABILITIES
Software: Cambridge Scientific Abstracts
Capabilities: keyword, Boolean, field searching, printing, downloading, field limiting, index searching, varied display formats, search saving, search statement retention and back referencing, proximity searching, truncation, nesting

PRINT/ONLINE/OTHER MEDIA COUNTERPARTS
Print: *Pollution Abstracts, Toxicology Abstracts, Ecology Abstracts, Health and Safety Science Abstracts, Food Science and Technology Abstracts, Aquatic Sciences & Fisheries Abstracts*
Online: Pollution Abstracts — DIALOG, BRS, Data-Star, ESA/IRS. Toxline - MEDLARS, BRS, DIALOG, Data-Star, DIMDI, Japan Information Center of Science and Technology. Life Sciences Collection — DIALOG. Enviroline — DIALOG, DIMDI, ESA/IRS, ORBIT. Health and Safety Science Abstracts — ORBIT, BRS. Food Science and Technology Abstracts — DIALOG, CAN/OLE, Data-Star, DIMDI, ESA/IRS, Gesellschaft fur Elektronische Medien mbH, Japan Information Center of Science and Technology, ORBIT. Aquatic Sciences & Fisheries Abstracts — DIALOG, CAN/OLE, DIMDI, ESA/IRS

NETWORK LICENSING ARRANGEMENTS
No additional charge

TITLE POLTOX II: POLLUTION AND TOXICOLOGY DATABASE ON CD-ROM

PUBLISHER Producer: Elsevier Science Publishers
Vendor: Cambridge Scientific Abstracts

SCOPE AND CONTENT
Compact Cambridge has added a new volume to its PolTox CD-ROM database, devoted to environmental pollution and toxicology. PolTox II: Excerpta Medica draws it source data from Excerpta Medica/EMBASE of Amsterdam, under an agreement with Elsevier Science Publishers. It offers a bibliographic database containing abstracts, citations, and indexes, representing over 260,000 records from the past ten years. Current material will be added on a quarterly basis.

PolTox II: Excerpta Medica joins two other "volumes" of the highly respected PolTox database, PolTox I: NLM, CSA, IFIS, and PolTox III: CAB. All three CDs constitute the PolTox Library: Pollution and Toxicology database from Compact Cambridge.

PolTox II's scope encompasses such pollution-related topics as: chemical pollution, and its effect on man, animals, plants, and microorganisms; environmental impact of chemical pollution, including measurement, treatment, prevention and control; radiation and thermal pollution; noise and vibration; dangerous goods; wastewater treatment and measurement; meteorological aspects of pollution; and legal and socioeconomic aspects of pollution.

Toxicology coverage in PolTox II: Excerpta Medica includes: pharmaceutical toxicology; foods, food additives, and contaminants; cosmetics, toiletries, and household products; occupational toxicology; waste material in air, soil and water; toxins and venoms; chemical teratogens, mutagens and carcinogens; phototoxicity; toxic mechanisms; predictive toxicology; regulatory toxicology; laboratory methods and techniques; and antidotes and symptomatic treatment.

More than 3,500 journals are screened comprehensively for material suitable for inclusion in PolTox II: Excerpta Medica—including 100 percent coverage of the top journals in the fields of toxicology and environmental pollution.

Like other CD-ROM databases from Compact Cambridge, all PolTox databases will share accessibility through Cambridge core software. Thus, any user already familiar with searching techniques and methods using another Cambridge product can use the same powerful software to search the new database. (Publisher's brochure)

Cambridge Scientific Abstracts is offering a unique subset of the world-renowned Excerpta Medica abstract journals covering the fields of pollution and toxicology, to serve as a complement to its other pollution and toxicology databases. In a time of increasing interest in environmental health research, this is a welcome addition to the CD-ROM world.

The excellent Cambridge interface provides all the necessary research capabilities for accessing this highly useful subject compilation. The abstracts included, the international scope, the lengthy backfile, and the breadth of the material covered by Excerpta Medica make this an important candidate for consideration by any environmental or health research facility. The only research drawback is the fact that the database covers only periodicals, but this still covers a large part of the literature in these fields.

Editor

EQUIPMENT AND SOFTWARE REQUIREMENTS
Computer: IBM PC, XT, AT, PS/2, or 100 percent compatible with hard disk, 640k RAM
Software: DOS 3.1 or higher, MS-DOS Extensions
CD-ROM Drive: any IBM-compatible

PRICE Annual price: $995; 15 percent discount if POLTOX I or III purchased

ARRANGEMENT AND CONTROL
Record fields: abstract, author, author affiliation, CAS Registry Number, category, CODEN, conference, country of publication, database name, descriptor, entry month, ISBN, ISSN, language, new material, number, original title, publication type, publication year, publisher, source, summary language, title, trade name, unique id
Searchable: all

SEARCH SOFTWARE AND CAPABILITIES
Software: Cambridge Scientific Abstracts
Capabilities: keyword, Boolean, field searching, printing, downloading, field limiting, index searching, varied display formats, search saving, search statement retention and back referencing, proximity searching, truncation, nesting

PRINT/ONLINE/OTHER MEDIA COUNTERPARTS
Print: *Excerpta Medica Abstract Journals*
Online: Embase — DIALOG, BRS, Data-Star, DIMDI, Japan Information Center of Science and Technology

NETWORK LICENSING ARRANGEMENTS
No additional charge

TITLE POLTOX III: POLLUTION AND TOXICOLOGY DATABASE ON CD-ROM

PUBLISHER Producer: Commonwealth Agricultural Bureau

Vendor: Cambridge Scientific Abstracts

SCOPE AND CONTENT

Compact Cambridge has expanded its line of PolTox CD-ROM databases to three with the addition of PolTox III: CAB, a major new database devoted to the agricultural dimensions of pollution and toxicology.

PolTox III draws its material from the comprehensive file of worldwide agricultural information produced by CAB International of Wallingford, U.K. It will join two other "volumes" of the highly respected PolTox database, PolTox I: NLM, CSA, IFIS, and PolTox II: Excerpta Medica. All three "volumes" constitute the PolTox Library: Pollution & Toxicology database from Compact Cambridge.

PolTox III: CAB provides access to the relevant contents of the CAB database, which corresponds to over fifty CABI abstract journals. Updated quarterly, the new CD will hold over 150,000 records from the past seven years.

Among the topics to be covered in PolTox III: CAB are: environmental agrochemicals, including insecticides, fungicides, pesticides, and fertilizers; groundwater contamination, run-off and leaching; heavy metals in soils, crops and animals; reclamation and re-vegetation of polluted sites; environmental impact of farming; waste management, treatment and disposal; toxicology, including toxic plants, wastes, food poisoning and toxic residues; food contamination; heavy metals as related to health; carcinogens; and health hazards of pesticides, drug residues, side effects of drugs, and steroids/hormones in animals.

All PolTox databases will use the Compact Cambridge "core" software, so that anyone already experienced in searching any other Cambridge database will be able to use the same powerful Cambridge software to search the new database. (Publisher's brochure)

Although many might not realize the possibilities for environmental, pollution, and toxicological literature in the agricultural area, it forms a substantial portion of the contents of CAB Abstracts. Ground water contamination, heavy metals in foods, contamination of food animals—all of these are important topics in environmental health.

The CAB database is known the world over for its immensity, its international scope, its useful abstracts, its coverage of a variety of material formats, and its excellent subject focus. The Compact Cambridge interface is more than adequate in its support of research capabilities. The backfile provided is of quite a useful length. This unique subset of the CAB Abstracts database will be of vital importance to environmental and health research organizations. It has no flaws as a research database.

Editor

EQUIPMENT AND SOFTWARE REQUIREMENTS

Computer: IBM PC, XT, AT, PS/2, or 100 percent compatible with hard disk, 640k RAM
Software: DOS 3.1 or higher, MS-DOS Extensions
CD-ROM Drive: any IBM-compatible

PRICE Annual price: $1,295; 15 percent discount if POLTOX I or II purchased

ARRANGEMENT AND CONTROL

Record fields: abstract, abstract/index source, author, author affiliation, corporate entry, database name, descriptor, entry month, ISBN, language, major subject heading, new material, notes, original title, publication type, publication year, publisher, source, subfile, summary language, title, unique id
Searchable: all

SEARCH SOFTWARE AND CAPABILITIES

Software: Cambridge Scientific Abstracts
Capabilities: keyword, Boolean, field searching, printing, downloading, field limiting, index searching, varied display formats, search saving, search statement retention and back referencing, proximity searching, truncation, nesting

PRINT/ONLINE/OTHER MEDIA COUNTERPARTS

Print: *AgBiotech News and Information*, *Agricultural Engineering Abstracts*, *Agroforestry Abstracts*, *Animal Breeding Abstracts*, *Biocontrol News and Information*, *Biodeterioration Abstracts*, *Crop Physiology Abstracts*, *Dairy Science Abstracts*, *Faba Bean Abstracts*, *Field Crop Abstracts*, *Forest Product Abstracts*, *Forestry Abstracts*, *Helminthological Abstracts*, *Herbage Abstracts*, *Horticultural Abstracts*, *Index Veterinarius*, *Irrigation and Drainage Abstracts*, *Leisure, Recreation and Tourism Abstracts*, *Maize Abstracts*, *Nematological Abstracts*, *Nutrition Abstracts and Reviews — Series A: Human and Experimental*, *Nutrition Abstracts and Reviews — Series B: Livestock Feeds and Feeding*, *Ornamental Horticulture*, *Pig News and Information*, *Plant Breeding Abstracts*, *Plant Growth Regulator Abstracts*, *Postharvest News and Information*, *Potato Abstracts*, *Poultry Abstracts*, *Protozoological Abstracts*, *Review of Agricultural Entomology*, *Review of Medical and Veterinary Entomology*, *Review of Medical and Veterinary Mycology*, *Review of*

Plant Pathology, Rice Abstracts, Rural Development Abstracts, Seed Abstracts, Soils and Fertilizers, Sorghum and Millets Abstracts, Soyabean Abstracts, Sugar Industry Abstracts, Veterinary Bulletin, Weed Abstracts, Wheat, Barley and Triticale Abstracts, World Agricultural Economics and Rural Sociology Abstracts
Online: CAB Abstracts — DIALOG, BRS, CAN/OLE, DIMDI, ESA/IRS, Japan Information Center of Science and Technology

NETWORK LICENSING ARRANGEMENTS
No additional charge

TITLE POPLINE

PUBLISHER Producer: Population Information Program, Center for Population and Family Health, Population Index, Carolina Population Center, National Library of Medicine
Vendor: SilverPlatter

SCOPE AND CONTENT
POPLINE is a bibliographic database containing more than 170,000 citations on population, family planning, and related health care, law, and policy issues. About 10,000 records are added each year, and updating is done three times a year. Specific topics include: research in human fertility, contraceptive methods, family planning services, maternal and child health, AIDS in developing countries, program operations and evaluations, community issues, demography, censuses, and vital statistics. The database reaches as far back as 1827 and includes citations and abstracts (averaging 250 words in length) to journal articles, monographs, technical reports, and unpublished works.

The POPLINE database presents citations and abstracts from fifteen types of publications. About 30 percent of the records represent difficult-to-obtain unpublished documents. The majority of items date from 1970. Ten percent of the records are from non-English language sources, but all POPLINE records are in English. The POPLINE Thesaurus, included as part of the CD-ROM product, provides specific subject indexing and serves as a guide to retrieving document records.

POPLINE is maintained by the Population Information Program at The Johns Hopkins University in collaboration with the Center for Population and Family Health at Columbia University, Population Index at Princeton University, and the Carolina Population Center at the University of North Carolina at Chapel Hill. POPLINE production is funded primarily by the United States Agency for International Development and by the National Institute of Child Health and Human Development. POPLINE is available online through the MEDLARS system of the National Library of Medicine. The CD-ROM version of POPLINE is funded by the United Nations Population Fund (UNFPA). (Publisher's brochure)

POPLINE is the world's most complete CD-ROM database on population, demography, family planning and related issues. It provides abstracts, covers a variety of material formats, goes back through an extended time period, provides international coverage, and is searched with SilverPlatter information retrieval software—all of which make it highly suitable for research in the areas it covers. As noted in the review cited below, it "addresses acute population and development problems by providing researchers with critical information on health care deficiencies in Third World countries." It has no real weaknesses as a research database. Institutions dealing with political science, public affairs, sociology, geography and other related areas should consider this database for research purposes.

Editor

REVIEWS

Foullon, Lee. "A High Tech Tool in Developing Countries." *CD-ROM End–User* 1 (February 1990): 48-51.

EQUIPMENT AND SOFTWARE REQUIREMENTS

Computer: IBM PC XT, AT, PS/2, or 100 percent compatible with hard disk, 640K RAM; Macintosh Plus, SE, or II
Software: DOS 2.1 or higher, may use MS-DOS Extensions
CD-ROM Drive: Toshiba, Hitachi, Philips, Sony, DEC, or Apple

PRICE Annual price: $750

ARRANGEMENT AND CONTROL

Record fields: abstract, address of author, author, country of publication, document number, entry month, language, major keywords, minor keywords, original title, publication type, title, source, year of publication
Searchable: all

SEARCH SOFTWARE AND CAPABILITIES

Software: SilverPlatter

Capabilities: keyword, Boolean, search statement retention and back referencing, field searching, field limiting, proximity searching, printing, downloading, index searching, thesaurus, search saving

PRINT/ONLINE/OTHER MEDIA COUNTERPARTS
Online: Popline— MEDLARS

NETWORK LICENSING ARRANGEMENTS
No additional charge

TITLE PSYCLIT

PUBLISHER Producer: American Psychological Association
Vendor: SilverPlatter

SCOPE AND CONTENT
Journal citations with abstracts to over 1,300 journals in psychology and behavioral sciences from the PsycINFO department of the American Psychological Association. This international database provides coverage from 1974 to present. Topics covered include all aspects of psychology, as well as the behavioral aspects of education, medicine, sociology, law, and management. The database is updated quarterly.

PsycLIT offers English-language summaries of articles from 50 countries on more than two dozen languages. PsycLIT contains over 470,000 records, with approximately 40,000 new entries added each year. Each article in PsycLIT is indexed by specialists using terms from the *Thesaurus of Psychological Index Terms* and is assigned a broad classification category to make searches quick and easy. (Publisher's brochure)

The Psychological Abstracts database is a research resource unmatched in the field of psychology. Psychological research simply cannot be done without resort to the information it contains, and the CD-ROM database vastly increases access to its contents. Becki Whitaker, information retrieval specialist at the Indiana Cooperative Library Services Authority, points out that Psyc–LIT is part of a "core of databases that have been online for almost twenty years and now find themselves on CD-ROM." Pat Riesenman, reference librarian at Indiana University, calls PsycLit "far and away the most heavily used of our CD-ROMs and in my view one of the best-constructed databases both online and on disc."

For the comprehensiveness of its subject coverage, its international scope, its excellent abstracts, the backfile available, and the SilverPlatter interface, it may be termed an essential research database for any institution supporting research in psychology and the behavioral sciences. Its only weakness for research is the fact that it indexes only one format of material, periodicals (dissertation citations are not included on the CD-ROM). This database is highly recommended for any basic research CD-ROM collection.

Fryer, Baratz, and Helenius, in evaluating PsycLIT as a medical database, concluded, "PsycLIT will be used by a wide range of people in psychology and mental health. Many patrons recommended that we purchase PsycLIT because it enabled them to perform complex searches quickly and efficiently."

Kathleen Voigt reviewed PsycLIT and found, "PsycLIT is useful for students at all levels as well as for professionals who will find in it the resources for their research and writing. One can use it in an unstructured or in a focused manner. The Quick Reference Guide provides enough information for the novice to search effectively and will not overwhelm the user with details. The user does not have to schedule appointments, pay hourly connect fees, or spend hours going through *Psychological Abstracts* to satisfy research needs in psychology. The user can do his own searching effectively at his convenience by using PsycLIT."

K. Salomon basically agreed, noting, "As with most CD-ROM software, the SilverPlatter software may seem cumbersome in the beginning, but gets easier over time. Once mastered, it can be a powerful tool, equaling the flexibility of an online search....The SHOW (display on screen) and PRINT commands are a bit unwieldy but again patience will be rewarded because of the flexibility SilverPlatter offers with these commands....All in all, a fine product; librarians may find that users who have not touched *Psychological Abstracts* will gravitate toward PsycLIT."

Editor

REVIEWS

Anders, Vicki, and Kathy M. Jackson. "Online Vs. CD-ROM—the Impact of CD-ROM Databases upon a Large Online Searching Program." *Online* 12 (December 1988): 24-32.

CD-ROM Librarian 2 (January/February 1990): 17-24.

CD-ROM Review 3 (July 1988): 32.

Fryer, R. K., N. Baratz, and M. Helenius. "Beyond Medline: a Review of Ten Non-Medline CD-ROM Databases for the Health Sciences." *Laserdisk Professional* 2 (May 1989): 27-39.

Information Today 2 (February 1987): 13, 35.

Salomon, K. "Databases: PsycLIT." *Choice* (December 1989): 618.

Voigt, Kathleen. "Optical Product Review: PsycLIT." *CD-ROM Librarian* 5 (February 1990): 45-48.

EQUIPMENT AND SOFTWARE REQUIREMENTS
Computer: IBM PC XT, AT, PS/2, or 100 percent compatible with hard disk, 640K RAM; Macintosh Plus, SE, or II
Software: DOS 2.1 or higher, may use MS-DOS Extensions
CD-ROM Drive: Toshiba, Hitachi, Philips, Sony, DEC, or Apple

PRICE Annual price: $3,995; multiple order discount: $2,99; special offer to *Psychological Abstracts* subscribers: $3,395; multiple order discounts for PA subscribers: $2,555

ARRANGEMENT AND CONTROL
Record fields: abstract, accession number, age group, author, classification code, CODEN, descriptors, institution, ISSN, journal code, journal name and bibliographic citation, key subject phrase, language, population, publication year, title, update code
Searchable: all

SEARCH SOFTWARE AND CAPABILITIES
Software: SilverPlatter
Capabilities: keyword, Boolean, search statement retention and back referencing, field searching, field limiting, proximity searching, printing, downloading, index searching, thesaurus, search saving

PRINT/ONLINE/OTHER MEDIA COUNTERPARTS
Print: *Psychological Abstracts*, *PsycSCAN*
Online: PsycINFO — DIALOG, BRS, Data-Star, DIMDI

NETWORK LICENSING ARRANGEMENTS
$5,995, $5,095 with subscription to *Psychological Abstracts*

TITLE PSYNDEX

PUBLISHER Producer: German Center for Documentation and Information in Psychology
Vendor: SilverPlatter

SCOPE AND CONTENT
Psyndex is the unique source for indepth coverage of German-language psychological literature. Psyndex CD-ROM contains more than 60,000 records on German-language psychology from 1977 to the present. Compiled by the German Center for Documentation and Information in Psychology at the University of Trier, Psyndex covers journal articles, books, chapters, reports, and dissertations from Germany, Austria, and Switzerland. Psyndex is bilingual: titles and descriptors are in German and in English, abstracts are in German (100 percent) and in English (30 percent). Psyndex is indexed with the *Thesaurus of Psychological Index Terms* by permission of the American Psychological Association. Psyndex is on one disc and includes a thesaurus. Updating is semiannual. (Publisher's brochure)

Germany is a world leader in psychology research and studies. Psyndex makes easily available material that was not widely accessible to world audiences previously. Psyndex covers a variety of material formats. Due to its scope, of course, it focuses on German-language material, but it does cover several countries. Psyndex uses an excellent psychological vocabulary for its indexing. For institutions supporting serious research in psychology, this database should be an excellent resource, opening up worlds of needed psychological literature. It is fortunate that the producers have chosen the useful SilverPlatter interface to support this potentially vital research tool.

Editor

EQUIPMENT AND SOFTWARE REQUIREMENTS
Computer: IBM PC XT, AT, PS/2, or 100 percent compatible with hard disk, 640K RAM; Macintosh Plus, SE, or II
Software: DOS 2.1 or higher, may use MS-DOS Extensions
CD-ROM Drive: Toshiba, Hitachi, Philips, Sony, DEC, or Apple

PRICE Annual price: $995

ARRANGEMENT AND CONTROL
Record fields: abstract, abstract (English), abstract (German), author, author's address, classification categories, classification categories in German, de-

scriptors, descriptors in German, doctoral supervisor, editor, free descriptors, free descriptors in German, institutional affiliation of first author, journal name, key phrase, source, title
Searchable: all

SEARCH SOFTWARE AND CAPABILITIES
Software: SilverPlatter
Capabilities: keyword, Boolean, search statement retention and back referencing, field searching, field limiting, proximity searching, printing, downloading, index searching, thesaurus, search saving

PRINT/ONLINE/OTHER MEDIA COUNTERPARTS
Print: *Psychologischer Index, Bibliographie Deutschsprachiger Psychologischer Dissertationen*
Online: Psyndex — DIMDI

NETWORK LICENSING ARRANGEMENTS
$1,492.50 for multiusers

TITLE RADLINE

PUBLISHER Producer: National Library of Medicine
Vendor: Aries Systems Corporation

SCOPE AND CONTENTS
Easy and rapid access to the biomedical journal literature most frequently used by radiologists. Each disc contains up to a third of a million journal article references from approximately 100 journals from the National Library of Medicine's Medline database for the current year and ten years prior. Features MeSH vocabulary and thesaurus file for a variety of flexible search options, including cross-references, subheads, and groupings of related terms.

The Radline Archive, which is updated annually, contains only the database for ten prior years. The current disc is updated quarterly or monthly, depending on the option chosen. (Publisher's brochure)

Paul Kahn, in comparing CD-ROM searching interfaces and looking at Aries' Knowledge Finder software, found that "Knowledge Finder is a unique blend of several innovations in information retrieval, wedded to a wonderfully designed user interface....When used in combination with a large bibliographic database on CD-ROM, these features redefine the task of searching for information." He also finds that, "Knowledge Finder makes excellent use of the window and pull-down menu features of the standard Macintosh interface." He concludes, "Knowledge Finder illustrates what possibilities unfold once the search application makes intelligent use of a full windowing system. Being a Macintosh application, it assumes the use of a mouse and inherits (and makes very good use of) the pull-down menus, full set of fonts, multiple windows, and general point-and-click features of the Macintosh interface."

As with the other subject-focused Medline subsets put out by Aries Systems Corporation, Radline provides a usefully narrowed grouping of Medline records for radiology researchers, to be used on an Apple platform. It is international in scope, and includes abstracts with many of its records; it covers only periodical literature, but this is adequate for fast-changing medical fields. It also has a fairly lengthy backfile. For organizations wanting a focus on radiology research for the Apple "world," this is a highly suitable product.

Editor

REVIEWS

Kahn, Paul. "Making a Difference: a Review of the User Interface Features in Six CD-ROM Databases." *Optical Information Systems* 8 (July/August 1988): 169-183.

EQUIPMENT AND SOFTWARE REQUIREMENTS

Computer: Macintosh Plus, SE, or II with 2MB RAM
Software: Apple System Software 6.02
CD-ROM Drive: SCSI CD-ROM drive

PRICE Annual price, current: $1,695, monthly updating $595 additional; annual price, archive: $1,195

ARRANGEMENT AND CONTROL

Record fields: abstract, article source, article title, author, CAS Registry Number, citation type, comments, grant ID number, indexing check tag, ISSN, journal group, language, major topical descriptor, Medline indexing date, minor topical descriptor, named subject, NLM call number, NLM jour-

nal code, publication type, secondary source identifier, vernacular title, unique NLM identifier
Searchable: all

SEARCH SOFTWARE AND CAPABILITIES
Software: Knowledge Finder
Capabilities: keyword, Boolean, field searching, proximity searching, printing, downloading, term explosion, truncation, thesaurus, relevance ranking, varied display formats, index searching

PRINT/ONLINE/OTHER MEDIA COUNTERPARTS
Print: *Index Medicus*, *International Nursing Index*, *Index to Dental Literature*
Online: Medline — DIALOG, BRS, MEDLARS, Data-Star, PaperChase, Mead Data Central, Questel, DIMDI, Australian Medline Network, Japan Information Center of Science and Technology, Karolinska Institutets Bibliotek och Informationscentral, MEDIS

NETWORK LICENSING ARRANGEMENTS
Contact vendor

TITLE RELIGION INDEXES

PUBLISHER Producer: American Theological Library Association
Vendor: H.W. Wilson

SCOPE AND CONTENT
Religion Indexes is the electronic version of the four indexes produced by the American Theological Library Association: *Religion Index One: Periodicals* (1949-1959; 1975-), *Religion Index Two: Multi-Author Works* (1960-), *Index to Book Reviews in Religion* (1975-) and *Research in Ministry* (1981-). The CD-ROM (325,000 plus records) corresponds to the printed indexes. A subscription to Religion Indexes on Wilsondisc includes unlimited searching (excluding telecommunications fees) of the online database on Wilsonline. The database is updated annually.

Religion Indexes cover Islam, Judaism, and the major Christian denominations, as well as Buddhism, Hinduism, and other non-Western religions. A unique resource for scholars, teachers, clergy, and students of religion and related fields, Religion Indexes provide accurate, indepth access to a broad range of subjects, including church history, Bible, theology, history of religions, sociology and psychology of religions, and liturgy.

In addition, Religion Indexes cover a multitude of related, interdisciplinary topics, such as anthropology, archaeology, art and religion, ethics, law and religion, medicine and religion, music, psychology and sociology. Materials covered include citations to journals, book reviews, monographs, dissertations, and multiple author works, including Festschriften, collected essays, proceedings, irregular series, and other publications on religion and theology.

Religion Index One: Periodicals indexes articles and features such as book reviews from over 450 periodicals (and selected articles from other journals) published worldwide.

Religion Index Two: Multi-Author Works indexes essays from collected works, Festschriften, conference proceedings and congresses (plus reprints of articles not included in other ATLA indexes).

Index to Book Reviews in Religion provides access to some 12,500 book reviews, review essays, and review articles from almost 500 journals and annuals.

Research in Ministry is an annotated guide to university and seminary-based research projects in contemporary ministry dating from 1981. RIM includes such topics as preaching, lay ministry, liturgy, church relations, and evangelism.

Sixty percent of the material covered is in English; the remainder (in order of descending frequency) is in German, French, Italian, Spanish, Swedish, Danish, Hebrew, Afrikaans, Norwegian, Portuguese, Finnish, Latin and Greek. Many citations include abstracts or extensive content notes. (Publisher's brochure)

Religion Indexes on Wilsondisc form an exemplary research resource for any institution interested in religion research—probably most institutions, in fact, should consider it. It has an extensive backfile, covers a wide variety of material formats, has excellent international scope, provides abstracts for many citations, and uses the Wilsondisc interface, which is acceptable for research.

The database's only drawbacks are that all of the records do not have abstracts, and the Wilsondisc interface can be awkward to use in some types of searches. This CD-ROM is, however, a must have for any organization supporting religion research.

Pat Riesenman, reference librarian at Indiana University, finds Religion Indexes "very useful...." She has noted in regard to Wilsondisc, "I am not a fan of the WILSON system—I especially loathe WILSEARCH, which I feel often confuses users—people need to know more than they really know to use it adequately and they therefore get unsatisfactory results."

As W. Fontaine notes (cited below), "In spite of its flaws, Religion Indexes on Wilsondisc... is a useful program for the novice, although many will require assistance. It is a very powerful tool for the advanced searcher, but improvements need to be made in the documentation, command language, and software. Recommended."

Mark Stover agrees, saying, "Religion Indexes is an excellent tool for those interested in religious studies and theological research." He finds that it is "...what is probably the finest religion bibliographic database in the world." Briefly comparing it to REX (see REX), he comments, "Its major competitor on CD-ROM, REX (REligious IndeX) cannot match Religion Indexes in either the number of titles indexed or the types of materials indexed. On the other hand, Religion Indexes only dates back to 1975 (REX indexes as far back as 1957) and Religion Indexes does not provide abstracts for most of its records (REX gives valuable abstracts for each article indexed)."

In a review done by Anne Womack at about the same time, the introduction appears, "Many theological libraries have been eagerly anticipating the advent of Religion Indexes on CD-ROM, a product which promised extensive periodical and analytic coverage of religious serial publications. The anticipation was justified. Religion Indexes furnishes a fast, accurate, user-friendly approach to a comprehensive range of religious information."

Womack concludes, "Religion Indexes is a CD-ROM product of invaluable use to any theological research library, including those outside the U.S. Religion Indexes will broaden the scope of resources patrons use for research. Quick and easy access to materials not found through the traditional library catalog opens a new dimension in paper-writing and project development for religion students. Encouraging the use of Religion Indexes should strengthen the quality of student research and increase access to under-utilized library resources."

"Other academic libraries, which already have more general CD-ROM indexes, should certainly consider purchase of Religion Indexes. Smaller colleges which emphasize religious studies would also benefit from this product. Religious publishers should find the annual subscription fee for Religion Indexes well worth the cost. Publishers could save considerable staff time on tasks such as confirming quotations and footnotes or building bibliographies. Clergy and local churches would not find this product economically feasible, yet they would certainly benefit from using this product at their local seminary or college."

Editor

REVIEWS

Fontaine, W. "Databases: Religion Indexes." *Choice* 28 (November 1990): 470.

Stover, Mark. "CD-ROM in Brief: Religion Indexes." *CD-ROM Professional* 3 (July 1990): 101.

Womack, Anne. "Religion Indexes on CD-ROM: a Review." *CD-ROM Professional* 3 (July 1990): 84-87.

EQUIPMENT AND SOFTWARE REQUIREMENTS

Computer: IBM PC, XT, AT, 386, PS/2, or compatible with hard disk with 1MB of space available and 640K RAM, Hercules graphics or better
Software: DOS 3.1 or higher, MS-DOS Extensions
CD-ROM Drive: Hitachi, Philips, Sony

PRICE Annual price: $795

ARRANGEMENT AND CONTROL

Record fields: abstract, accession number, article contents, Biblical citation note, date of entry, derived file indicator, Dewey Decimal classification number, ISBN, ISSN, journal title, language code, LC card number, LC classification number, out-of-print indicator, personal name author, physical description, publisher name, record type, subject heading, title, title series note, year of publication, year of publication of book being reviewed
Searchable: all

SEARCH SOFTWARE AND CAPABILITIES

Software: Wilsondisc
Capabilities: keyword, Boolean, search statement retention and back referencing, field searching, proximity searching, printing, downloading, trunca-

tion, thesaurus, online updating, novice search mode, search saving, automatic singular and plural, nesting, local holdings display

PRINT/ONLINE/OTHER MEDIA COUNTERPARTS
Print: *Religion Index One: Periodicals, Religion Index Two: Multi-Author Works, Index to Book Reviews in Religion, Research in Ministry*
Online: Religion Index — DIALOG, BRS, Wilsonline

NETWORK LICENSING ARRANGEMENTS
No additional charge for inbuilding access; contact Wilson for remote access charges

---

TITLE REX (RELIGIOUS INDEX) ON CD-ROM

PUBLISHER Producer: American Theological Library Association
Vendor: Foundation for Advanced Biblical Studies International

SCOPE AND CONTENT
This disc indexes all abstracts contained in *Religion One Index, New Testament Abstracts, Old Testament Abstracts, Religious and Theological Abstracts.* REX contains a cumulative index of all periodical abstracts from the beginning of each publication through and including 1986. Over 550 journals are indexed. Abstracts may be searched for author, title, journal, year, or keyword. REX does not contain the text of the abstracts indexed. (Publisher's brochure)

The REX CD-ROM database provides an excellent combination of resources for researchers in religion, theology, and philosophy. This database combines international coverage, an excellent subject focus, abstracts, and a good-sized backfile. It covers only periodicals, however. The interface has been found to be weak by reviewers.

Mark Stover reviewed REX before Wilson's Religion Index was available, concluding, "REX is a helpful database that should prove quite useful to those involved in academic research in religious studies. Its strengths include incredibly fast searching capabilities and continual access to one or more of the indexes during the actual search. Also, the search interface, though not as easy to learn as some other CD-ROM products, is not difficult...."

He continued, "REX's weaknesses include: a small database (less than 70,000 records) and an inability to perform truncation or use adjacency operators. Some may consider the Reteaco search interface a liability since it takes a fair amount of time before the user is comfortable searching the database. I would suggest that ease of use is somehow related to a system's power and sophistication....REX seems to fall somewhere in the middle when judging it by its user-friendliness, but the same could be said for its sophistication...."

The article in *College & Research Libraries* covered REX, and concluded, "On the negative side, one must note the absence of any tutorial program, fairly generic documentation, a noticeable number of typographical errors, and less than comprehensive coverage of many subject areas and issues. The recent appearance of the larger Religion Index in CD-ROM represents a serious challenge to REX's monopoly status in the field, and the latter's producers are now expanding the number of journals abstracted in order to provide comparable coverage; it is reported that an additional seventy-five periodicals will be included in the new version of the disc produced this August [1989]. It remains to be seen, moreover, whether the new Religion Index will match REX's retrospective coverage, and REX's provision of abstracting and faster searching speed will continue to be factors to consider."

Paul Nicholls, cited below, gives REX two stars out of a possible four stars, giving it two stars for data quality, search power, and ease of use.

Editor

REVIEWS

McIlvaine, E. "Selected Reference Books of 1988-89." *College and Research Libraries* 50 (September 1989): 559-60.

Nicholls, Paul T. *CD-ROM Collection Builder's Toolkit: the Complete Handbook of Tools for Evaluating CD-ROMs.* Weston, CT: Pemberton Press, 1990.

Preview 2 (issue 2, 1989): 31.

Stover, Mark. "Optical Product Review: REX on CD-ROM." *CD-ROM Librarian* 4 (February 1989): 17-20.

EQUIPMENT AND SOFTWARE REQUIREMENTS
Computer: IBM PC, XT, AT, PS/2, or compatible with 30MB hard disk and 640K RAM
Software: DOS 3.1 or higher, MS-DOS Extensions
CD-ROM Drive: any IBM-compatible

PRICE Annual price: $695; update: $595

ARRANGEMENT AND CONTROL
Record fields: abstract number, author, body of abstract, division heading, journal title, journal volume number, pages in journal, rta volume number, section heading, source, subject heading, title of article, year of publication
Searchable: all

SEARCH SOFTWARE AND CAPABILITIES
Software: Findit
Capabilities: keyword, Boolean, printing, index searching, nesting, field searching, downloading

PRINT/ONLINE/OTHER MEDIA COUNTERPARTS
Print: *Religion One Index*, *New Testament Abstracts*, *Old Testament Abstracts*, *Religious and Theological Abstracts*
Online: Religion Index — DIALOG, BRS, Wilsonline

NETWORK LICENSING ARRANGEMENTS
Contact vendor

TITLE SCIENCE CITATION INDEX COMPACT DISC EDITION

PUBLISHER Producer: Institute for Scientific Information
Vendor: Institute for Scientific Information

SCOPE AND CONTENT
As a complement to the existing print SCI and the SciSearch online database, the SCI Compact Disc Edition was designed specifically for end-user searching of the literature of science and technology. Searchers can browse through lists or dictionaries of cited authors and cited patents, cited works, title words,

author names, author addresses, and journal titles. They can move between dictionaries to choose qualifying search terms, to examine variant or similar terms, or to check intermediate hit counts. They can also enter search strategies directly.

Once users find a record of interest, they can call up other relevant articles with a few key strokes—without developing a new search strategy. These related articles are identified by the fact that their bibliographies share one or more references. Searchers can use this feature to investigate new areas of interest related to their original search, without knowing specialized terminology or publishing authors. Over 4,500 journals are indexed, including cover-to-cover indexing of 3,100 science journals from over 100 subject disciplines. Coverage is available back to 1980. Over 10 million new source items and references are added yearly. Updating is done quarterly. (Publisher's brochure)

The citation index CD-ROM databases of the Institute for Scientific Information exemplify the advanced and new research capabilities that can be provided for databases using the power of the microcomputer workstation. Any institution supporting scientific research should consider acquisition of this database, Science Citation Index, with its hypertext-like linking of records by their common citations.

The breadth of its coverage is without equal in the sciences. The international focus is excellent, and, although journals are the focus, some other materials are covered. The lengthy backfile is also highly useful. The research capabilities of the interface are quite valuable. The only research drawback is the lack of abstracts, but the unique citation coverage and linking make this a wonderful research tool. As Becki Whitaker, information retrieval specialist at the Indiana Cooperative Library Services Authority, points out, SCI is part of a "core of databases that have been online for almost twenty years and now find themselves on CD-ROM."

Martin Courtois, science librarian at Michigan State University, notes that SCI "...is firmly established as a major research tool in the sciences. Its strongest point and most unique feature is the ability to do citation searching, and searchers who have struggled with the print equivalent will appreciate the speed and legibility of the CD-ROM edition. Although ISI claims to cover the world's scientific and technical literature with SCI, most researchers will get better coverage by using a database in a particular subject area, e.g., Biological Abstracts, Medline, Compendex, etc. SCI lacks abstracts, but now that abstracts are being added to the online equivalent Scisearch, they may be made available in the CD edition."

In looking at the searching interface, however, Barbara Burke (cited below) finds that "Like the little girl who had a little curl, right in the middle of her forehead, the ISI CD-ROM products are very good when they are good; but when they are bad, they are horrid....Although...experienced searchers may find them more decipherable, they often appear just too complex and daunting for the novice end-user to master without additional assistance and/or education."

She finds Science Citation Index "valuable for...broad coverage of the sciences...a boon for libraries that cannot afford a large number of more specialized products. The ISI "Citation" indexing features, which include the ability to identify related references, adds a unique and valuable dimension to the identification of similar material and/or the verification of obscure nontrade publications which do show up in bibliographies of articles. The online dictionaries, once mastered, provide a browsing function which can greatly facilitate searching and help to overcome the negative impact of unusual formats and abbreviations. Unfortunately, these products are unreasonably challenging for the effort in some cases....[ISI's] databases are too valuable to go underutilized because of a poor user interface."

Fran Brahmi reviewed SCI in a medical context. She concluded, "SCI CD Edition is an excellent new CD-ROM product. It conforms to High Sierra Standards and ISI high quality. Its unique feature, related records, is useful in tracing similar articles which use different keywords. It links citations by virtue of their common references. If they share one or more references, they are considered related records. It is easy to use because no new search strategy is necessary. One relevant article simply leads to another with a few keystrokes. SCI CD Edition offers a unique approach to literature linkage which is now easily accessible."

Robert Michaelson in his review of SCI comments, "A primary criterion in picking a CD-ROM database is whether it provides 'value added.' The Science Citation Index CD-ROM exemplifies 'value added' better than any other CD-ROM I've seen. Once a relevant article is located by searching for citations of a known article or from searching by title words or author, the database allows retrieval of 'related records': other records on the database which share common references. This unique feature...allows researchers to browse and turn up relevant articles, which might not be found by traditional searches. Since, in addition, Science Citation Index indexes the most important journals from the entire range of science and engineering areas, I consider it the top priority CD-ROM product for a science or engineering library."

He concludes, "The print version of SCI is the most frequently consulted index in most science libraries in large part because researchers recognize the benefits and advantages of citation indexing. The added convenience of citation indexing on CD-ROM will of course be evident to every user. But in addition, I believe that the 'related records' feature of the CD-ROM version of SCI will have an impact similar to the original citation indexing revolution: SCI on CD-ROM allows the researcher to browse in ways not possible before and to find unanticipated connections. SCI is the first bibliographic CD-ROM product I have seen which is not just a search aid, but a true interactive research tool."

Colborne and Nicholls look at SCI in the context of life sciences research tools. They feel that "The major drawback of SCI on CD-ROM is the number of discs that can be involved in doing a comprehensive search. Searching the database from 1986 to the present would require searching at least four discs, and if both citation and address fields were required it could involve as many as eight discs. For the life sciences collection the strengths of SCI lies in its comprehensive coverage of the literature and its coverage of other sciences. To exploit this, end-users will require training in the use of Boolean logic and citation searching." They conclude that it is one of two products which "...offer the most comprehensive global coverage of all areas comprising the life sciences."

Fryer, Baratz, and Helenius look at SCI as a medical database. They find, in the area of ease of use, "SCI is easy to use and has very good context-sensitive help screens, as well as a clearly written manual." They conclude, "This CD-ROM with two unique features, cited author searching and 'related records' searching, is an important resource for any medical or science library. SCI Compact Disc Edition will be a key information tool for students, faculty, and staff involved in medical or basic science research."

A. E. Cawkell studied the related records feature of the ISI CD-ROM databases, and concluded, "The effectiveness of Related Records or Automatches obviously cannot be judged from a single search, but they do have the potential of being useful, particularly during the cycling backwards and forwards in time type of search enabled by the design of citation indexes. Such a search carried out with the printed volumes is very time consuming—it would take a long time to get to the point of identifying the significant articles in the 'Automatic Indexing' example given....Using the CD-ROM and one Automatch, this information was identified in minutes."

What is essentially a press release in *Technicalities* points out that SCI-CD has been released in an enhanced version. "Enhancements include improved search software that increases retrieval speed and supports multiple CD-ROM drives, and the incorporation of data compression techniques that will enable an entire year's worth of data to fit on a single disc."

Editor

REVIEWS

Brahmi, F. A. "SCI CD Edition: ISI's New CD-ROM Product." *Medical Reference Services Quarterly* 8 (Summer 1989): 1-13.

Burke, Barbara L. "Optical Product Review: SCI/SSCI on CD-ROM." *CD-ROM Librarian* 5 (October 1990): 31, 34-40.

Cawkell, A. E. "Automatic Indexing in the Science and Social Science Citation Index CD-ROM." *Electronic Library* 7 (December 1989): 345-350.

Colborne, David and Paul Nicholls. "Biology on Disk: CD-ROM Databases for the Non-Medical Academic Life Sciences Collection." *Laserdisk Professional* 3 (January 1990): 91-96.

Fryer, R. K., N. Baratz, and M. Helenius. "Beyond Medline: a Review of Ten Non-Medline CD-ROM Databases for the Health Sciences." *Laserdisk Professional* 2 (May 1989): 27-39.

Herther, Nancy K. "The Silver Disk: Laserdisk Product of the Year: a Matter of Significance." *Online* 13 (January 1989): 108+.

Michaelson, Robert. "Science Citation Index." *Laserdisk Professional* 2 (January 1989): 69-70.

Rosen, Theresa H. "Coming Soon: the Science Citation Index on CD-ROM." *Inspel* 22 (issue 3, 1988): 208-211.

"Social Sciences Citation Index on CD," *Technicalities* 9 (June 1989): 2.

EQUIPMENT AND SOFTWARE REQUIREMENTS
Computer: IBM PC, XT, AT, PS/2 Model 30, or 100 percent compatible with hard disk, 640K RAM
Software: Current DOS, MS-DOS Extensions
CD-ROM Drive: any IBM-compatible

PRICE 1991 disc price: $10,200; 1990 disc price: $9,900; 1989 disc price: $9,000; 1988 disc price: $8,400; 1987 disc price: $7,000; 1986 disc price: $4,500; 1985 disc price: $3,800; 1980-1984 disc price: $2,700; all print subscribers receive a 50 percent discount

ARRANGEMENT AND CONTROL
Record fields: Author, title, language, document type, journal citation, number of cited references, number of related records, cited references
Searchable: all

SEARCH SOFTWARE AND CAPABILITIES
Software: Institute for Scientific Information
Capabilities: keyword, Boolean, search statement retention and back referencing, field searching, proximity searching, varied display formats, printing, downloading, index searching, truncation, citation searching, related record searching, search saving

PRINT/ONLINE/OTHER MEDIA COUNTERPARTS
Print: *Science Citation Index*
Online: Scisearch — DIALOG, Data-Star, DIMDI, ORBIT

NETWORK LICENSING ARRANGEMENTS
Contact vendor

TITLE SEDBASE

PUBLISHER Producer: Excerpta Medica
Vendor: SilverPlatter

SCOPE AND CONTENT

SEDBASE on CD-ROM is an exciting new way to access one of the world's leading sources on the safety of a drug, its side effects or interactions.

SEDBASE contains current, full-text drug information from the last twelve years. It consists of *Meyler's Side Effects of Drugs & Duke's Side Effects of Drugs Annuals*, containing over 40,000 synopses of clinically relevant drug adverse reactions and interactions; a thesaurus of 9,000 side-effects terms and synonyms, taken from *Marler's Pharmacological and Chemical Synonyms* to ensure you find all the relevant records you're looking for; and references to journal articles from EMBASE, with abstracts where appropriate. Topics covered include adverse drug reactions, drug interactions, drug toxicity, pharmacological or patient-dependent factors associated with the occurrence of side effects, and special risk situations. The disc is updated semiannually.

SEDBASE provides not only the literature abstracts, but impartial clinical evaluations of the often conflicting evidence. It tells you whether a reaction is proven or only suspected, whether it is serious, how often it occurs, and how the risks can be kept to a minimum.

SilverPlatter has designed a special menu driven interface that makes it easy to find any given drug combination and side-effect in seconds. Search by any of the following: all side-effects, specific side effects of a drug or class of drugs, specific drug interactions, any interactions involving a specific drug, and interactions causing a specific side effect.

As you view your results, you can toggle with ease between a summary and the full record. A special de-duping routine ensures efficient display.

SEDBASE should be of great value to researchers in pharmacology and drugs, especially because of its unique full-text coverage. SilverPlatter asked two information specialists to compare finding information on drug side effects on SEDBASE, Martindale Online, De Haen Drug Data, and Drug Information Fulltext. In at least five cases, the searchers found information in SEDBASE that they did not find in other sources, found more precise, complete information and/or found SEDBASE easier and more convenient to use.

The database does provide much abstract and full-text coverage, is international in focus, and has a good-sized backfile. It covers some book and periodical information. It not only uses the useful SilverPlatter search interface, but also has specialized features that make searching for drug information easier. As a research database, it is an excellent resource.

Editor

EQUIPMENT AND SOFTWARE REQUIREMENTS
Computer: IBM PC XT, AT, PS/2, or 100 percent compatible with hard disk, 640K RAM; Macintosh Plus, SE, or II
Software: DOS 2.1 or higher, may use MS-DOS Extensions
CD-ROM Drive: Toshiba, Hitachi, Philips, Sony, DEC, or Apple

PRICE Annual price: $995

ARRANGEMENT AND CONTROL
Record fields: cross reference to another drug name, document number, drug classification code, drug name, effect classification code, effect name, factors of influence, interacting drug name, reference, subject, synonyms for drug, synonyms for effect, synonyms for interacting drug, text
Searchable: all

SEARCH SOFTWARE AND CAPABILITIES
Software: SilverPlatter
Capabilities: keyword, Boolean, search statement retention and back referencing, field searching, field limiting, proximity searching, printing, downloading, index searching, novice mode, truncation, search saving, nesting, varied display formats

PRINT/ONLINE/OTHER MEDIA COUNTERPARTS
Print: *Meyler's Side Effects of Drugs & Duke's Side Effects of Drugs Annuals, Marler's Pharmacological and Chemical Synonyms, Excerpta Medica Abstract Journal — Drugs and Pharmacology*
Online: SEDBASE — DIALOG, Data-Star

NETWORK LICENSING ARRANGEMENTS
$1,495 for multiusers

TITLE SOCIAL SCIENCES CITATION INDEX COMPACT DISC EDITION

PUBLISHER Producer: Institute for Scientific Information

Vendor: Institute for Scientific Information

SCOPE AND CONTENT

Social Sciences Citation Index provides access to 1,400 of the world's leading social science journals representing over fifty subject disciplines and selected items from 3,300 science journals by cited work, title word, journal title, author name and author address. Search terms may be entered directly or selected from dictionaries. Using the related records feature, one record of interest can lead to others that have references in common; no additional searching is needed. Display, print, or save results, individually or in sets. Coverage is back to 1980. Over 1.5 million new source items and references are added yearly; updating is provided quarterly. (Publisher's brochure)

The Social Sciences Citation Index provides the best coverage of the broad expanse of the social science periodical literature. It is especially excellent for research topics that cross discipline boundaries in the social science area. The searching capabilities ISI has provided for its CD-ROM products are also the epitome of the value that can be added to a database when it is put on CD-ROM by increasing access capabilities in new and different ways. The ability to search by citation and, especially, by linking related records through their citations is invaluable in research.

Social Sciences Citation Index covers a large number of journals in a broad subject area, provides excellent international coverage, has a good-sized backfile, and has the excellent research searching interface mentioned above.

On the other hand, SSCI does not provide abstracts, and it covers only periodical literature. As it is, though, it is an invaluable research tool for almost any institution. Becki Whitaker, information retrieval specialist at the Indiana Cooperative Library Services Authority, calls SSCI part of a "core of databases that have been online for almost twenty years and now find themselves on CD-ROM."

Pat Riesenman, reference librarian at Indiana University, notes that SSCI "...online...is a fairly 'dirty' product, and its price, like the online version, is outrageous, but it is the 'only show in town' for some disciplines (e.g., anthropology, women's studies) the only computerized source of which I am aware...."

In looking at the searching interface, however, Barbara Burke (cited below) finds that "Like the little girl who had a little curl, right in the middle of her forehead, the ISI CD-ROM products are very good when they are good, but when they are bad, they are horrid....Although...experienced searchers may find them more decipherable, they often appear just too complex and daunting for the novice end-user to master without additional assistance and/or education."

She finds Social Science Citation Index "valuable for...broad coverage of the...social sciences...a boon for libraries that cannot afford a large number of more specialized products. The ISI "Citation" indexing features, which include the ability to identify related references, adds a unique and valuable dimension to the identification of similar material and/or the verification of obscure nontrade publications which do show up in bibliographies of articles. The online dictionaries, once mastered, provide a browsing function which can greatly facilitate searching and help to overcome the negative impact of unusual formats and abbreviations.

She continues, though, "Unfortunately, these products are unreasonably challenging for the effort in some cases. Many individuals will give up in frustration and go to other products or back to the old familiar printed resources.... [ISI's] databases are too valuable to go underutilized because of a poor user interface."

Nancy Clemmons, evaluating SSCI from a health sciences library point of view, says, "...we have found it a valuable complement to SCI in areas such as medical ethics, medical psychology, health economics, etc." She concludes, "The flexibility of SSCI on CD-ROM and its ability to connect related records are exciting enhancements, but each library will have to weigh the anticipated use of these features against the costs involved."

A.E. Cawkell studied the related records feature of the ISI CD-ROM databases, and concluded, "The effectiveness of Related Records or Automatches obviously cannot be judged from a single search, but they do have the potential of being useful, particularly during the cycling backwards and forwards in time type of search enabled by the design of citation indexes. Such a search carried out with the printed volumes is very time consuming—it would take a long time to get to the point of identifying the significant articles in the 'Automatic Indexing' example given....Using the CD-ROM and one Automatch, this information was identified in minutes."

A very current review of SSCI by Paula Rothstein comments, "Nearly every social scientist and social science librarian has been waiting for this product to appear. It is the first CD-ROM that has more information than its parent online database. The unique Related Records feature as well as citation indexing offer all that is needed to build a comprehensive bibliography in a specific area of expertise." She concludes, "The SSCI Compact Disc Edition is recommended for academic libraries, special libraries with a social science focus and public libraries serving college students and serious researchers."

What is essentially a press release in *Technicalities* points out that SSCI-CD has enhancements to the original ISI CD-ROM presentation of their first product, SCI-CD. "Enhancements include improved search software that increases retrieval speed and supports multiple CD-ROM drives, and the incorporation of data compression techniques that will enable an entire year's worth of data to fit on a single disc."

Editor

REVIEWS

Burke, Barbara L. "Optical Product Review: SCI/SSCI on CD-ROM." *CD-ROM Librarian* 5 (October 1990): 31, 34-40.

Cawkell, A. E. "Automatic Indexing in the Science and Social Science Citation Index CD-ROM." *Electronic Library* 7 (December 1989): 345-350.

Clemmons, Nancy W. "Databases: Social Sciences Citation Index." *RQ* 29 (Spring 1990): 423-425.

Rothstein, Pauline M. "Social Sciences Citation Index Compact Disc Edition." *CD-ROM Professional* 4 (January 1991): 79-80.

"Social Sciences Citation Index on CD," *Technicalities* 9 (June 1989): 2.

EQUIPMENT AND SOFTWARE REQUIREMENTS

Computer: IBM PC, XT, AT, PS/2 Model 30, or 100 percent compatible with hard disk, 640K RAM
Software: Current DOS, MS-DOS Extensions
CD-ROM Drive: any IBM-compatible

PRICE 1991 disc price: $4,500; 1990 disc price: $4,300; 1989 disc price: $4,100; 1988 disc price: $3,700; 1987 disc price: $2,800; 1986 disc price: $2,200; 1980-1985 disc price: $10,500; all print subscribers receive a 50 percent discount

ARRANGEMENT AND CONTROL

Record fields: author, title, language, document type, journal citation, number

ber of cited references, number of related records, cited references
Searchable: All

SEARCH SOFTWARE AND CAPABILITIES
Software: Institute for Scientific Information
Capabilities: keyword, Boolean, search statement retention and back referencing, field searching, proximity searching, varied display formats, printing, downloading, index searching, truncation, citation searching, related record searching, search saving

PRINT/ONLINE/OTHER MEDIA COUNTERPARTS
Print: *Social Sciences Citation Index*
Online: Social Scisearch — DIALOG, Data-Star, DIMDI, ORBIT

NETWORK LICENSING ARRANGEMENTS
Contact vendor

TITLE SOCIAL WORK ABSTRACTS PLUS

PUBLISHER Producer: National Association of Social Workers
Vendor: National Association of Social Workers

SCOPE AND CONTENT
Social Work Abstracts Plus, the first CD-ROM offering of the National Association of Social Workers, houses the country's most complete social work abstracts database—plus items on social work practice, education, research, policy, and legislation—on compact disc.

Social Work Abstracts Plus provides social workers and other human service professionals with easy, instantaneous access to Social Work Abstracts (SWAB—previously available only online), the complete 1991 Register of Clinical Social Workers, listings of major social work publications, and specialized full-text information, such as professional standards, legal regulations, state licensing laws, position papers and career information.

This small but impressive disc brings the power, durability, and clean simplicity of the compact disk to social work. Social Work Abstracts Plus contains the entire social work abstracts database and provides descriptions of over 23,000 journal articles and citations of social work literature dating back to 1977—plus listings of over 600 major social work books.

Social Work Abstracts Plus is easy to install, learn, and use. Search by descriptor, title, author, or any combination of natural language. Flexible Boolean logic lets the user broaden or narrow the scope of any search—then display, print, or save information as needed. The database is updated annually. (Publisher's brochure)

Social Work Abstracts has long been the foremost source of research information in the field of social work. Available for several years online on BRS, SWA is now available on CD-ROM and should be an invaluable source of information for social workers, counselors, and other human service workers.

The database has abstracts, covers a variety of formats of materials, has some full text and directory information, has a lengthy backfile, and provides usable research capabilities in its interface. The only research "drawback" is the fact that the database focuses mostly on the United States. It will be an essential source, however, for social work research.

Editor

EQUIPMENT AND SOFTWARE REQUIREMENTS
Computer: IBM PC XT, AT, PS/2, or 100 percent compatible with hard disk, 640K RAM
Software: DOS 2.1 or higher, may use MS-DOS Extensions
CD-ROM Drive: any IBM-compatible

PRICE Annual price: $1,000

SEARCH SOFTWARE AND CAPABILITIES
Software: KAware2
Capabilities: keyword, Boolean, search statement retention and back referencing, field searching, index searching, printing, varied display formats

PRINT/ONLINE/OTHER MEDIA COUNTERPARTS
Print: *Social Work Abstracts, Register of Clinical Social Workers*
Online: Social Work Abstracts — BRS

NETWORK LICENSING ARRANGEMENTS
Contact vendor

TITLE SOCIOFILE

PUBLISHER Producer: Sociological Abstracts Inc.
Vendor: SilverPlatter

SCOPE AND CONTENT
Sociofile on CD-ROM offers abstracts of articles from 240 core sociology journals and 1,600 discipline-related journals published worldwide. This eclectic information resource provides a window to both the theoretical and applied areas of sociology, and touches on topics, such as education, medicine, anthropology, social policy, gender studies, social work, community development, law and penology, social psychology, disaster studies, gerontology, marriage and family studies, substance abuse, and racial interactions. Specific descriptors and broad classification categories give access to exactly the information needed.

Sociofile contains abstracts of journal articles published in *Sociological Abstracts* since 1974 and the enhanced bibliographic citations for dissertations in sociology and related disciplines that have been added to the database since 1986. Sociofile contains over 144,000 records, with about 10,000 entries added each year. The database is updated three times annually. (Publisher's brochure)

Pat Riesenman, reference librarian at Indiana University, calls sociofile, "quite useful; some of the problems which (in my view) beset the printed and online versions are avoided here, since it excludes the generally frustrating because relatively inaccessible papers given at conferences. Other problems remain—e.g., there has been no global change in indexing terms, so it is necessary to use both terms from the 1986 thesaurus and from the earlier authority list."

Charlene York, in evaluating sociofile, as cited below, notes that "Librarians and patrons familiar with the sometimes painstaking task of manually searching *Sociological Abstracts* in print will discover the many benefits sociofile has to offer, especially with the several searching and output options available." She concludes, "Sociologists, faculty, and students at all levels will find sociofile useful to their research without the worry of online costs or time. It provides plenty of help, both online and in print, so that even novice users will be quickly comfortable in using it once they get beyond understanding the use of Boolean operators. When they discover that they can tailor their search and output they will find sociofile a great asset to their research needs."

Paul Kahn, in looking at sociofile on SilverPlatter and generally comparing different CD-ROM searching interfaces, finds that, "The user interface of the SilverPlatter product is much simpler than any of the other products discussed....The user has only one interface to deal with and only the CD-ROM source for the database." However, "Unlike the Wilson databases, which are nearly all created by a single vendor, there is no commonality in the design of the databases offered by SilverPlatter. Even so, SilverPlatter has succeeded in creating a relatively simple and entirely uniform interface, but this has been done at the expense of offering the user a minimum amount of information about the contents of each database."

Sociological Abstracts is a renowned source of information in sociology and related fields. Its availability in CD-ROM format makes it much more useful and accessible for researchers. The comprehensive subject coverage, the international focus, the inclusion of journal articles and dissertations, the lengthy backfile, and the valuable abstracts all make it an essential research database in its field. As Becki Whitaker, information retrieval specialist at the Indiana Cooperative Library Services Authority, points out, sociofile is part of a "core of databases that have been online for almost twenty years and now find themselves on CD-ROM."

The use of the SilverPlatter information retrieval interface to make sociofile accessible entirely suits it for research purposes. The coverage of even more formats of materials, as its online counterpart has, would increase its research comprehensiveness, but this is the only weakness in this area. Any institution supporting sociological research should be interested in this database.

L. Friend, also cited below, notes about sociofile, "A rich source of information on other cultures, both historic and modern, the system can also be a gold mine for contemporary topics. Successful searches were conducted on male contraceptives, wives in the Japanese patrilineal kinship system, the concept of "machismo," glossolalia, and teenage suicide; a classroom simulation model of the spread of AIDS among heterosexuals was identified." Friend concludes, "Mid-range in price and somewhat specialized, sociofile cannot be recommended as a primary purchase for undergraduate libraries, but it is a major improvement over the printed counterpart because it permits full-text searches in almost all fields of a record and the use of Boolean logic. It is recommended for any library with many requests for information in sociology or related disciplines, or for those looking to expand their CD-ROM holdings in the social sciences."

Editor

REVIEWS

CD-ROM Review 3 (July 1988): 32.

Friend, L. "Databases: Sociofile." *Choice* 27 (September 1989): 98.

Kahn, Paul. "Making a Difference: a Review of the User Interface Features in Six CD-ROM Database Products." *Optical Information Systems* 8 (July/August 1988): 169-183.

York, Charlene C. "Optical Product Review: Sociofile." *CD-ROM Librarian* 5 (July/August 1990): 30-33.

EQUIPMENT AND SOFTWARE REQUIREMENTS

Computer: IBM PC XT, AT, PS/2, or 100 percent compatible with hard disk, 640K RAM; Macintosh Plus, SE, or II
Software: DOS 2.1 or higher, may use MS-DOS Extensions
CD-ROM Drive: Toshiba, Hitachi, Philips, Sony, DEC, or Apple

PRICE Annual price: $1,950; with subscription to other SilverPlatter databases: $1,750

ARRANGEMENT AND CONTROL

Record fields: abstract, accession number, author, availability code, availability information, classification code, CODEN, country of publication, descriptors and codes, document type, index phrase, institutional affiliation of first author, journal name, language, notes, publication year, subject heading, subset, title
Searchable: all but availability information

SEARCH SOFTWARE AND CAPABILITIES

Software: SilverPlatter
Capabilities: keyword, Boolean, search statement retention and back referencing, field searching, field limiting, proximity searching, printing, downloading, index searching, truncation, search saving, nesting, varied display formats

PRINT/ONLINE/OTHER MEDIA COUNTERPARTS

Print: *Sociological Abstracts*, *Social Planning/Policy & Development Abstracts*
Online: Sociofile, Social Planning/Policy & Development
Abstracts: DIALOG, BRS, Data-Star, DIMDI

NETWORK LICENSING ARRANGEMENTS
$2,995 for multiusers

TITLE SPORT DISCUS

PUBLISHER Producer: Sport Information Resource Centre
Vendor: SilverPlatter

SCOPE AND CONTENT
The international sports database corresponding to the printed publication *Sport Bibliography.* SPORT DISCUS covers the world's practical and research literature dealing with all sport and fitness disciplines. SPORT DISCUS annually indexes over 1,000 international sport periodicals along with many medical and other related journals. Books, conference proceedings, dissertations, reports, and other monographs on sport are also included. The database covers areas, such as exercise physiology, medicine, biomechanics, coaching, counseling, psychology, training, physical education, physical fitness, history, facilities, equipment, recreation, and sports medicine. The periodicals in the database date from 1975, with monograph and thesis coverage back to 1949; based on more than 2,000 international sources. Languages include German, French, and English. Updating is provided semiannually. (Publisher's brochure)

SPORT DISCUS is a unique database in its coverage of sports and physical fitness. No serious athletic, sport, or recreation research program should be without it. The comprehensiveness of its subject coverage, the range of material formats it covers, its international scope, the date range covered, and the inclusion of abstracts with many of its records make SPORT DISCUS essential for research in its field.

Its weaknesses include the lack of abstracts for many of its entries, the difficulty of obtaining some of the materials cited, and a lag in currency. There is, however, no other source to rival it in this subject area.

In a review cited below, Cindy Slater comments, "The CD-ROM product has the same strengths as the online version—it is comprehensive and provides international coverage of sport related literature that includes theses, proceedings papers, and other usually un-indexed material. But, it also exacerbates the confusing indexing in Sport by not including the Sport Thesaurus. SilverPlatter's v.1.5 search software is quick to learn, easy to use, well-documented, and supported by friendly and very knowledgeable customer service representatives."

A more current review, by Winiarz and Sullivan, was also generally favorable, concluding, "SPORT DISCUS offers a number of advantages to the users compared to its papercopy counterparts. It saves considerable time and effort by cumulating several disjointed sources into one CD-ROM database. Users may identify related subject headings and codes right on the screen in a relevant citation and select these directly."

"Some of the outstanding features of SPORT DISCUS include: identification of the level of the article, listing its availability at the Sport Information Resource Centre for interlibrary loan purposes and the inclusion of abstracts for many research level records, even when the original article is in a foreign language. For those organizations which already use SilverPlatter CD-ROM products, the installation of SPORT DISCUS will be straightforward."

"The initial reactions of first-time student users suggest that it will be well received in libraries or other organizations with an interest in sports issues. Users were happy with the results of their searches and felt that with practice they would become even better searchers. Since the time of our survey, popularity of the SPORT DISCUS has grown and a series of introductory instructional sessions has been provided. We expect to incorporate the use of SPORT DISCUS into a freshman level bibliographic instruction program in the immediate future."

Editor

REVIEWS

Slater, Cindy. "CD-ROM in Brief: Sport Discus." *Laserdisk Professional* 2 (September 1989): 80-83.

Preview 2 (issue 2, 1989): 36.

Winiarz, Elizabeth and S. John Sullivan. "Let's Discuss Sport Discus: Sports Information on CD-ROM." *CD-ROM Professional* 4 (January 1991): 47-48.

EQUIPMENT AND SOFTWARE REQUIREMENTS

Computer: IBM PC XT, AT, PS/2, or 100 percent compatible with hard disk, 640K RAM; Macintosh Plus, SE, or II
Software: DOS 2.1 or higher, may use MS-DOS Extensions
CD-ROM Drive: Toshiba, Hitachi, Philips, Sony, DEC, or Apple

PRICE Annual price: $1,500

ARRANGEMENT AND CONTROL
Record fields: abstract, accession number, author, classification number, corporate author, conference name, country of publication, descriptors, document number, document type, handicapped subject headings, journal, language, language of original, level, notes, publication year, series, source, subfile, subject codes, subject headings, title
Searchable: all

SEARCH SOFTWARE AND CAPABILITIES
Software: SilverPlatter
Capabilities: keyword, Boolean, search statement retention and back referencing, field searching, field limiting, proximity searching, printing, downloading, index searching, truncation, search saving, nesting, varied display formats

PRINT/ONLINE/OTHER MEDIA COUNTERPARTS
Print: *Sport Bibliography*
Online: Sport Database — DIALOG, BRS, DIMDI

NETWORK LICENSING ARRANGEMENTS
$2,250

TITLE SUPERTECH ABSTRACTS PLUS

PUBLISHER Producer: Bowker A&I Publishing
Vendor: R.R. Bowker

SCOPE AND CONTENT
Consolidation of all retrospective and current records from *Artificial Intelligence Abstracts*, *CAD/CAM Abstracts*, *Telecommunications Abstracts*, and *Robotics Abstracts* (over 35,000 citations and abstracts) onto one CD-ROM disc. In addition to core academic and professional journals, Bowker scans U.S. and foreign government reports, conference proceedings, newspapers and consumer magazines, books, corporate research papers, special commission reports, special laboratory studies, patents and other materials with limited or no distribution. The database is updated quarterly.

Supertech Abstracts Plus encompasses the entire computer and technology fields with retrospective and current data. It provides instant access to nearly a decade of worldwide research on artificial intelligence, CAD/CAM and robotics collected in three major interdisciplinary databases. The databases are searchable separately or together. Coverage of both theoretical concepts and practical applications serves a broad range of users. Advanced CD-ROM technology allowing keyword and subject searching enhances the interrelationship among subject areas and issues. Coverage includes software programs, hardware design, computer architecture, graphic displays, and manufacturing technology with browsable indexes of citations and abstracts for more than 40,000 records provides ongoing coverage plus easy and direct access to backfiles to 1983.

Review categories in artificial intelligence include specialty applications (medical, military, transportation, chemical analysis, etc.), automation and robotics, knowledge-based systems, computer architecture, programming and software, sensors, human-machine interface, cognitive sciences, neural networks, plus business and economics, international news, human factors, and general coverage.

Review categories in CAD/CAM include graphics and imaging, computer-aided engineering, inspection and work monitoring, product design, product assembly, integrated factory systems, specialty applications (office automation, map making, business graphics, textiles, etc.), graphic displays, human-machine interface, control systems and software, automation design, plus business and economics, international news, human factors and general coverage.

Review categories in robotics include specialty applications (aerospace, agriculture, education, etc.), computer-aided manufacturing, inspection and optical systems, materials handling, process-oriented applications, product assembly, transport, artificial intelligence and planning software, sensors, control, locomotion, mechanical design, plus business and economics, international news, human factors, and general coverage. (Publisher's brochure)

This combination of databases on CD-ROM provides some much-needed focus on rapidly changing, "hot" technology fields: AI, CAD/CAM, telecommunications, and robotics. This CD-ROM combines the databases in a useful way, contains abstracts, covers international material, includes a variety of formats, has a lengthy backfile, and uses an interface that is at least capable of supporting research. The primary drawback is that the Bowker searching interface is somewhat clumsy for lengthy, complicated searches that might be desirable in an abstracting database. This database does, however, merit strong consideration by any institution supporting technology research.

Editor

EQUIPMENT AND SOFTWARE REQUIREMENTS
Computer: IBM PC, XT, AT, PS/2, or compatible with hard disk (strongly suggested) or two 5.25- or one 3.5-inch floppy diskette drive, 640K RAM
Software: DOS 3.0 or higher, MS-DOS Extensions
CD-ROM Drive: any IBM-compatible

PRICE Annual price: $1,295, $3,690 for three-year subscription; for subscribers to Bowker A&I microfiche: $695, $1,410 for three-year subscription.

ARRANGEMENT AND CONTROL
Record fields: database, review classification, accession number, title, author, author affiliation, source, date, number of pages, document type, abstract, subjects, SIC codes, special features
Searchable: all except number of pages

SEARCH SOFTWARE AND CAPABILITIES
Software: Bowker
Capabilities: keyword, Boolean, search statement retention and back referencing, field searching, proximity searching, printing, downloading, index searching, truncation, novice search mode, thesaurus, OCLC-type 4,4 author, title searching, online vendor ordering, varied display formats

PRINT/ONLINE/OTHER MEDIA COUNTERPARTS
Print: *Artificial Intelligence Abstracts, CAD/CAM Abstracts, Robotics Abstracts*
Online: Supertech — Data-Star, DIALOG, ESA/IRS, ORBIT
Other media: Bowker A&I microfiche

NETWORK LICENSING ARRANGEMENTS
$3,885 for multiusers; $11,073 for multiusers, three years

TITLE TOXLINE
PUBLISHER Producer: National Library of Medicine
Vendor: SilverPlatter

SCOPE AND CONTENT
TOXLINE on SilverPlatter is a collection of toxicological information from

the U.S. National Library of Medicine, containing references to published material and research in progress in the areas of adverse drug reactions, air pollution, carcinogenesis via chemicals, drug toxicity, food contamination, occupational hazards, pesticides and herbicides, toxicological analysis, water treatment and more. TOXLINE on SilverPlatter CD-ROM will include the public domain records in the NLM file from 1981 to present. Updating is provided quarterly. (Publisher's brochure)

Toxline is one of the most important toxicological databases in the CD-ROM field. Its extensive subject coverage, the variety of formats indexed, the availability of abstracts, the time period covered, and the capabilities of the SilverPlatter searching interface make it extremely useful for research in the environment, occupational safety, biochemistry, food science, and more. Its primary weakness is the American focus. Another important point to note for research purposes is the database's inclusion of research in progress.

Martin Courtois, of Michigan State University's Science Library, says of Toxline, "Produced by the National Library of Medicine, Toxline is made up of over a dozen separate files covering citations to the literature in biomedicine, toxicology, pesticides, waste management, hazardous substances, and occupational safety and health. Toxline also includes files such as the Toxic Substances Control Act Test Submissions, which covers data on the environmental and health effects of over 35,000 chemical substances."

"Long available only through MEDLARS, Toxline may not have been readily accessible to those outside a medical research setting. Toxline was recently made available on BRS, and now with a CD version priced at under $1,000, researchers in other areas of the biosciences will have access to an important database."

Editor

EQUIPMENT AND SOFTWARE REQUIREMENTS
Computer: IBM PC XT, AT, PS/2, or 100 percent compatible with hard disk, 640K RAM; Macintosh Plus, SE, or II
Software: DOS 2.1 or higher, may use MS-DOS Extensions
CD-ROM Drive: Toshiba, Hitachi, Philips, Sony, DEC, or Apple

PRICE Annual price: $950

ARRANGEMENT AND CONTROL
Record fields: abstract, accession number, address of author, author, availabili-

ty, award type, CAS registry number, classification code, CODEN, contract/identification numbers, corporate source, country of intellectual origin, ISSN, keywords, language, major MeSH headings, Medical Subject Headings, publication type, publication year, source, subfile, subjects, title, update code
Searchable: all but availability

SEARCH SOFTWARE AND CAPABILITIES
Software: SilverPlatter
Capabilities: keyword, Boolean, search statement retention and back referencing, field searching, field limiting, proximity searching, printing, downloading, index searching, truncation, search saving, nesting, varied display formats

PRINT/ONLINE/OTHER MEDIA COUNTERPARTS
Online: Toxline — MEDLARS, BRS, DIMDI, Japan Information Center of Science and Technology

NETWORK LICENSING ARRANGEMENTS
No additional charge

TITLE TROPAG & RURAL

PUBLISHER Producer: Royal Tropical Institute
Vendor: SilverPlatter

SCOPE AND CONTENT
This data covers literature related to the practical aspects of agriculture in rural and tropical and subtropical regions, with attention to crop production, crop protection, farming systems, post-harvest systems, cultural practices, environmental relationships, economic policy and planning, agricultural development, nutrition and food, and health care. Coverage is back to 1975 for tropical topics and 1985 for rural topics. Approximately 6,000 journals are indexed. Updating is provided annually. (Publisher's brochure)

Although its focus is comparatively narrow, Tropag & Rural is quite useful to support research in topics relating to rural and tropical development. The rural aspect of coverage has especially far reaching implications, since more than just agriculture is covered. This database is international in coverage, does have abstracts, has a fairly good-sized backfile, and covers its subject exhaustively. Institutions with research interests in agriculture, the tropics, rural sociology, the environment and other related areas should consider this database for subscription.

Editor

EQUIPMENT AND SOFTWARE REQUIREMENTS
Computer: IBM PC XT, AT, PS/2, or 100 percent compatible with hard disk, 640K RAM; Macintosh Plus, SE, or II
Software: DOS 2.1 or higher, may use MS-DOS Extensions
CD-ROM Drive: Toshiba, Hitachi, Philips, Sony, DEC, or Apple

PRICE Annual price: $750

ARRANGEMENT AND CONTROL
Record fields: abstract, accession number, address of author, author, availability, category code, database, descriptors, ISSN, ISBN, language, location, original non-English title, project name, publication type, publication year, source, taxonomic name, title, update code
Searchable: all

SEARCH SOFTWARE AND CAPABILITIES
Software: SilverPlatter
Capabilities: keyword, Boolean, search statement retention and back referencing, field searching, field limiting, proximity searching, printing, downloading, index searching, truncation, search saving, nesting, varied display formats

PRINT/ONLINE/OTHER MEDIA COUNTERPARTS
Print: *Abstracts on Tropical Agriculture, Abstracts on Rural Development in the Tropics*
Online: Tropag — ORBIT

NETWORK LICENSING ARRANGEMENTS
Contact vendor

TITLE UKOP: THE CATALOGUE OF UNITED KINGDOM OFFICIAL PUBLICATIONS ON CD-ROM

PUBLISHER Producer: HMSO (Her Majesty's Stationers Office) Books
Vendor: Chadwyck-Healey

SCOPE AND CONTENT

UKOP, the Catalogue of United Kingdom Official Publications on CD-ROM, is the first complete catalogue of all official publications including both HMSO publications and departmental or "Non-HMSO" publications. The Catalogue contains all such publications from 1980 to the present, together with the publications of twelve important international organizations for which HMSO is the U.K. agent. It is a major advance in the bibliographic control of government documents and the public's access to them.

Just under half of U.K. official publications are published by HMSO. These include Parliamentary publications and the publications of other official bodies. The remainder are published by more than 500 government agencies. Many official organizations publish both through HMSO and directly on their own behalf. UKOP removes this artificial distinction and provides for the first time a single catalogue of all U.K. official publications, regardless of their publisher.

UKOP is a joint publication of Chadwyck-Healey and HMSO books, which amalgamates HMSO's Publications Catalogues and Chadwyck-Healey's *Catalogue of British Official Publications Not Published by HMSO*. It covers the period from 1980 and currently contains more than 160,000 records.

HMSO publications include Parliamentary Publications; Hansard (Commons and Lords); Debates of Standing Committees; House of Commons and House of Lords Journals; House of Commons Weekly Information Bulletin; House of Commons Bills; House of Commons Papers; House of Lords Papers; House of Lords Bills; Command Papers; Acts of Parliament; non-Parliamentary publications published on behalf of government departments or agencies; Statutory Instruments; and Statutes in Force.

Non-HMSO publications include titles published directly (not through HMSO) by more than 500 official organizations—over half of all U.K. official publications. Publications of international organizations available through HMSO include those from the Council of Europe; Customs Co-operation Council; European Communities; Food and Agricultural Organization; General Agreement on Tariffs and Trade; International Atomic Energy Agency; International Monetary Fund; Organisation for Economic Co-operation and Development; United Nations; United Nations Educational, Scientific and Cultural Organization; United Nations University; and World Health Organization.

UKOP is published quarterly, within four weeks of the latest quarter it records. Each new disc accumulates the complete file back to 1980 and replaces the previous disc. Information on prices and the availability of publications is updated regularly. (Publisher's brochure)

UKOP is a treasure trove for researchers in political science, public affairs, economics, and history. Anyone who researches topics that concern the United Kingdom, countries of the Commonwealth, or any nations' relations with them will find this database very useful. It also contains document citations from a large variety of international organizations. It is, of course, international in scope, provides bibliographic access to a group of related publications that have never been brought together in this way before; it has a good-sized backfile, and the interface used with it provides reasonable access to record contents for research purposes.

On the down side, much of the material indexed may be difficult to obtain for some libraries. Abstracts are not provided. In addition, although the interface is acceptable, especially for a bibliographic database like this one, it can sometimes be a bit awkward to use for complicated research. Any institution, however, with major subject research interests in the areas listed above, should consider this vital CD-ROM.

Editor

EQUIPMENT AND SOFTWARE REQUIREMENTS
Computer: IBM PC, XT, AT, PS/2, or compatible with hard disk and 640K RAM
Software: DOS 3.1 or higher, MS-DOS Extensions
CD-ROM Drive: any IBM-compatible

PRICE Annual price: $1,400

ARRANGEMENT AND CONTROL
Record fields: author, title, series title, publisher, publication year, corporate author, country of publication, bibliographic information, session year, subject, ISBN, ISSN
Searchable: all

SEARCH SOFTWARE AND CAPABILITIES
Software: Chadwyck-Healey
Capabilities: keyword, Boolean, search statement retention and back refer-

encing, field searching, field limiting, printing, downloading, index searching, truncation, varied display formats, nesting, thesaurus

PRINT/ONLINE/OTHER MEDIA COUNTERPARTS
Print: *HMSO's Publications Catalogues, Catalogue of British Official Publications Not Published by HMSO*

NETWORK LICENSING ARRANGEMENT
No additional charge for multiusers

TITLE ULRICH'S PLUS

PUBLISHER Producer: R.R. Bowker
Vendor: R.R. Bowker

SCOPE AND CONTENT
Here's the one database you can depend on for accurate details about virtually every periodical, serial, and annual—regular and irregular—published in the U.S. and around the world. With a wealth of data on some 145,000 publications—including over 25,000 cessations since 1979—this unmatched database provides full purchasing information plus names, addresses, and phone numbers for the 61,000 publishers from 184 countries represented throughout.

What's more, twenty-three search criteria give you the power to trace titles by first year of publication, price, publisher, circulation, abstracting/indexing service and more. (Even look-up serials published from a specified zip code!) With keyword searching you can boost Ulrich's 542 subject categories to find titles on everything from anatomy to the zodiac. New to Ulrich's Plus are concise editorial annotations of selected periodicals (with each word in every annotation searchable), LC Classification Numbers for some 16,000 titles, CODEN designations for over 7,000 sci-tech publications, vendor file names and numbers for titles available online, and notations for serials available on CD-ROM. The database is updated quarterly. (Publisher's brochure)

In addition to the traditional research avenues of searching databases for books, periodical articles, technical reports, and so on, is the method of searching for entire periodicals to support research. This can be necessary to assess research collections to decide where to look for material, to support ongoing research by subscribing to certain periodicals, to find where journals of interest are indexed to help in choosing research tools, and for other related reasons. Ulrich's has long been recognized as the foremost periodical directory in the world, and having it available on CD-ROM has increased access to its contents immensely. Pat Riesenman, reference librarian at Indiana University, finds Ulrich's "far less bothersome for this essentially directory-type of product than the (relatively) same software applied to PAIS [original version]."

In reviews along with Anthony J. Ferraro's description of Ulrich's Plus (Ferraro also describes Ulrich's in *Serials Librarian*), Mary Jane Donnelly finds "Ulrich's PLUS is a valuable, time-saving source for information on serials. Since I started to use this database, I have been continually impressed by its many features. These features provide various options that can lead to fast efficient searching. The opportunity to access various sources at one time, the advantage of cross-referencing subject-headings, and the ability to apply Boolean-logic in a search makes my job...easier."

She continues, "I am enthusiastic about Ulrich's PLUS....The documentation is good and the support from Bowker has been positive. The system is menu driven and does contain embedded-training and help screens; both features should be useful for public access. The total visual interface of Ulrich's PLUS including the use of 'window' displays, is very effective." She concludes, "Ulrich's PLUS is not perfect and will not, of course, answer everyone's needs, but it provides a source of easily accessible information. It is a versatile tool...."

Kirchmann and Ashford, in a review attached to the same article, agree, saying, "We are very pleased with the system. Our compliments are many; our complaints are few." They conclude, "In summary, we are very pleased with the Ulrich's PLUS system. The documentation is superb and the window menu system makes Ulrich's a breeze to use. The search capabilities provide access to information that was not possible with the print format. Ulrich's PLUS is well worth the price and pays for itself many times over in speed and access of information."

In an another early look at Ulrich's, Carson Holloway concluded that Ulrich's Plus is "...among the better CD-ROM products currently on the market. The search software works well and the products are adequately supported by the Bowker Company; further development of these products, such as resolving the delays in retrieving records for the indexes and brief displays could make them even more useful....the ability to provide these databases in a powerful automated form and to provide users with an up-to-the-minute information technology is very appealing. The high quality of the databases on which the CD-ROMs are based and their appeal to a broad range of users, ensure that Ulrich's Plus...will find a place in many library settings."

In a more recent review, Linda Karch finds Ulrich's "...produced excellent retrieval in sample searches. User aids provide clear, concise explanations of search options and strategies. On-screen 'Help' facilities provide additional assistance for users...." It "...provide[s] screens that are menu-driven and user-friendly." It offers "...extensive, comprehensive bibliographic information." It is a "...useful tool for providing serials information."

Meta Nissley also evaluated Ulrich's, and commented, "Ulrich's Plus has many advantages over the print product: it is more current; it offers flexibility in manipulating citations; there are numerous ways of retrieving citations including the application of Boolean logic; groups of citations can be printed out; and it is easy on the eyes. The documentation, which has a table of contents and an index, is very clear and offers good examples. The inclusion of serials and annuals provides a new and important dimension. In spite of a few minor annoyances, it is an excellent product overall and well-used in the Meriam Library." Norman Desmarais wrote an indepth description several years ago of Ulrich's Plus, describing the functioning of the database in extensive detail.

Ulrich's provides excellent international coverage, especially of the types of journals likely to be used for research, its coverage is broad and inclusive, it is current, it provides some annotations, and the Bowker interface is usable for searching a directory type database. It is the most extensive CD-ROM periodicals directory. It supports research in every conceivable subject area.

By its very nature, of course, Ulrich's covers only periodicals and many of the records are not annotated. It also is not complete in telling where all of its periodicals are indexed. It is, however, still an incredibly valuable research tool.

Editor

REVIEWS

CD-ROM Lab Report 1 (June 1988): 18-19.

Desmarais, Norman. "An Examination of Ulrich's Plus." *CD-ROM Librarian* 3 (April 1988): 24-31.

Ferraro, Anthony J. "Ulrich's PLUS: a High-Performance, Low-Cost Alternative to Online Serials Reference Systems." *Serials Librarian* 14 (issue 3-4, 1988): 121-125.

Ferraro, Anthony J., Mary Jane Donnelly, Jennifer Kirchmann, and Connie Ashford. "Ulrich's PLUS: a New Serials Reference Technology." *Serials Review* 13 (Fall 1987): 19-23.

Holloway, Carson. "Books in Print and Ulrich's on CD-ROM: a Preliminary Review." *Online* 11 (September 1987): 57-61.

Karch, Linda S. "Serials Information on CD-ROM: a Reference Perspective." *Reference Services Review* 18 (Summer 1990): 81-88.

Nissley, Meta. "Ulrich's Plus." *Laserdisk Professional* 1 (November 1988): 80-81.

Urbanski, Verna. "Resources & Technical Services News: CD-ROM Takes Center Stage." *Library Resources & Technical Services* 32 (issue 1, 1988): 13.

EQUIPMENT AND SOFTWARE REQUIREMENTS
Computer: IBM PC, XT, AT, PS/2, or compatible with hard disk (strongly suggested) or two 5.25- or one 3.5-inch floppy diskette drive, 640K RAM; Macintosh Plus, SE, II, IIx, or equivalent with at least 1MB of memory. Minimum 2MB of memory required to run program under Multifinder.
Software: DOS 3.0 or higher, MS-DOS Extensions
CD-ROM Drive: Any, including Apple CD SC CD-ROM drive

PRICE Annual price: $465, $1,126 for three-year subscription

ARRANGEMENT AND CONTROL
Record fields: Dewey classification, LC classification, country of publication, ISSN, CODEN, title, year first published, frequency, price, publisher, address, telephone number, editor, special features, circulation, abstracted index, subject headings, status, media code, online/CD-ROM availability, annotation.
Searchable: all

SEARCH SOFTWARE AND CAPABILITIES
Software: Bowker
Capabilities: keyword, Boolean, search statement retention and back referencing, field searching, proximity searching, printing, downloading, index searching, truncation, novice search mode, OCLC-type 4,4 author, title and 3,2,2,1 title searching, online vendor ordering, varied display formats

PRINT/ONLINE/OTHER MEDIA COUNTERPARTS
Print: *Ulrich's International Periodicals Directory and Irregular Serials and Annuals*
Online: Ulrich's Plus — DIALOG, BRS, ESA/IRS

NETWORK LICENSING ARRANGEMENTS
$1,395 for multiusers; $3,378 for multiusers, three years

TITLE WATER RESOURCES ABSTRACTS

PUBLISHER Producer: Water Resources Scientific Information Center
Vendor: NISC—National Information Services Corporation, OCLC

SCOPE AND CONTENT
Water Resources Abstracts provides water information from 380 journals compiled by the Water Resources Scientific Information Center of the U.S. Geological Survey. It contains about 200,000 citations, with abstracts, to scientific as well as technical literature, on water resource aspects of physical, social, and life sciences. It also covers related legal and engineering aspects of conservation, control, use and management of water resources. The database corresponds in part to Selected Water Resources and Water Resources Abstracts online databases. The disc's coverage is back to 1967. The NISC version is updated semiannually, the OCLC version quarterly. (Publisher's brochure)

Water Resources Abstracts is a premiere resource database on all aspects of water use and management. It is of possible interest to some programs in engineering, public affairs, environmental health, and other related areas. It provides abstracts, of course, has a lengthy backfile, provides a useful subject focus, and the OCLC interface is quite useful for research.

On the other hand, the coverage is just of periodicals, and the focus is not really international. Water Resources Abstracts is a vital support, however, for research in its subject area.

Martin Courtois, science librarian at Michigan State University, notes that Water Resources Abstracts is "A very specialized database, but it is the most comprehensive coverage of the scientific and technical literature on water and water resource management. I do not have experience with the CD-ROM version, but I have worked with researchers in searching this database on DI-

ALOG, and have been impressed with how pleased the researchers are with the results. Few libraries will be interested in such a specialized database, but at only $625 for the NISC version, and with coverage back to 1967, is this the database that the individual researcher buys to search on his/her own PC? If other databases were priced in this range, would the vendors open a whole new market?"

Katie Clark reviewed the NISC version of Water Resources Abstracts, and concluded, "Most novice searchers will find the Water Resources Abstracts from NISC easy to use and certainly an improvement over searching twenty-two years of the printed index. The response time is quite fast...and it is convenient to have the entire database on one rather than two discs. The system has several nice features, such as year range searching and a thesaurus of keywords."

"I preferred the Novice mode over the Expert mode and most first-time users will probably agree. As an experienced searcher, there were several features of the software that I found lacking. The retrieval software does not have some of the powerful features of online systems, such as DIALOG, or of the more sophisticated CD-ROM databases, such as those from SilverPlatter. I found it cumbersome to use Boolean operators between fields—too many steps were required."

"It was inconvenient not to have a search history with individual sets; every time I started a new search I had to erase the previous one. While there are advantages to having a search history, I have observed that most CD-ROM users are actually confused by multiple sets. The average end-user will not be bothered by this feature, but librarians and other sophisticated end-users may wish the retrieval software of Water Resources Abstracts allowed them to do the kinds of complex searches to which they have become accustomed. Overall, end-users will like searching this CD-ROM database from NISC and will not realize the limitations of the software."

Editor

REVIEWS

Clark, K. E. "Water Resources Abstracts: a Review." *CD-ROM Professional* 3 (May 1990): 102-107.

EQUIPMENT AND SOFTWARE REQUIREMENTS

NISC
Computer: IBM PC, XT, AT, PS/2, or 100 percent compatible with hard disk, 640K RAM
Software: DOS 3.1 or 3.3, MS-DOS Extensions
CD-ROM Drive: any IBM-compatible

OCLC
Computer: IBM PC or compatible with hard disk and 640K RAM; Macintosh
Software: DOS 3.2 or higher, MS-DOS Extensions
CD-ROM Drive: Any IBM-compatible, Apple

PRICE *NISC* annual price: $625; *OCLC* annual price: $750, $700 for OCLC members

ARRANGEMENT AND CONTROL

NISC
Record fields: abstract, author, corporate author, field and group, major keywords, minor keywords, record ID, source/citation, title, year
Searchable: all

OCLC
Record fields: abstract, accession number, author, corporate source, journal volume and issue codes, major descriptors, minor descriptors, source, subject field codes, title
Searchable: all but journal volume and issue codes

SEARCH SOFTWARE AND CAPABILITIES

NISC
Software: Dataware
Capabilities: keyword, Boolean, novice search mode, field searching, proximity searching, truncation, nesting, index searching, search saving, sorting, printing, downloading

OCLC
Software: Search CD450
Capabilities: keyword, Boolean, search statement retention and back referencing, field searching, field limiting, proximity searching, printing, downloading, index searching, truncation, nesting, varied display formats

PRINT/ONLINE/OTHER MEDIA COUNTERPARTS
Print: *Water Resources Abstracts*
Online: Water Resources Abstracts — DIALOG

NETWORK LICENSING ARRANGEMENTS

NISC
Contact vendor

OCLC
No additional charge

TITLE WAVES CD-ROM VAGUES

PUBLISHER Producer: Canada Department of Fisheries and Oceans
Vendor: Optim Corporation

SCOPE AND CONTENT
WAVES CD-ROM VAGUES provides easy access to report literature in the field of fisheries and marine science. An added feature is the ability to identify Canadian scientists, consultants and engineers working in this field. It is updated on a quarterly basis.

Demonstrated at the annual conference of the International Association of Marine Science Libraries and Information Centres in Seattle, Washington, October 1 through 5, the WAVES CD-ROM VAGUES received rave reviews. WAVES CD-ROM VAGUES contains two databases: the WAVES Database, a bibliographic database of approximately 75,000 records produced by the libraries of the Department of Fisheries and Oceans (DFO), and the Directory of Marine and Freshwater Scientists in Canada 1989. The WAVES Database represents the holdings from all the regional libraries of the Department of Fisheries and Oceans. Although focusing especially on report literature of interest to Canada, the database also covers international literature. Until now the database has only been available within DFO itself; the WAVES CD-ROM VAGUES will make it accessible to a wider audience.

WAVES CD-ROM VAGUES is searchable in both English and French. It offers an easy-to-use but powerful search system, context-sensitive help screens, and on-disc interactive tutorials to guide new users.

The WAVES CD-ROM VAGUES is of primary interest to the fisheries and marine sciences community, but it will also be a useful resource to many other audiences including government information centres, universities, and industry. The database is the result of a co-publishing agreement between OPTIM, the Department of Fisheries and Oceans, and the Canadian Government Publishing Centre.

What effects do hatchery salmon have on wild salmon stocks? Is acid rain affecting the marine fisheries? Who is doing research in pelagic ecology in British Columbia? WAVES CD-ROM VAGUES can provide the answers!

Anyone looking for reports (published and unpublished) on fisheries and aquatic sciences will find the WAVES Database an important tool. The database contains references to consultants' reports, working papers, internal studies commission reports and much more, with an emphasis on Canadian works and items relevant to Canadian interests. Documents listed in the database are held by DFO libraries across the country.

Those interested in finding out who is doing what in the field of marine and aquatic research in Canada, should consult the Directory of Marine and Freshwater Scientists in Canada, which lists research institutions, scientists and engineers, their specialties and activities. The power and flexibility of CD-ROM technology makes these databases easily accessible through a PC. (Publisher's brochure)

Although certainly specialized, this database will be of interest to institutions supporting Canadian environmental or marine, aquatic, and fisheries research. It covers a variety of material formats, some of them for hard-to-find items, but they should be available through Canadian DFO libraries. The database provides international coverage, and focuses in helpfully on a research area. Although it does not provide abstracts, the uniqueness of coverage of this database make it worthy of consideration by institutions in these subject areas.

Editor

EQUIPMENT AND SOFTWARE REQUIREMENTS
Computer: IBM PC, XT, AT, PS/2, or compatible with hard disk and 512K RAM
Software: DOS 3.0 or higher, MS-DOS Extensions
CD-ROM Drive: any IBM-compatible

PRICE Annual price: $995

SEARCH SOFTWARE AND CAPABILITIES
Software: Dataware CD-Answer
Capabilities: keyword, Boolean, novice search mode, field searching, proximity searching, truncation, nesting, index searching, search saving, sorting, printing, downloading

PRINT/ONLINE/OTHER MEDIA COUNTERPARTS
Print: *Directory of Marine and Freshwater Scientists in Canada 1989*

NETWORK LICENSING ARRANGEMENTS
Contact vendor

TITLE WILDLIFE & FISH WORLDWIDE

PUBLISHER Producer: U.S. Fish and Wildlife Service
Vendor: NISC—National Information Services

SCOPE AND CONTENT
This disc covers the world's literature on mammals, birds, reptiles, amphibians, and fish. Thousands of journal articles, monographs, conference proceedings, symposia, government reports, theses, dissertations, and scientific periodicals are included in this bibliographic database. This CD-ROM provides coverage of many non-traditional information sources which the existing commercial databases seldom are able to tap. Wildlife coverage ranges from studies of individual species to specific habitat types, hunting, economics, wildlife behavior, management techniques, diseases, and parasites. Fish coverage includes culture and propagation, limnology and oceanography, genetics and behavior, natural history, parasites, diseases, and general research and management topics. Updated semiannually; coverage extends back to 1971.

Never before has this database been available for direct electronic access by the general public. NISC is pleased to help make the valuable information contained in *Wildlife Review* and *Fisheries Review* available to the scientific community on CD-ROM. "It took us many weeks to reconstruct a solid bibliographic database from the files which were sent to us—the programming job became a complex, expert rule system—but we feel that once researchers become familiar with this NISC DISC, the effort we made will have been worthwhile. There simply is no other database like it which is available for as little as a $695.00 annual subscription," said Fred Durr, President and CEO, NISC. "The taxonomic and geographic identifiers are extremely well done. The user can query by species in locations as specific as a province, state, county, or even a community, park, lake, or stream!" he said. The geographic identifiers span the globe and searches can be done on a broad, regional basis as well as specific localities. (Publisher's brochure)

This CD-ROM makes easily available a highly useful database in the area of animal studies. For any institution with programs involving fish, wildlife, and other zoological research, Wildlife & Fish Worldwide could be invaluable as a resource. It has a useful subject focus, covers a wide variety of material formats, has a lengthy backfile, and provides good international coverage. Its main drawback is the lack of abstracts. This can still be an excellent research resource in its subject areas.

Martin Courtois, of Michigan State University's Science Library, notes, "This database corresponds to *Fisheries Review* and *Wildlife Review*, which are produced by the Fish and Wildlife Service of the U.S. Department of the Interior. Sources covered include over 1,300 journals and more than 500 books and conference proceedings in the areas of wildlife, fisheries, and management of natural resources. These indexes are not available through an online vendor, so Wildlife and Fish Worldwide provides unique electronic access to this literature."

"Researchers in this field commonly need to search for a particular animal within a specified geographical area, which is difficult to do in the print index, but will be easier to do with the Boolean search capabilities of the CD-ROM version."

Editor

EQUIPMENT AND SOFTWARE REQUIREMENTS
Computer: IBM PC, XT, AT, PS/2, or compatible with 512K RAM
Software: DOS 3.1 or higher, MS-DOS Extensions
CD-ROM Drive: any IBM-compatible

PRICE Annual price: $695

SEARCH SOFTWARE AND CAPABILITIES
Software: Dataware CD-Answer
Capabilities: keyword, Boolean, novice search mode, field searching, proxim-

ity searching, truncation, nesting, index searching, search saving, sorting, printing, downloading

PRINT/ONLINE/OTHER MEDIA COUNTERPARTS
Print: *Wildlife Review*, *Fisheries Review*

NETWORK LICENSING ARRANGEMENTS
Contact vendor

Subject Index

Aerospace

Agriculture

Biography

Biology and Life Sciences

Geography and Anthropology

Government Information

Humanities

Language and Literature

Law

Publishers and Producers Index

Publisher Addresses

American Mathematical Society
P.O. Box 6248, 201 Charles St.
Providence, RI 02940
Telephone: (401) 455-4000
Telex: 797192
Fax: (401) 331-3842

American Psychological Association
1400 N. Uhle St.
Arlington, VA 22201
Telephone: (800) 336-4980;
(703) 247-7829
Fax: (703) 524-1205

American Society of Hospital Pharmacists
4630 Montgomery Ave.
Betheseda, MD 20814
Telephone: (301) 657-3000
Fax: (301) 657-1641

Aries Systems Corporation
One Dundee Park
Andover, MA 01810
Telephone: (508) 475-7200
Fax: (508) 474-8860

Bibliotheque Nationale
2 rue Vivienne
Paris
CEDEX 02 F-75084 France
Telephone: 33-1-47-03-87-79

BIOSIS, Marketing Section
2100 Arch St.
Philadelphia, PA 19103-1399
Telephone: (215) 587-4800
Fax: (215) 587-2016

Bowker Electronic Publishing
245 West 17th Street
New York, NY 10011
Telephone: (212) 337-6989

The British Library
Bibliographic Services
2 Sheraton St.
London
W1V 4BH U.K.
Telephone: 01-323-7073

Buchhandler Vereinigung GmbH
Grosser Hirschgraben 17-21
Postfach 100442
Frankfurt am Main
1 6000 Germany
Telephone: 069-13060

Cambridge Scientific Abstracts
7200 Wisconson Ave.
Betheseda, MD 20814
Telephone: (301) 961-6738
Fax: (301) 961-6720

CD Plus, Inc.
951 Amsterdam Ave., #2C
New York, NY 10025
Telephone: (212) 932-1485
Fax: (212) 865-0899

Chadwyck-Healey
1101 King St.
Alexandria, VA 22314
Telephone: (703) 683-4890;
(800) 752-0515
Fax: (703) 683-7589

Chadwyck-Healey France S.A.R.L.
(Group)
3 Rue De Marivaux
Paris
75002 France
Telephone: (1) 42-86-80-20
Telex: 9312102283 DG G
Fax: (1) 42-61-33-87

Chadwyck-Healey, Ltd.
Cambridge Place
Cambridge
CB2 1NR U.K.
Telephone: 0223 311-479
Fax: 44-223-66-440

Chicano Studies Library, UC Berkeley
3404 Dwinelle Hall
Berkeley, CA 94720

Telephone: (415) 642-3859
Fax: (415) 642-6456

CINAHL Information Systems
P.O. Box 871, 1509 Wilson Terrace
Glendale, CA 91209-0871
Telephone: (818) 409-8005

CITIS
2 Rosemont Terrace, Black Rock
Dublin
Ireland
Telephone: 011-353-1-886227;
(212) 683-9221 NY Office
Fax: 011-353-1-885971

Congressional Information Service, Inc.
4520 East-West Highway
Suite 800
Betheseda, MD 20814-3389
Telephone: (301) 654-1550

Dialog Information Services, Inc.
3460 Hillview Ave.
Palo Alto, CA 94304
Telephone: (415) 858-3785;
(800) 334-2564
Telex: 334499 (DIALOG)
Fax: (415) 858-7069

Dialog/France
75 avenue Parmentier
Paris
75011 France
Telephone: 1-40-21-24-24

DNASTAR Inc.
1228 South Park St.
Madison, WI 53715
Telephone: (608) 258-7420
Fax: (608) 258-7439

DNASTAR, Ltd.
St. James House
105-113 The Broadway
London
W13 9BL U.K.
Telephone: 081-566-1200

EBSCO Electronic Information
P.O. Box 325
461 Old Boston Rd. Suite E4
Topsfield, MA 01983
Telephone: (508) 887-6667

EBSCO Subscriber Services Europe
P.O. Box 204
Aalsmeer
1430 AE The Netherlands
Telephone: 31 2977 23949

Excerpta Medica Publishing Group
Molenwerf 1
Amsterdam
1014 AG The Netherlands
Telephone: (020) 5803524
Telex: 18582
Fax: (020) 5803222

Human Relations Area Files, Inc.
755 Prospect St.
New Haven, CT 06511
Telephone: (203) 777-2334
Fax: (203) 777-2337

Institute de l'Information Scientifique et Technique (INST)
2, Allee du Parc de Brabois
Vandoeuvre-Les-Nancy
Cedex 54514 France
Telephone: (33) 83-50-46-00
Fax: (33) 83-50-46-50

Institute for Scientific Information
3501 Market St.
Philadelphia, PA 19104
Telephone: (215) 386-0100 x1290
Fax: (215) 386-6362

International Food Information Service GmbH
Melibocusstr. 52
Frankfurt am Main
71 6000 Germany
Telephone: (069) 669007-0
Fax: (069) 669007-10

Library Association Publishing, Ltd.
23 Ridgmount St.
London
WC1E 7AE U.K.
Telephone: 636-7543

Telex: 21897 LALDN G
Fax: 636-3627

Library of Congress
Cataloging Distribution Service
2nd & Independence Ave. SE
Washington, DC 20541
Telephone: (202) 707-1308

Maxwell Electronic Publishing
124 Mount Auburn St.
Cambridge, MA 02138
Telephone: (617) 661-2955;
(800) 342-1338

The Medical Publishing Group
1440 Main St.
Waltham, MA 02166
Telephone: (617) 893-3800
Fax: (617) 893-8103

Medical Publishing Group
Saxon Way, Melbourn
Royston
HERTS SG8 6NJ U.K.
Telephone: 44-7636-2368
Fax: 44-7636-2040

Micromedex, Inc.
600 Grant St.
Denver, CO 80203-3527
Telephone: (303) 831-1400
Telex: 703618 Medex UD
Fax: (303) 837-1717

Micromedia Limited
158 Pearl St.
Toronto, ON M5H 1L3
Canada
Telephone: (416) 593-5211
Fax: (416) 593-1760

National Information Services Corp.
(NISC)
Suite 6, Wyman Towers, 3100 St. Paul
St.
Baltimore, MD 21218
Telephone: (301) 243-0797;
(301) 243-0798
Fax: (301) 243-0982

Online Computer Library Center, Inc.
(OCLC)
6565 Frantz Rd.
Dublin, OH 43017-0702
Telephone: (800) 848-5878
Fax: (614) 764-6096

OPTIM Corporation
338 Somerset St. West
Ottawa, ON K2P 0J9
Canada
Telephone: (613) 232-3766
Fax: (613) 232-8413

Population Information Program, Center
for Communication Programs
Johns Hopkins University
527 St. Paul Place
Baltimore, MD 21202
Telephone: (301) 659-6341
Fax: (301) 659-6266

Predicasts
11001 Cedar Ave.
Cleveland, OH 44106
Telephone: (800) 321-6388;
(216) 795-3000
Telex: 985 604
Fax: (216) 229-9944

Public Affairs Information Service, Inc.
521 W. 43rd St.
New York, NY 10022
Telephone: (212) 736-6629
Fax: (212) 643-2848

Quanta Press, Inc.
2550 University Ave. West
Saint Paul, MN 55114
Telephone: (612) 641-0714
Fax: (612) 644-8811

Research Publications, Inc.
12 Lunar Drive, Drawer AB
Woodbridge, CT 06525
Telephone: (203) 397-2600
Telex: 710 465-6345
Fax: (203) 397-3893

Research Publications, Ltd.
P.O. Box 45

Reading
RG1 8HF U.K.
Telephone: 0734-583247
Fax: 0734-591325

SAZTEC Europe, Ltd.
London House
26-40 Kensington High St.
London
W8 4PT U.K.
Telephone: 01-938-2222

SAZTEC International
6700 Corporate Drive
Lakeside Building II, Suite 100
Kansas City, MO 64120
Telephone: (816) 483-6900
Fax: (816) 214-4966

SilverPlatter Information Service, Inc.
10 Barley Mow Passage
Chiswick
London W4 4PH U.K.
Telephone: 01-994-8242
Fax: 44-1-995-5159

SilverPlatter Information, Inc.
One Newton Executive Park
Newton Lower Falls, MA 02162-1449
Telephone: (800) 343-0064;
(617) 969-5554
Fax: (617) 969-5554

Sociological Abstracts, Inc.
P.O. Box 22206
San Diego, CA 92122
Telephone: (619) 695-8803
Fax: (619) 695-0416

Sport Information Resource Centre
1600 James Naismith Dr.
Gloucester, ON K1B 5N4
Canada
Telephone: (613) 748-5658
Telex: 053-3660 Sportrec Ott
Fax: (613) 748-5701

United Nations Food and Agriculture Organization
Fisheries Department
Via delle Terme di Caracalla
Rome
00100 Italy
Telephone: 39-6-579-74993
Fax: 39-6-679-9563

For further information on CD-ROM publishers and distributors, readers are urged to consult the annual directories *CD-ROMS IN PRINT* and *CD-ROM Market Place* (both Meckler).